A NEW AFRICAN ELITE

A New African Elite
Place in the Making of a Bridge Generation

Deborah Pellow

First published in 2022 by

Berghahn Books

www.berghahnbooks.com

© 2022, 2026 Deborah Pellow
First paperback edition published in 2026

All rights reserved. Except for the quotation of short passages for the purposes of criticism and review, no part of this book may be reproduced in any form or by any means, electronic or mechanical, including photocopying, recording, or any information storage and retrieval system now known or to be invented, without written permission of the publisher.

Library of Congress Cataloging-in-Publication Data

A C.I.P. cataloging record is available from the Library of Congress
Library of Congress Cataloging in Publication Control Number: 2021062574

British Library Cataloguing in Publication Data

A catalogue record for this book is available from the British Library

EU GPSR Authorized Representative

LOGOS EUROPE, 9 rue Nicolas Poussin, 17000, LA ROCHELLE, France
Email: Contact@logoseurope.eu

ISBN 978-1-80073-378-7 hardback
ISBN 978-1-83695-409-5 paperback
ISBN 978-1-83695-410-1 epub
ISBN 978-1-80073-379-4 web pdf

https://doi.org/10.3167/9781800733787

CONTENTS

List of Illustrations	vi
Acknowledgments	viii
Prologue	xi
Introduction	1
Chapter 1. Dagbon in Context	27
Chapter 2. Childhood Home	62
Chapter 3. Getting Educated	92
Chapter 4. Paths to Careers	131
Chapter 5. Living in Between: Patronage and Hybrid Modernity	168
Chapter 6. Conflict at Home, Enflamed from Afar	202
Conclusion	220
Epilogue	228
Glossary	232
References	233
Index	249

ILLUSTRATIONS

Figures

1.1. The route of succession to Ya-Na (created by Deborah Pellow). 43

2.1. Da Tchuma Luna, Baba Fuseini (photo by Deborah Pellow). 71

2.2. The warriors of one of the Dagomba chiefs, Yendi, April 2006 (photo by Deborah Pellow). 76

2.3. The caretaker of the shrine at Katariga with her elders (photo by Deborah Pellow). 79

2.4. Drawing of a Dagomba compound (Al-Hassan 1980, 180b, redrawn by Liu Qi). 83

2.5. Courtyard of Sunson-Na's compound (photo by Deborah Pellow). 84

3.1. Salamatu Abdulai (photo by Deborah Pellow). 125

4.1. Dr. David Abdulai, the "mad doctor" (photo by Deborah Pellow). 156

4.2. Fati Isaka with some of the children in her orphanage Amfani (photo by Deborah Pellow). 159

5.1. Courtyard at a home in North Legon, Accra (photo by Deborah Pellow). 175

5.2. Ad for The Vteng Mall, Tamale, in process (photo by Deborah Pellow). 182

5.3. An informal photograph of the Sunson-Na, Na Mahama Shani Hamidu (photo by Deborah Pellow). 184

5.4. The interconnection of Henry Kaleem, Tamale *dakpema*, Huudu Yahaya, and Fati Isaka (created by Deborah Pellow, computerized by Matt Coulter). 186

5.5. Chief Abdulai, three of his wives, two of his brothers, and the interconnection of their offspring (created by Deborah Pellow, computerized by Matt Coulter). 187

5.6. Three generations of Issifu Sumani's patrilineal descent group (created by Deborah Pellow, computerized by Matt Coulter). 188

5.7. Dr. Yahuza Gomda's royal connections (created by Deborah Pellow, computerized by Matt Coulter). 189

5.8. Iliasu Adam and his familial connections (created by Deborah Pellow, computerized by Matt Coulter). 190

6.1. Ya-Na Yakubu Andani II (Mahama Alhassan, aka Americana). 209

6.2. The military presence near the old palace, Yendi (photo by Deborah Pellow). 212

6.3. Diagram of houses burnt adjacent to the Ya-Na's palace, March 27, 2002 (Kampakuya-Na, Regent of Yendi). 214

8.1. Ya-Na Abubakari Mahama II (Mohammed Adam Gariba). 230

Map

0.1. Map of Ghana, showing regions (© Joseph W. Stoll). xvi

ACKNOWLEDGMENTS

When I began to cast about for a new project, I became interested in the north of Ghana, for personal and intellectual reasons. The Dagomba are the largest of the chiefly groups in the north, and their socio-political significance notwithstanding, there was very little written about them. I also did not know the north at all—I had spent a week in Tamale decades earlier. I have also never worked among an elite population. This was intriguing to me. As I began to design my study, I saw this as a chance to do multi-sited research, drawing together the north (that I did not know) and Accra (that I did), exploring the solidifying of a new elite, who came from the former and now live in the latter.

It was a somewhat worrying time to do research among the Dagomba. Their king Ya-Na Yakubu Andani II had been murdered two years before I began my field research. He had not yet been buried, because there was no agreement on who would next sit on the skin. Passions were high. There was acrimony if not hatred between members of the two Dagomba gates (clans). I had to tread lightly.

I alternated time spent between the Tamale-Yendi axis where my study population hailed from and the suburbs of Accra, where they had relocated. It was a very different kind of research for me, because there was no physically delineated community of elite Dagomba in Accra where I could hang out and interact with them—as well-to-do people, they can live where they wish, in locales scattered throughout the metro region. I started out talking to members of the Accra contingent. In Accra, I used snow ball sampling to create a study population. It was remarkably easy, as one person would either call another on my behalf or give me the person's phone number. I first met A. E. Abdulai summer 2004 through a local friend who is a dental patient of his. My apartment during 2005–2006 in Tudu/Adabraka was just three blocks from A. E.'s office. I often went over late afternoon to cool off and it was in his waiting room that I met a variety of Dagomba men who agreed to talk to me. Along with not wanting to bias my study in the direction of one gate (clan) or the other, I wanted to bring in as many women as possible. Because of cultural biases, as I discuss in the book, there were simply very few women who fit the criteria of educated professionals. Alhaji Mahama Iddrisu, who hails from Wa in the Upper West and as a former politician knew many northerners, sat with me one day early on in my research and gave me the names of most of the women I ultimately brought into the study.

All of the Accra study participants are active professionals with busy schedules. Some travel frequently and extensively. I am ever grateful to all of them for the time they gave me, and in many cases, the friendship they extended.

While I easily met Dagomba, one through another, and enjoyed their hospitality, I missed the intimacy and togetherness of an enclosed community. And then I went north. It was a thirteen-hour bus ride to Tamale. Tamale is a city, said to be the fastest growing in West Africa, but it does not seem anonymous; it was warm and friendly and easy to get around in. It reminded me a lot of Accra in the 1970s—a few traffic lights, some storied buildings, and everyone seemed to know where one another lived. I am ever grateful to Father Jon Kirby, the founder of and soul behind TICCS (Tamale Institute of Cross-Cultural Studies). He gave me a home whenever I was in town, and I enjoyed the camaraderie with him and others who stayed at TICCS. He knows the Northern Region well and he gave me great pointers. It was also in Tamale that I met Janet Mohammed. Janet was the head of the Tamale office of the Christian Council. A deeply committed member of the peace network, Janet introduced me around that community; one of those she introduced me to was Vincent Boi-Nai, a southerner who was the Bishop of Yendi and a significant peace-broker.

Yendi is like a village, and there I found the physical community that I missed in Accra. Bishop Boi-Nai gave me a home when I was visiting in the area. He spent hours with me, delineating the cast of characters in the drama of the Ya-Na's murder and the road to peace, reciting tales of the meetings he had with members of the two gates.

In the north, there were others without whom I simply could not have done this research. The Dagomba chiefs were all welcoming. Some I got to know rather well. Every time I came north, I visited the Sunson-Na, a remarkably progressive man. Kampakuya-Na, the Regent in Yendi, and his elders, allowed me fairly unfettered access to him; I learned a great deal from him about growing up the son of a Ya-Na, of how he was coping following his father's murder, of how he saw the future of Dagbon. My driver Shirazu Harona was not just a driver; he assisted me in finding people to talk to, in suggesting day trips to acquaint myself with the Dagomba towns and villages, and he was a great companion. He introduced me to his friend Zibilila Alida. Zibs, as I call him, is smart as a whip, extraordinarily helpful and really well-connected. He became my research assistant the first day I met him. From the royal butcher family, he introduced me to Kampakuya-

Na when he was in quasi-hiding following his father's death and before being chosen to sit on the skin. Zibs helped me walk the line between the two gates. Henry Kaleem, a Tamale dweller, was the son of the famous educator J. S. Kaleem. He returned to Tamale after living in the UK for thirty years, spending much of his time putting together an archive of things Dagomba. He represented Kuga-Na, the Dagomba kingmaker, at the Eminent Chiefs Committee in the creation of a road map to peace. He was ever available to answer questions and help fill in some of the holes. Iliasu Adam, one of the youngest members of my study population, is one of the first people I met when I went to Tamale summer 2004 to plot out a project. He was a journalist and worked as a stringer for the BBC, reporting on the situation in Dagbon. He is remarkably articulate and smart and gave me a context for much of what I found myself confronting, given the tensions in Dagbon. Through time spent with the new elite Dagomba in the north—six of them retired and having moved back, and four who stayed north and are working—I gained a real appreciation for the attachment that all of my study population have maintained for the place Dagbon. Mohammed Adam Gariba, official state secretary to the Dagbon Traditional Council, paved the way to my first formal meeting with the new Ya-Na, Abubakari Mahama II.

Colleagues around the country read and commented on drafts, chapters, snippets of what became this book. Over the long haul of this research project, I gave talks and published papers dealing with aspects of my Dagomba focus. Discussants and listeners asked questions and gave pointers that helped me sharpen my analysis. I am extremely grateful to Denise Lawrence-Zuniga, Bob Rotenberg, Danny Hoffman, Adeline Masquelier and Setha Low for their wisdom and sharp critique on earlier drafts of this manuscript.

Reviewers for the IIE Fulbright Scholar Program saw the worth of the project; their funding made all the difference and I am very thankful to them for it.

Matt Coulter, in The Maxwell School's ICT group, and friend and former colleague Bob Gates made the final push with photos and figures less painful. My editor Tom Bonnington has been ever patient and helpful in the production process.

I would normally acknowledge my husband for his support. David became chronically ill and died six years ago. While it paralyzed me for a time, his illness and death also convinced me that I had to finish this book. My partner Bill Rahling has been nothing less than encouraging, which during this solitary plague year has gotten me over the hump of inertia to tell the tale of these remarkable people.

For Bill, forever

PROLOGUE

The Death of a King

From March 25–27, 2002, there were three days of upheaval in Yendi, Ghana, seat of the Dagomba kingship in Dagbon. Members of the Abudu and Andani clans, known as "gates," once again fought over their kingship. The mayhem culminated in the murder of the king, Na-Yakubu Andani II, of the Andani gate and twenty-eight of his followers died at the hands of their Abudu brothers. The population of Ghana, from north to south, was shaken by the violence of the act. From within the palace, the scene was frightening and personal. There were rioting and killings, looting and defilement of the palace and the Ya-Na's mosque. There was arson and bodily mutilation (dismemberment and decapitation). Several types of weapons and ammunition were used in the attack at the palace, including 7.62 mm assault rifles, assault rifles and Special Game 12 GA live shotgun cartridges. Most warriors used locally made guns fitted for G3 or AK 47 ammunition. The bullet pock marks on the palace walls were made by shotguns and assault rifles (Pellow 2016).

The murder intensified attachment to the Dagomba homeland and its chieftaincy of Abudu and Andani living hundreds of miles south in the capital of Accra. It also heightened the smoldering resentments between members of the two gates. Some said it was set in motion by Abudu and Andani elite living in Accra, who cared so much they funded fighters on both sides.

An intimate view of the turmoil comes from the last people to see the king alive, three of his wives, all Andani.[1] This is clearly their story. It is a story they have told to others. I have incorporated their words into the chronicle of events, because it exacerbated Dagomba emotions and reactions. The tale they told began February–March 2002, the time for *Id al Adha*, celebrated by Muslims throughout the world at the conclusion of the *hajj* (pilgrimage). Among the Dagomba of northern Ghana, their king, the Ya-Na, traditionally leads the *Id* festivities and then those of *Bugum*, the Fire Festival. According to King Yakubu Andani II's three widows, at *Id al Adha* 2002, the king, a member of the Andani clan, was advised by letter that he was to vacate the palace so that members of the Abudu clan could perform the royal funeral of his predecessor, Ya-Na Mahamadu Abdulai IV. King Mahamadu had been de-skinned (de-throned) in 1974, thus when he died in 1988, he was no longer king. For the king, the Dagomba celebrate the burial and the funeral separately. Mahamadu was given a royal burial but not a royal funeral. This has roiled his clan members ever since.

The Abudu request planted the seeds of the fight at hand. Ya-Na Yakubu Andani refused the request. "So there was disruption around the palace and [soldiers] advised the chief to tell his people not to go that way, because all the places were occupied by soldiers."

> The *salla* festivity was about to start, and people were at the palace dancing. And it came to a point that stones were being thrown toward the palace from the crowd. The chief did not come out on that day because of what he had heard. So people entered and told them that people were throwing the stones. That very day, the room of the Ya-Na was being destroyed by stones. (Daalabi October 5, 2005)

The king called in the divisional police; they said it was "small small children" who were throwing the stones. Things returned to normal.

Four weeks later, a group from the Abudu decided to celebrate *Bugum*, for the first time separately from and before the king did. The elders to the Abudu Regent, son of the deceased and de-skinned Mahamadu, positioned him to oversee the unofficial set of festivities. A letter came from Mohammed Tijiani, the District Chief Executive (DCE) in Yendi, stating that the Fire Festival was indefinitely postponed. "The [king] told the officers to take the letter back to whoever gave it to him, to bring it through the correct channel. So the three of them took back the letter and never brought it again."

Security agencies worried and the government imposed a curfew. An elder of the chief phoned the Regional Minister Prince Andani and said, "If there is any abnormality going on, I am inviting you to tell me what is going on. And there is a curfew, so kindly call the DCE to the palace here." The regional minister "couldn't find the DCE Tijani until he found him at the small boy's palace, the Abudu Regent. He went there and met him and a lot of people were there."[2] The DCE declined the regional minister's request to meet with the king.

The situation was an affront to the sitting Ya-Na. Some believe that Abudu defiance derived from challenge and "undermined the authority of the reigning king, Ya-Na Andani II" (Tonah 2011:10). Others believe that individual Abudu big-men pushed for the auxiliary celebration as retaliation for old hurts. And yet others believe that Abudu defiance derived from their sense that with a sympathetic national government, they could challenge and "undermine the authority of the reigning king, Ya-Na Andani II" (Tonah 2011, 10).

Those responsible for tradition advised the king not to perform the festival. Others advised the king not to allow a curfew and to continue with the festival. Wanting to bolster his status, the Ya-Na prevailed upon the regional minister and had the curfew suspended. The festival went forward under his watch and a fight broke out among the revelers (Pellow 2016, 41). The chief linguist of the Ya-Na had sent his son to fetch a man for the reading of the Quran. The man lived in former Ya-Na Mahamadu's area, the so-called Abudu side. The man refused. As the boy was leaving, he was beaten. The new bicycle he was riding was broken by local boys. He left it on the road. The chief imam and his people went to the palace where they read the Quran. When others came toward the palace "from the other side" (of the Abudu Regent), everyone dispersed. This was on Monday, March 25. A boy and then an elder coming to the palace were both hit by bullets.

> So it began seriously on that Monday. All those who had come from different houses went back to their houses, leaving us alone. Tuesday morning. There was one other house that belonged to the palace, standing behind the palace, it was burnt. Another that tom-tom beaters [drummers] went to, it was burnt. (Daalabi October 5, 2005)

The king stood outside and looked at the houses that were burnt. "'Hey my grand people Abudu side, is it me you have burnt?' While the 'chief' [king] was speaking, bullets were falling in front of [him]. Elders who were inside the palace advised the 'chief' to come in" (Daalabi October 5, 2005).

Early Wednesday morning, around 3 am, the women said a helicopter landed. Everything stopped—it was quiet. At this time, the king came out and advised his wives to send the children to his mother's house. One of the elders called the king and told him to vacate the palace.

> The king asked, "Why? What is happening?"
> "Some soldiers came to my place in the night—their armored car had a problem with the battery. When the soldiers came and I was repairing their battery, I asked why they had come to town—'is there a problem in town? Did you come to separate the fight that was in town?' They said if I was from the Andani side, I should leave Yendi." The man said, this is why I have called you [the King]—to tell you about the development—because I have heard it from a soldier man.
> The king said, "This is why I should vacate the palace? I have been on the seat for 28 years now—and I have included the Abudus too. I

will not vacate the palace. They should kill me in the palace." (Daalabi October 5, 2005)

The King told his wives to leave. Garbong, Litwang and Dalaabi stayed. "We refused to go to anyplace."

One of the children looked outside the palace and told the three women to climb—the children all said, *"Alahu Akhbar."*

> We the women asked the boy what he saw. The boy said we should all cry, *Alahu Akhbar*. We are all going to be killed. They have surrounded the palace. As I was saying these words, the bullets came toward my direction and fell in front of me. The elder shouted at me to get away. I went in another direction. I was crying. Another bullet fell from where I was and another. Three times. We could see the soldiers. A helicopter. We saw them. Shooting. They were inside the yard, nowhere to pass. All of us women came in one direction. They said we should climb the wall. I was so heavy I could not climb. Three of the women carried me over and I jumped down—I fell on the ground. Soldiers were on the ground and they were crawling to the mosque.
>
> We were 11 in number who jumped the wall . . .
>
> We the three [wives] ran to where the military people were. There's a fence all around. They all put their guns on their arms. All the gates were locked. We couldn't enter. We were even holding leaves as a symbol of surrender and we were talking to the solders. We asked them to come and rescue our chief. They did not mind us. We asked if they had no sympathy for us, didn't they fear God? At that time, a brother who was passing, I asked him to interpret. The brother said if I was standing there, they would kill me. That if they got to know we were the wives of the "chief", they would kill us. Better to run away. We thought we would go back—we could not leave our husband. It was only the "Chief" who was there. We got to a church... they were beating an instrument and the tom-tom. And a war song—*bangoma*. When we heard that, we started running. We went to a nearby house, lay down and cried. When we were in that house, we thought we'd go back to the fire and they would kill us all rather than leaving. A church leader talked us into going back. We didn't see what the "Chief" [who wouldn't leave] had seen. We said we were going purposely to see if the "Chief" was injured, I'd carry him on my back. That's why we were going. What they did to spoil, we'd do to regain everything. They brought in a car but we the three refused. We wanted to see him to tell his people. If we leave, his people would ask us, what has happened to the "Chief"? The church elder was begging us—we should be patient.
>
> People came and carried us into the car and brought us to Tamale [the largest northern city]. (Daalabi October 5, 2005)

"We had no quarrel with the late 'chief' and he was our husband, so how do you run to your peoples' house? There was confusion in town. So that led to the murder of our husband. And we've come to live with his people" (Daalabi October 5, 2005). "Lawyer" Ibrahim Mahama, uncle and lawyer to the murdered Ya-Na, housed them and the other twenty-three widows with his sister during the four years they spent in Tamale until their deceased husband could be buried.

The fact of the Ya-Na's murder and the problems of chiefly succession frame the time period of the story of the Dagomba new educated elite which I tell. The drama of what happened hooked the Dagomba new elite living in Accra—the Andani who mourned the death of *their* clansman, the Abudu who sought to defend *theirs*.

NOTES

1. The murdered king left twenty-six widows. The three women are Galiban, wife #4 ("I was the first person the chief would consult, concerning how to cater with all those coming for the festival, as far as the women were concerned"), Katini, wife #3 ("I was responsible for what the chief ate, morning, noon, night") and Daalabi, wife #9 ("When there are strangers, I control the food"). I spent three hours with the three on October 5, 2005. Daalabi narrated the events that led to the Yendi crisis, her story punctuated by remarks from the other two, particularly Katini. Galiban wept openly.
2. Abdulai Mahamadu. This is the thirty-something son of the de-skinned Ya-Na Mahamadu, who has been made a place-holder by Abudu elders, in particular the *mbadugu* (linguist) Alhassan Iddrisu.

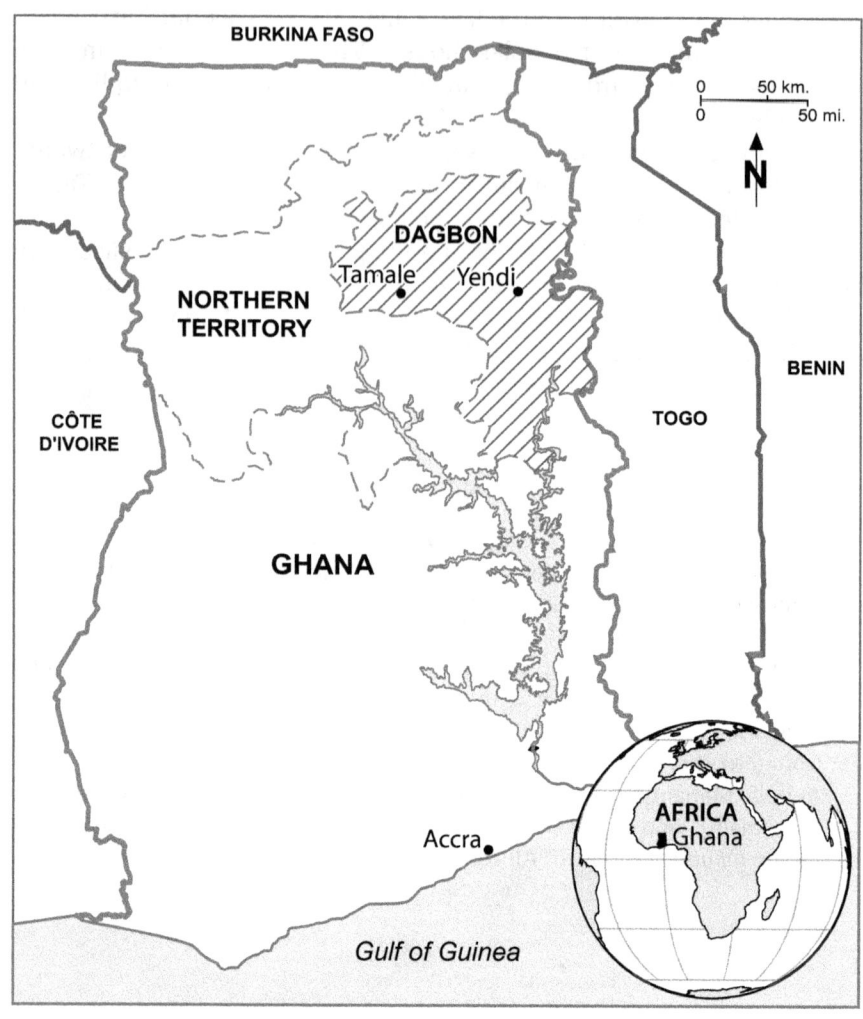

Map 0.1. Map of Ghana, showing regions (© Joseph W. Stoll).

INTRODUCTION

This book narrates a tale of attachment to old, of becoming new, of adaptation between. It tells the tale of the creation of a new African elite, tracing its members' beginnings, influences, movement, and change; of their relocation from "home" to a new place, across space and levels of social and economic development. It sketches out their visceral attachment to that natal home, and ultimately, how that attachment has led to their involvement in hometown affairs. This new elite composes a sub-section of the Dagomba (Dagbamba), an ethnic group that itself is composed of two clans (known as "gates"), the Abudu and the Andani. Offshoots of two brothers, they have been at odds for decades, fighting over the rights of succession to kingship and disrupting Dagomba solidarity. The Dagomba new elite were born and bred in Dagbon in Ghana's Northern Region. The Northern Region, together with the Upper West and Upper East, account for about forty-one percent of Ghana's land mass and house twenty percent of its population. The north suffers from Ghana's north-south inequality, which represents one of the most politically salient socioeconomic divisions in Ghana (Abdulai 2012). This has produced a narrative of deprivation affecting most of the north, but which the new Dagomba elite have succeeded in escaping.

In this book, I consider how this new elite became a bridge generation—what they have taken along, what they have left behind, how they have achieved new status, and how their manipulation of that status has impacted the Dagomba as a whole. I tell the story of the new Dagomba elite, both Andani and Abudu, how they came to be patrons, highly educated professionals living and working mainly in urban southern Ghana (Pellow 2011). As members of the modernizing world they have gained power, which as patrons they use to influence the world they left. The book covers a period of seventeen years, bookended by two events: the murder of the Ya-Na in 2002, so chillingly described by three of his widows in the Prologue, and the installation of a new king in 2019. The men (and a few women) of this bridge generation are bicultural and multilingual. They easily identify with both Western and home culture according to the situation they find themselves in. They live graciously in the "modern" south without relinquishing but rather adapting many customs and practices of the "traditional" north. They are members of a between-generation, called 1.5ers, who have one foot in the less-developed north and one in the modernizing south and who have become patrons for those less fortunate who hope to follow in their steps. They themselves characterize their success as serendipitous.

They may live at a distance, but their attachment to the homeland, and to gate, is palpable and intense, made even more so with the death of the king. The kingship of the Dagomba, the *ya-na*, defines their ties to that place. Their ultimate influence is on who succeeds to chieftaincy in Dagbon. They have also a new sense of home in the south, creating, remodeling, renovating and maintaining their homes. Their place attachment, whether to their natal homes in the north or to their new homes in the south, is tied to bundles of social relations. The materiality of home plays a part in the production of their social life. One might say that their dual existence or ties epitomize what McIntyre labels a new kind of dwellingness, "specifically dwelling in multiple places" (2006, 8). One might also assert that their dwellingness—how they dwell and what the dwelling accommodates (behaviors, aesthetics)—varies with the place.

Memorable Attachment

All societies share collectively held memories. As Halbwachs (1992) has written, the group has the capacity to remember and, like culture and personality, one might argue that individual memory correlates with group memory, "a totality of thoughts common to a group, the group of people with whom we have a relation at this moment, or with whom we have had a relation on the preceding day or days" (p. 52). Memories include the idea of a type of life, a reconstructed picture of what was, of what might have been. Place memory plays a powerful role in "the construction of a social and cultural identity" (Bahloul 1996, 2). Ideas of society incorporate collective memories; they are embodied in persons or groups and individual memory relies on them. "Those groups and persons exist in the passage of time and leave their traces in the memory of people. In this sense, there is no social idea that would not at the same time be a recollection of the society" (Halbwachs 1992,188). Halbwachs speaks of locating such memories through social landmarks that people carry within themselves.

The power of place, of hometown, of memory, of Dagbon, has played out in Accra, hundreds of miles south. During the Ya-Na murder trial in the capital, "violence and a near bloodbath" occurred between rival factions ("Six injured . . ." 2010). I would argue that salient landmarks include the home, that memories "build" that site and are also anchored there. Homes are built with ideas of lifestyle and status—they enable behaviors and activities—and in turn provide a significant locus of sentiment and meaning for the self (Cuba and Hummon 1993). Bahloul, born and raised in France, focuses on her extended family's home in Setif, Algeria, in the years 1937–62, to understand the cultural history of the Jewish community. She argues that the house is an architecture of memory, and that it is through the house's meaning system that an uprooted people such as her own share a collective memory (Bahloul 1996): "the domestic and family world makes up the woof of remembrance, of memory. The house is 'inhabited'" (p. 29). Remembered objects and places may be carried materially or be stored in memory. "Remembrance of the house evolves as a narrative interpretation of the past" (Bahloul 1996, 126). As she reminds us, the house is where everyone begins life, it is there that the developmental cycle unwinds. It is the first spatial environment that the child inhabits. The embedding of memories is non-verbal—or pre-verbal—and experiential. It is those memories of home (or place) in a village (place) that are commonly held. The memories and attachments of those spaces evoke the place relationships.

The dwelling place that the Dagomba elite living in Accra, and even Tamale, remember and revisit, in their memory and on the occasional trek north, helps provide their identity. The person and the group use environmental meaning to symbolize or situate identity (Cuba and Hummon 1993, 112). Place identity understands locales for the creation, maintenance and transformation of identity, as "it answers the question —Who am I?—by countering—Where am I? or Where do I belong?" (Cuba and Hummon 1993, 112). This is because culture is spatialized and spaces in the physical and social world are linked (Low and Lawrence-Zuniga 2003).

Beyond home, there is community and even region, through which collective memory speaks and is performed, at festivals, reunions, marriages and funerals. Indeed, to understand the significance of place to the re-located new Dagomba elite, I have found valuable the approach of place attachment, "an affective bond or link between people and specific places," and more specifically, "the tendency of the individual to maintain closeness to such a place" (Hidalgo and Hernandez 2001, 274). There are myriad ways in which people form meaningful relations with places— place attachment helps us understand that people "invest places with meaning and behave accordingly" (Lawrence 1992, 212).

Place attachment involves both the social and physical dimension and reflects and helps cultivate group and individual identity (Brown et al.

2003). There are four processes associated with the formation/maintenance of place attachments: the biological, psychological, environmental and sociocultural. It is nourished by interaction with others from the same socio-physical background, as they reproduce their collective identity through their common attachment by recreating memories, festivities and occasions. Phenomenologists were among the first to write about place attachment, emphasizing its emotional component. Bachelard (1964), for example, ruminated on the importance of memories, and "the more securely they are fixed in space, the sounder they are" (p. 9), constituting a "poetics of space."

Environment-behavior studies emphasized individual psychology, such as understanding of the environment, and later emotional and cultural attachment perspectives. The space-place field was enriched by the entry of cross-cultural research perspective from environmental psychology (Altman and Low 1992). Louise Chawla wrote of the value of continuity with important environments and people of the past—that they anchor people to times, people and places (1992, 68)—and that this occurs through memories. In her research among the Swazi, Hilda Kuper (1972) has written about the symbolic values of certain indigenous places, as compared to those established by the British, and the difference in meanings that attach to them respectively. The Swazi shared a symbolic relationship with these institutionalized places. Through their attachment to these culturally salient places, the Swazi kept the past alive, "maintaining a sense of continuity, fostering identity . . ." (Rubinstein and Parmalee 1992, 140).[1] In their introduction to the volume *Place Attachment*, Altman and Low (1991, 7) characterize places as "repositories and context within which interpersonal, community, and cultural relationships occur" and thus place attachment "*is to those social relationships*, not just to place qua place, to which people are attached" (emphasis added). Writing about the urban compound house in Accra, Ghana, I argued that people's attachment to place emerges from their experience living there, that it socializes them into the urban system and teaches them new roles and ways of being (1992). Thus, while there is a psychological element to place attachment, there is also a social one, and it is the latter that I am pursuing to better comprehend the Dagomba new elite who have left the hometown but yearn for it.

Furthermore, strong residential bonds need not equate to aesthetics or style. In a classic article on neighborhood relocation in Boston, Fried (1963) illustrates the strong place attachments and community viability, despite deteriorated housing. I found the same affective connection of residents with their dilapidated community in my work in Sabon Zongo, Accra (2008).

Hidalgo and Hernandez point out (2001, 273) that as important as are the "feelings that people develop toward the places where they were born and brought up," there is much that we do not know. In this book, I am arguing that it is through symbol and ritual, sociality and practice, that the Dagomba elite who have relocated to the big city are bonded to places (their hometowns in the north, the family house). These inscribe identity and meaning (chieftaincy, festivals, holidays, family occasions) and spatialize culture (indigeneity). While the hallmark of attachment is the affect, emotion and feeling that one associates with certain places, such as childhood haunts, the attachment people feel is enacted and performed, through the relationships and encounters that they created and in those places where they created them. The attachment is social—it is generated through social practice. It can be by the individual or by a collective group. For some people, places are bridges to the past that provide continuity. They may suggest nostalgia, sentimentality or inspiration as a result of their infused meaning" (Lawrence 1992, 212). For example, in Yendi, the seat of Dagbon, every Friday and Monday, the king comes out and sits in state. His enactment of kingship, the ritual of his emergence, is observed by his people and allows them to engage in deference to him, which also reinforces the power of that space as the seat of the kingdom.

Hometown Disruption

The Dagomba, numbering about 985,000 people, make up 8 percent of the Ghanaian population at large, 32.9 percent of Ghana's Northern Region, which is twice as much as the next largest group, the Konkomba. In Accra, the Dagomba as a whole constitute 5 percent of the population, the fourth largest ethnic group following the three main southern groups of Akan, Ga-Adangbe and Ewe.

The Dagomba patrons are a tiny sub-set of this Dagomba whole and occupy a unique and privileged position within the Dagomba community. They have inspiring and compelling personal stories. All come from humble beginnings, growing up in homes without electricity and running water, in polygynous families with many siblings, and with parents who were almost universally illiterate. Their linkages to both customary and state offices have given them the power to influence home politics, both of state and chieftaincy. They exercise what I call "leadership by remote control." This was exemplified by the killing of the Dagomba king, Ya-Na Yakubu Andani II. By all accounts the regicide was fueled and funded by Dagomba patrons living in Accra. The murder further defined the ties of the patrons to the place, to the Kingdom of Dagbon.

This book tells the story of an elite group's journey to eliteness: from humble homes in an underdeveloped, illiterate region in the north, to the cosmopolitan and modern south, but holding on to the north as imaginary. In the course of this book, I detail their life histories, how these people came of age as education was opening up in the north, and in many cases, their sheer luck at gaining access to secondary schooling. Northern Ghana has been relatively underdeveloped since the colonial period and purposely so. (I will give a more detailed accounting in Chapter 1.) The north and south of what would become Ghana were constituted by the British as two regions with different policies (Bening 1975). In the south, the investment of money and attention paid off; in contrast, "the colonial takeover of the north of Ghana prepared the way for several decades of neglect and stagnation . . ." (Eades 1993, 26). The northern third of the country was delineated as the Northern Territories in the late nineteenth century. The belief of the Governor, F.M. Hodgson was that the north was commercially unimportant, thus there was no reason to open it up (Eades 1993)—despite successful pre-colonial trade with Asante and to points north and east, and the potential of a shea nut industry that could have been developed. This also meant little investment in infrastructure.

The north was developed by the British to be far poorer than the south. The two regions also exhibited inequalities in terms of population density, modernization, and residential amenities. The north was not to be developed economically beyond its role as supplier of labor for The Colony and Ashanti (Grischow 2006). Moreover, northerners were considered to be war-like and thus military recruitment was disproportionately from the north (Abdulai 2012).

When modernization started under the colonial administration, resources and political will went largely to the south. Accra has been Ghana's primate city since 1877, when the British moved their administrative headquarters there from Cape Coast. When they arrived, it was a trading town; the modern city took shape under British town planning. Until 1940, the educational system in the country developed slowly and was confined largely to Asante and The Colony (i.e. the south). Secondary school education had already come to the south, with the establishment of Mfantsipim in Cape Coast in 1876. Another premier school, The Achimota School, opened in 1927 on the outskirts of Accra with the encouragement of the British Governor Guggisberg. As of 1943, the Northern Territories had only twenty schools, not one at the secondary level. Tamale Secondary School was only established in 1951, due to the persistence of Kwame Nkrumah, elected six years later as the country's first president.

Accra today has five-star hotels, divided highways, shopping malls, fancy restaurants, and beautiful suburbs. It is the country's commercial center. Tamale, the big city in the north, has little to compare. It is not "bush," i.e. the village but it is also not particularly cosmopolitan. It is looked down upon by southerners. For those who have professional training, Tamale offers few opportunities, Accra offers many.

Tamale today is the political center of Dagbon, the territory of the Dagomba people, and it is the regional capital of the Northern Region. It is a provincial city, with hotels, restaurants, wide boulevards and a couple of traffic lights. The landscape is constituted by round houses, with more recently built rectangular structures interspersed. Dagbon is estimated at 8,082 square miles and has a population of 650,000. Yendi is the traditional capital of Dagbon, the seat of the Dagomba kingship. It lies fifty miles east of Tamale. Twenty-nine miles north of Tamale is Yendi Dabari, the original capital of the Dagomba.

Key to understanding Dagomba worldview is to bear in mind what many observed to me: Dagombas appreciate leadership—they are very hierarchical: "[by] seniority and merit, in family and community, and sometimes by wits" (Issa Naseri September 28, 2005). And if hierarchy, and succession and progression collapse, "I bet you Dagbon will collapse. There will be no Dagbon state" (Inusah A.B. Fuseini, aka "Lawyer" Inussa May 2, 2006). Many have said to me, "one can't talk about Dagbon without talking about chiefs—central in Dagomba life" (Issa Naseri September 28, 2005); because "chieftaincy is the state" (Lawyer Inussa May 2, 2006). A Member of Parliament, and former Minister for Lands and Natural Resources, "Lawyer" Inussa of course is referring to the Dagomba state, with the king at its core. The new elite have ties to both the tradition-based state and also federal state-based rules and laws. Most are not chiefs (*na*) and they are not spiritual custodians of the land (*tindana*). Most are not state politicians, such as Members of Parliament. But they have had access to new kinds of resources—education in a region with a 20 percent literacy rate, and after relocation, professional status, social connections, urban cosmopolitan linkages. They have become patrons, creating new rules and resources for themselves and their clients, the less fortunate Dagomba. As is the case throughout Africa, patron-client relations are pivotal in structuring access to power and resources (Diamond 1987). Members of this Dagomba elite are regularly approached by northerners who know of them through the network, in hopes that they can help them go to school, find a place to live, get a job. The patron-clientage structure fits the Dagomba appreciation of hierarchy. The patrons fit into a different form of structure than the leaders in Dagbon—that of the modern urban society. It fits the needs of those who request help. Many of their clients want to relocate in part because the opportunities do not exist in the north, in part because they do not want to stay there.

The latter was particularly true during the four years after the Ya-Na was murdered, until he was buried and his son installed as Regent of Yendi.

On March 27, 2002, Malik Yakubu, the then-Minister of Information was quoted in the *Daily Graphic* as saying that Yendi was "calm." And yet, a military occupation took over. When I began this project, the Ya-Na Yakubu Andani II had not yet been buried. Both Tamale and Yendi bristled with tension. To drive to Yendi from Tamale in 2004, we had to go through several checkpoints. There were periodic disturbances, such as the incineration of NDC's political headquarters in Tamale. Yendi in particular was on edge. I had wanted to see the new "temporary" palace that the government built; the area was off-limits. A priest walking by the new palace to church on a Sunday had been remanded for twenty-four hours before he was released. The then-MP Malik Yakubu allowed a soldier to drive me by, but nothing more. The market in Yendi during the seventeen years after the Ya-Na's murder was barely functioning.

During the four-plus years between the king's death and burial, many of the Dagomba new elite did not go up to Dagbon out of fear of reprisal (especially those who were Abudu, since it was Abudu who murdered the king) or just discomfort. One man told me he was afraid his car would be incinerated. The larger Dagomba community in Accra was riven in two. The coherence of the Dagomba, and of the Dagomba new elite in Accra, born of common provenance and socio-spatial attachments, was shattered. Gifty Mahama, a senior civil servant, remembers that in the past, people did not know about the gate differences. "Those days, we didn't have Andani, Abudu—we could go to the chief's house and they'd feed you . . . I miss the unity, because when we were growing up we were one. Now we're afraid of each other" (March 27, 2013). Fuseini Baba was one of the few I know who did not stop visiting his hometown Yendi during the four-year break, but like Gifty, he missed the unity of the past. As a child, he did not travel from Yendi to Tamale, he says, because it was a day's journey (today with a paved road it takes one hour) and because Yendi was so lovely. "In those days, Yendi had a whole street of trees planted by the Germans. Kapok trees. And they're gone" (April 28, 2006).

As a result of the murder, much of what the Dagomba hold dear was put on hold: festivals were suspended, drumming and dancing were banned and the *luntse* did not recite. The luntse have always mattered, because Dagomba like to hear about their ancestors. Normally the "tom-tom beaters" recite the history. During the four-year cessation between the murder and the burial, the children "were not learning it-o, they're not learning anything" (BA Fuseini 2008). The sense was that between the time of Na Yakubu's murder and the return to some degree of normality, people lost their culture: "The things we saw and valued we haven't preserved or paid attention to. If the Ya-Na hadn't died, fewer people would know about Dagbon history and culture" (Abdul Majid October 22, 2005). Members of the two gates did not interact, and inter-gate marriages broke down.

Following the so-called Road Map to Peace enacted after the Ya-Na's burial in April 2006, tensions subsided. The drumming recommenced with a vengeance. Laughing, the Kunbun-Na told me that when the drumming resumed, the dogs at his palace all ran to hide; they became frightened, having not heard the music for four years, or, for the young dogs, ever. Not only do the drummers make music; according to A. A. Iliasu, they constitute an "elaborate, accessible and efficient machinery" to propagate history (quoted in MacGaffey 2013, 39). This machinery is particularly evident at festivals, celebrations, and traditional events such as the installation of the king and chiefs.

After the burial, the Accra Dagomba elite began returning to visit. They stayed in their respective father's home, mother's home, family house. The houses now have plumbing and electricity, but they look little different from when the men and women of this bridge generation were growing up. Like Ghanaians from the south, these northerners say that they want to retire to the north, to return to their roots. Many own plots in the hometown or Tamale, and some have begun to build. Several have farms. Dr. Muta Iddrisu has combined the two: he has built a home on the Yendi road, where he has a cashew farm. While his home only has two bedrooms, he said guests can all sleep together: "Even I can have 100 people sleep in my house here—just put mats on the floor" (March 9, 2013).

The town of Yendi has a renewed spirit. Many people are on the streets, and there is even an express bus to Accra. The local market is bustling. The military barriers are gone (security cost the state millions of dollars), though the military presence in Yendi near the king's palace has remained until today. In July 2019, I made a formal visit to the palace in Yendi to greet the new Ya-Na, who had been enskinned in February. He was surrounded by highly armed state military.

A Dagomba Sample

I spent time with thirty-two Dagomba professionals in Accra and seventeen in the Tamale area, as well as seventeen traditionalists—chiefs, linguists, imams—in Accra and the north. I interviewed both Andani and Abudu. The Accra group included lawyers, politicians, economists, engineers/contractors, people in the medical field, researchers, university faculty, civil servants, architects, administrators, accountants, journalists and the military. The Accra elite group is fairly homogeneous in the sense that all but one of its members were born in Dagbon. They span a generation, between forty to sixty-five years of age—all coming of school age after 1951, when Tamale Secondary opened.

The voices of women are not prominent in this book. As important as the women are, as a labor resource, for procreation, there just are not many of them of this generational cohort who have been educated. Their sphere of agency was largely internal to the family, helping their husbands and as traders. But they were also influential in their sons' success in school—supporting them in material and non-material ways. I discuss this at some length in both Chapters Three and Four.

The bicultural and multilingual Dagomba professionals have compelling personal stories that encompass north and south, hometown and new town. In this book, they tell them—the discrimination and deprivation they experienced but how through luck, ability, indecipherable parental motivation, and the accidents of life, the (largely) sons gained good educations, became successful professionals, and created lifeways that are socially and materially different from those of their childhood. They live in various affluent Accra suburbs and work in venues closed off to their fathers and grandfathers. Given the distance and difference between their hometown and place of relocation, I consider them internal transnational migrants or transmigrants (Pellow 2011).

This term, transnationalism, is defined as "the processes by which immigrants forge and sustain multi-stranded social relations that link together their societies of origin and settlement" (Basch et al. 1994, 8), to their development of networks, activities, patterns of living and ideologies that spanning home and their host society. In this way "[t]ransnational communities commonly refer to migrant communities spanning two nations" (Kearney 1995, 559). The word "transmigrant" has been coined to refer to those transnational individuals who "develop networks and engage in activities that span home and host society" (Mahler 1998, 87). Southern Ghana is so socially, economically and spatially distant and different from the homeland in the north that residents of each operate in environments perceived as being worlds apart. I am accordingly arguing that elite Dagomba internal migration is similar to international migration. This transnational framework captures the processes of deterritorialization and reterritorialization (Brettell 2016, 50; Appadurai 1996). Deterritorialization refers to the transformation migrants produce in new places as technology progresses, while in reterritorialization, they reproduce the homeland in new places. In the case at hand, they easily shuttle back and forth between two very different material and social existences, identifying with their Westernized quotidian while also venerating their home culture.

Bridging Place

In a very real sense, the new Dagomba elite are a bridge: culturally, between the norms and values of the north and those of the south, socially, for a new generation of northerners to whom they perform as models for migration, and materially, to take on the appearances of those they are desirous of resembling. They are internal transmigrants to the big city, ever a crucible for socio-spatial change, but they are also connected to the rural hometown. They are exposed to and absorb modernity, but they manipulate it to fit their wants and needs, creating a hybrid modernity.

As neither first generation migrants nor second generation people who were born in the new place, they were born and bred in the north and maintain strong ties to their respective hometowns. Even as they may have gone through a life change, they have also actively maintained strong ties to the hometown area. Thus, to a large extent, they have developed dual loyalties.

Sociologists have coined the term "1.5 generation" to describe such an in-between generation of immigrants, for example Latinos who came to the United States as children or teens (Holloway-Friesen 2008, 38), distinguishing such immigrants from first generation migrants, or those who came as adults, and second generation people, those who were born in the new place (see also Danico 2004 for Korean migrants). "It recognizes potential differences between [the] adaptation processes and experiences of this population of immigrants and first and second generation immigrants" (Holloway-Friesen 2008, 38). The 1.5ers represent, in theory, a bridge or in-between generation between the home and host nations.

The Dagomba 1.5ers have social and economic links with their home area, which contribute to the development of community both among themselves and with those "at home." While they live graciously in the south, they hold onto the north: "You don't want to forget your roots," one of them, an accountant, told me (Yakubu Andani October 18, 2005).

According to the literature, three main characteristics shape and construct the 1.5 identity. First, 1.5ers are conscious of being bicultural. A biculturally competent person is one who "understands, appreciates, and internalizes the basic tenets of two cultures or societies [and has an] awareness of gender roles, religious practices, political issues, and societal conventions that govern the way people carry themselves within each culture" (Holloway-Friesen 2008,45). Geography or locality plays a large role in how such ethnic identity and understanding is formulated, how adaptation proceeds, and how ethnic or hometown connectedness is maintained. For members of a 1.5 generation "[a] strong connection to either or both cultures indicates a deep appreciation, admiration, and identification with elements of the culture(s), including values, languages, and socially acceptable roles" (Ibid., 48). Bicultural competence appears to buffer such immigrants from acculturative stress and as well as to protect their self-esteem (Holloway-Friesen 2008, 58).

A second characteristic of 1.5ers is the tendency to identify with both their new and their home cultures and values in varying ways, but with the ability also to switch identities in different situations, becoming what is appropriate in different situations. And finally, 1.5ers have a tendency towards bilingualism, and particularly, the ability to code-switch (Danico 2004). While 1.5ers are foreign-born, due to fluency in the language of their host society they are able to "pass" as locals while also having a home language, which can help buffer their experience of acculturative stress, the problems of self-identification resulting from transnational migration. Language is particularly important for such identity formation.

In her conversations with Vietnamese who fled Vietnam and came to America, Sucheng Chan (2006) reports that many speak of discrimination as newcomers due to language issues. There were also tensions in the home as immigrant parents missed the home culture and were saddened by changes in the immediate family, as the children became Americanized and lost their heritage. But the children themselves gained recognition for their success in school despite coming from a poor country, which gave them pride. "Living in America, I am also an Asian American. Being Asian American does not mean we have to lose the Asian parts of our identity. I am trying to be a person with a broader view, open to the loftier parts of [my home] and American cultures" (Chan 2006, 142).

The 1.5ers are more adaptive than the first generation while still being connected to the homeland. While the age at immigration is not necessarily the key factor in typifying the 1.5er, "what is key are the process, the experience, and the socio-cultural environment—specifically, the role of family, education, and community in forming and constructing a 1.5 ethnic identity" (Danico 2004, 5). These foreign-born individuals must have "memories of [ ] and an understanding of the culture" they left behind (Danico 2004, 5), while also internalizing new norms and values in their new home and identifying with both.

The Dagomba 1.5ers, "foreign" born though from the same country, succeeded against all odds and in only one-plus generation. Educational and occupational successes are fundamental to their identity. Many are cosmopolitan, what Appiah (2006, xviii) characterizes as "being a part of the place you were and a part of the broader human community." He tells the charming story of visiting the Asantehene, the Asante king, with his mother. Appiah is from the royal Asante family but he himself lives in

New York City and at the time of writing was teaching at Princeton University. His mother, a British woman whose father Sir Stafford Cripps was a diplomat and politician, met A. K. Appiah's father in London, married him and lived in Kumase until her death fifty years later. There is an empty throne, two columns of people in traditional cloth sitting on stools, with their cloth baring their shoulders out of respect. People are on their cell phones. After some time, a horn player blows the ram's horn, informing those gathered that the Asantehene has arrived. Everyone stands. Once seated there is music making. When it is Appiah's turn to greet the king, he is formally introduced, and he present the Asantehene with bottles of Schnapps and cash. They speak briefly, the Asantehene asks how things are in America, and he informs Appiah he will soon be travelling there to meet with the head of the World Bank (2006, 88–89). As Appiah points out, around the world people are rooted in old traditions, even as they are connected to places at a distance. While Appiah grew up in Kumase, he lives thousands of miles away. But he notes, "like many, when I am there, I feel I both do and that I don't belong" (2006, 91). He does fit and knows how to behave. He also recognizes unfamiliarity and can become comfortable with it.

I have seen this with the Dagomba 1.5ers especially in their split between home in Accra and home up north. They live in Western contemporary homes in in the Accra suburbs. They entertain in living rooms or modern equivalents—for example, a roofed porch or pergola outside by a swimming pool. When spending time in the family house in Tamale or one of the other towns, they socialize in the compound yard or drag chairs outside of the compound. Working in a bank in Accra, the bank president wears a Western suit. At home in Sarnargu, or among family and close friends in his Accra home, he dresses in a *batakari* (a Dagomba smock) or Hausa tunic and pants. The split is not confusing. The activity, behavior, and accoutrements match the locale.

Their cosmopolitanism does not necessarily connote "Western," as there may be "multiple modalities of cosmopolitanism" (Leichtman and Schulz 2012, 2). We may think of cosmopolitanism "as a set of practices, a disposition, and a specific cultural and social condition that allows [individuals] to inhabit the contemporary world" (Leichtman and Schulz 2012, 2). They "live and position themselves in the world in ways that cross borders, involve complex positionalities and experiences, and require a mastery of different registers, languages and forms of interaction" (Schielke 2012, 29). For Appiah, this includes as a Kumase man (although not living there) knowing how being enmeshed in a web of relationships in Kumase translates into a particular status. If one has the social standing which translates into helping someone acquire what he needs, he becomes a patron— "it's a sign that you think he has the status to get things done" (2006, 92).

The Dagomba new-elite fit this characterization. They are individuals who are seeking to be "up-to-date," combining a modern life-style with hometown tradition, leading satisfying lives and enjoying the material fruits of their labor. We might say they are more consumption-oriented, insofar as (Western) consumables are so available and so much a part of the lifestyle to which they aspire. At the same time, even as they live in Western suburban homes and work as professionals, they simultaneously maintain active, affectionate and strong ties to the hometown area. Thus, to a large extent, they have developed dual loyalties. In their lives in Accra, they blend and juxtapose elements of modernity with elements of tradition in modes of doing business, raising a family, and designing new spaces for living.

They help newly arrived countrymen lacking education, money and contacts, to get settled, find work, educate their children. They also influence hometown politics from afar, using tools gained through education and social connections. The patrons have also become the power behind the throne. Succession to chieftaincy, and especially the kingship, has been a flashpoint of conflict for more than a century. This speaks to their continuing attachment to the Kingdom of Dagbon.

Like transnational migrants, their links with the place they come from are not fixed but are reworked from place to place through practice. And like 1.5ers elsewhere, no matter where they go, they remain attached to the place they hail from, the place where they were socialized. Attachment is generated through social practice. This is embodied in the material environment, for example taking in dwellingness and place. Place memory plays a powerful role in "the construction of a social and cultural identity." The Dagomba patrons remember nostalgically the place they grew up, elements in their surroundings, activities they engaged in, and social institutions, in particular chieftaincy. A repository of culture, chieftaincy is located socially and spatially. There are socio-cultural and political dimensions and benefits of migrant communities and their impact on the home community (Danico 2004).

Although they may seem otherwise, members of this group are not unique. Such communities exist throughout the developing world, bi-cultural bridges between the rural and the urban, the illiterate and the professional, the past and the present, creating through their social and spatial positionality unique new communities across differences and distances.

Emigrants from a particular place are often conscious of the need to maintain links with the home country, which "is at the core of the transnational global landscape" (Orozco 2005, 4). Transmigrants, the foreign-born members of these communities, have social and economic links with their home countries which contribute to the development of community both among transmigrants themselves, and over the great distance to the homeland.

Their communities in the host society are often referred to as diasporas. The paradigmatic case is the Jewish diaspora. The narrative implied by this usage often focuses on "negative interpretation of displacement, discrimination, and oppression" (Totoricaguena 2007, 13). But diasporas have been categorized and defined according to various other criteria (e.g. Cohen 1995; Safran 1991; Sheffer 1986). When I speak of diaspora, I follow the definition of Patterson (2006, 1896):

> a people dispersed from their original homeland, a people possessing a collective memory and myth about and sentimental and/or material links to that homeland, which fosters a sense of sympathy and solidarity with co-ethnic diasporans and with putative brethren in the ancestral homeland.

This fits the West African scene, where for hundreds of years, people moved from one area to another, one country to another, creating stranger communities (Pellow 1991, 422; Shack and Skinner 1979). In his book on Hausa communities in Chad, Works (1976, 1) used diaspora as follows:

> Outside Hausaland, emigrants have exploited simultaneously their high degree of cultural unity and their ethnic flexibility, which are the hallmarks of their homeland, to create a new form of community, the outpost.

The territorialization of such communities with networks are bound by shared morality and attachment to home (Mohan 2006), and the creation of a diaspora is contingent on an identity that ties it to home. The Hausa have created a migrant culture throughout West Africa, which is part of a "wider diaspora . . .: the Hausa communities in Cameroon, the Central African Republic, Gabon, Congo, and Zaire . . . " (Works 1976, 2). Their links with the Hausa homeland have encouraged their unique activities, such as long-distance trade and the transport business.

One can also speak of diasporic citizenship and cosmopolitanism. Multiple identities abound in modernizing society, most defying national (internal) boundaries. Transnationals, including internal transnationals, are simultaneously embedded in more than one social group. Migration, obligation and development link the diaspora to the homeland, through kinship, community and the state. The active help of prosperous migrants cements their status. For southern Ghanaians, to gain respect, the relocated person must take care of the extended family and contribute to the welfare of the community. Town investment in the southern hometown communities include infrastructure and beautification. The patron's pursuit of respect is tied to place. The Dagomba patrons are different from the southerners, as their support for the hometown area is far more family or network based. As with communities throughout Ghana, associational life is rich, and for the Dagomba like the Akan, this includes chieftaincy structures.

The Dagomba new elite living in Accra are a diaspora community specifically because they self-identify as a diaspora and both form and maintain, among themselves, networks of sociality and community, while also remaining integrally connected to the homeland in the north (see Sökefeld 2006). Indeed, this group exists and maintains itself because of the homeland and the obligations members of this small group of educated elites feel towards their networks in the north and due to their normative place within the traditional "moral matrix" of power and authority (Schatzberg 1993). They constitute a community with critical mass, outside of the homeland, whose members embrace a solidarity with and affection for the hometown area, but a diaspora nonetheless, located *within* Ghana (Pellow 2011). Elite Dagomba have belonged to diaspora associations, their affiliations linked to internal disagreement—not with Ghanaian society as a whole, not with Dagomba as a whole, but to class, gate and chiefly succession. Their diaspora is largely a collection of social (sub) units, constituting one node in a network of obligation and responsibility that ties it to the north.

I propose, in short, to lower the target zone of migration from trans-*national* to trans-*regional*, as Abner Cohen (1969) has done for the Hausa network of communities in Nigeria but outside of Hausaland. Thus, like the Yorubaland Hausa, I view the Accra Dagomba as living in a diaspora. Members of this diaspora fit the category "1.5 generation." I purposefully reconceptualize the 1.5 perspective, applying it to the Dagomba new elite: namely, a sub-national diaspora group, which is a migrant community. It is made up of cosmopolitan elites, is engaged in the process and experience of globalization, but it is located *within* the same nation from which the members originate and continue to identify and engage with, and indeed some members have returned to, their home community.

While educational and occupational successes are fundamental to their identity, Dagomba 1.5 status is more than that. Each of this group of elite men and women has gone through a "process" whereby they "became" 1.5ers: growing up and getting their basic education in one place, establishing themselves in a qualitatively very different place, and nurturing split loyalties. This is typical of Ghanaian internal migrants generally: even though they may have gone through a life change, they have also actively maintained strong ties to the hometown area. Thus, to a large extent they have developed dual loyalties.

Like others throughout the global south, the Dagomba internal transmigrants both straddle and serve as a bridge between the rural, impoverished and underserved, and the urban, privileged and cosmopolitan. Unlike migrants to the United States, their adaptation is easier in a very important way, that of language: "culturally pervasive multilingualism that involves a high degree of individual participation is one of the most distinctive characteristics of urbanism in West Africa" (Dakubu 1997, 22).

Multiple Modernities

An important element in their 1.5 becomingness, and indeed their spatial relocation, is the Dagomba new elite's engagement with modernity. While modernity is a vague term, with many meanings and a vast literature, generally it "serves to draw our attention to long-term processes of social change, to the multidimensional yet often systematic interconnections between a variety of cultural, political and economic structures" (Felski, quoted in Hodgson 2001, 3). It refers to modes of social life or organization that emerged in Europe as a product of the Enlightenment, an eighteenth-century intellectual project to demystify knowledge and rationalize relationships and modes of thought. It set out to use science in particular to develop technological innovations and free people from "irrational practices," reorder the built environment to save time, create efficiencies, and through material and social forms to change people's perceptions and behavior. This is not true of traditional design or designers/builders. They have not sought to change the built environment. If anything, they wanted to express and reinforce collective understandings.

Yet the traditional-modern binary is far too simplistic. For years, Africanists have worked to negotiate this, attempting to counter the knee-jerk association of "tradition" with indigeneity and "modernity" with Europeanization, as there are continuities between the two (see for example Appiah 1992; Ferguson 1999; Mudimbe 1988; Piot 1999). When a Dagomba villager leaves his home up north for the city in the south, he does not dispose of his identity or kinship connections. He does not forget hometown festivals or ignore obligations of a family member's death. Nor does he dispose of material elements, such as clothing for ritual occasions or utensils for cooking. He amalgamates the traditional and the modern. While they are different, one cannot contrast them sharply.

Modernity carries a Western bias (Giddens 1990, 174; Menon 2001), because it is typically associated with structures that have their roots in specific characteristics of European history; indeed, considering modernity "less a historical condition than a political project, whose aim has always been to center the West and marginalized the rest" (Piot 1999, 173), the modern comes in a variety of forms, not simply Western (Tsing 2005). Moreover, non-Western societies have not received modernity in identical ways. "Multiple modernities" (Hodgson 2001, 7) have been produced by the fusion of different colonial traditions with indigenous traditions and newer global forms, "the continual reinterpretation of the cultural program of modernity . . . [and] attempts by various groups and movements to reappropriate and redefine the discourse of modernity in their own new terms" (Eisenstadt 2002, 23; Knauft 2002).

Multiple modernities suggests that "being modern" means different things in different places and to different populations; that cultural programs have been continually constituted and reconstituted in line with actors and movements. While non-Western peoples may struggle to create their own cultural versions of modernity, they improvise culturally and indigenize modernity. And through circular migration, they are part of an "on-going creation of new forms in the modern world Culture of cultures" (Sahlins 2000, 57).

Modernity(ies) is especially evident in the urban context. The African city is what Graeber might call a space of "intercultural improvisation" (Graeber 2008, 289). In the post-Independence period, which stretches from the mid-1950s in West Africa to the early 1990s in Southern Africa, it is the city where changes in subjectivity, status, and lifestyle are most evident. In the African city, as people encounter others from diverse sociocultural backgrounds and experience, they "engage the ideologies and institutions of a so-called modernizing world . . ." (Knauft 2002: 4). Individuals become aware of the world beyond their village or town—through schooling, seeking a better life in cities understood as centers of modernity, and the nation-building efforts of the state (Nyamnjoh 2002, 116). The two locations and sensibilities, while socially and spatially distant from one another, are mutually influencing, embodying what Appadurai terms "tangled modernities" (1996). As among the Dagomba translocal community, many seek to become "up-to-date" in lifestyle and taste, to "appropriate the power and wealth of other places" (Donham 2002, 246) and consumption. Their thoughts and consciousnesses change, and they adapt their practices and their taste in things, indices to a change in their social position (Bourdieu 1984).

Their adaptation represents an African cosmopolitanism which is, empirically, the openness to, acquisition of and use of knowledge gained across sociocultural and spatial boundaries—often boundaries shared with the West, but certainly not restricted to these. Like the Dagara educated elite in the Upper West of Ghana whom Lentz (1994) has written about, their distinguishing mark of self and social involvement is that they straddle modernity. Their aspirational role is in part as mediators between "traditional" and "modern" ways. Among the Dagara, the elite are culture brokers in solidifying ethnic ties. Among the Dagomba, I would argue that the new elite solidify *sub*-ethnic (gate) ties. There is a popular association of cosmopolitanism with the elite. But cosmopolitans need not be elite. Stuart Hall (2008, 347) has observed that historically, there have been different forms of cosmopolitanism and that today, globalization enforces a "'cosmopolitanism from below'," what we might call "vernacular cosmopolitanism": people learning to survive by moving to a new place and engaging in new practices.

The actions and interactions among individual people as well as groups of people across space and time result in the sharing of knowledge and practice across boundaries of difference. Throughout sub-Saharan Africa, people have moved from one area to another for hundreds of years, often living in diasporic communities (Cohen 1969; Works 1976). They form and maintain among themselves networks of community, often feeling connected to a distant or historical homeland. At the same time, by relocating to communities very different from the ones they grew up in, where they are exposed to culturally heterogeneous populations, they are exposed to the lifeways of others, their horizons expand, and their relationships with others widen (Pellow 2011).

In Ghana, the hometown area is the source of a primal identity, kinship, community, and while there may be a gulf between the hometown residence and a "cosmopolitan home" elsewhere, there is often an interdependence between the two. In the "cosmopolitan home," people produce new creations, local adaptations to the modern. I call these cultural hybrids. They are creations of mixed ancestry in all realms, from the aesthetic and symbolic to the behavioral. Cultural hybridity matters, because it can produce social, political, and economic conditions for cultural reflexivity and for change (Werbner 1997).

My use of hybridity does not imply a kind of enlightened diversity, oppositional behavior or a way to describe developing countries with unsophisticated tastes, but rather connotes those who have learned from contact with different social, cultural, and geographically located populations. As Werbner has written, "the history of all cultures is the history of cultural borrowing" (1997, 15). Hybridity "contributes to the understanding of mixing cultural phenomena, regardless of their origins, and refers to the transformation of objects, values and cultural institutions . . ." (Hahn 2012, 27). It is constituted by artifacts, practices and people/groups. The item or practice itself may or may not remain unchanged, but its transferal into another context, with differing cosmologies and local agency, produces its hybridity. And globalization matters. Western goods, for example, constitute a cluster with appeal. In nineteenth century South Africa, Christian converts appropriated Western clothing but wore them differently than the Europeans they were copying (Hahn 2012).

As I observed for modernity, *"locales of encounter* particularly favorable to cultural exchange, and this hybridization, are the metropolis, the port and the frontier" (Werbner 1997, 19). This is what I found among the Dagomba new elite.[2] In Ghana, it also speaks to those I have called cosmopolitans—intellectually and aesthetically open to divergent cultural experiences and able to make their way into other cultures (Hannerz 2005, 201).

African cosmopolites do far more than embrace foreign aspects of culture and politics; they also express innovative identities and belongingness. While we can argue that s/he who is usually taken to be the cosmopolitan African may have been educated in Europe or elsewhere in the non-Western world and thus is affected by particular traditions from abroad, we must also acknowledge that s/he is simultaneously tied to the traditions into which s/he was socialized, themselves products of deep historical interconnection. Connections are made, continuity experienced, modernity negotiated (De Brujin et al. 2001) across a multitude of internal and external boundaries of difference and rootedness. They blend and juxtapose elements of modernity with elements of tradition, expressing cultural hybridity through alternative or vernacular modernities in modes of doing business, raising a family, designing new spaces for living (Knauft 2002).

Most members of the Dagomba new elite who were born and bred in the homeland area and became professionals migrated south, primarily to Accra. Like other members of Ghana's urban elite, they have embraced modernity—in the aesthetics of their lifestyles and of their everyday life. Their social relations are embodied in goods (Mauss 1990[1950]), a materiality that is also achieved through houses built and occupied. Within their respective sociocultural context, the changes in house style carry positive status, reflecting positively on the homeowner. For example, these Dagomba, as members of the professional elite, move into houses that are "new spaces of transaction" and configure "a new 'place' for places" (Simone 2001, 16). The spheres of activity delineated in the spatial layout embody orientations and sensibilities, which can constitute a mixture, not always easy, "of external imposition and local redeployment of selective appropriations of that imposition" (Simone 2001, 18; see also Coquery-Vidrovitch 1991) along with spatial elements of traditional sensibilities and orientations. So just as Zambian villagers are not complete prisoners of Ferguson's "localism" (1999) as they open up to a wider world, the Dagomba urbanites I am writing about have not thrown out all northern traditions and materialities even as they have taken on cosmopolitan ways.

These urbanites, like other transplanted newcomers, have imported elements of Western modernity, both material and sociological. But while they may showcase them—for example the furnishings in their contemporary homes—they may often also sidestep these modern elements in favor of the "traditional," which is core to who they are. Bourdieu asserts that "taste classifies" (1984, 6), that the system of classification generates "practices adjusted to the regularities inherent in a condition . . . it generates the set of 'choices' constituting life-styles, which derive their meaning, i.e. their value, from their position in a system of oppositions and correlations" and with a change in social position, taste "commands the practices objectively adjusted to these resources" (Bourdieu 1984, 175). The new elite to some extent are copying from the new locale, exhibiting what they understand as "tasteful" or "modern" or whatever it is that they aspire to. It is a kind of sympathetic magic: if so and so has a garage and he appears to belong to a higher social group, then if I build a garage, I too can be a member of that class.

The Dagomba new elite merge their new social status and connection in a very different world than the one from which they hail, and they wear the mantle of "patron." They are not chiefs, a hallowed role in traditional society; they are not *tindamba* (sing, *tindana*, custodians of the land). They do not wield the power of chief or *tindana*, both of which are "communal political leadership positions sanctified by cultural mores and values" and carry legitimacy (Manboah-Rockson 2007, 6), but they are often in the position of making chiefs and supporting the *tindana* in their connection to the land. They represent a new form of advisor with access to a new kind of resources—new social connections, urban cosmopolitan linkages—which they link to the old. In one respect, they are not completely new: someone like Ibrahim Mahama has played the advisory and king-maker role. Mahama is a maternal grandson of Ya-Na Andani III and a powerful traditional elder. He is also a Tamale lawyer, who served as Joint General Secretary of the NAL (National Alliance of Liberals), was elected to parliament in the August 1968 election and was appointed Commissioner for Information by Prime Minister Kofi Busia. After the coup that overthrew Busia's administration, Mahama was expelled and became directly involved in chiefly politics, going to work for Ya-Na Andani IV. People listened to him and he gained power, becoming the lawyer of the murdered king, Yakubu Andani II (who was his nephew). Over the years he has been involved in political brokering, his influence legendary. The lead-up to the choice of a new Ya-Na in 2019 produced two Andani factions: Andani One are the supporters of the current Savelugu chief (the former Kampakuya-Na, Regent of Dagbon) and Andani Two are the supporters of Ibrahim Mahama and the man selected as Ya-Na, the former Savelugu-Na). Thus Ibrahim Mahama's patronage continues to matter.[3]

The new patrons are different. While their position fits a well-worn model, they have created new rules for themselves. Patronage is integral to the social organization of societies throughout West Africa, where authority is based "on a complex and largely unarticulated moral matrix" that pivots on the balance between patron and client or on the "image and language of father and family" (Schatzberg 1993,451–52). Elites, such as the Dagomba described here, acquire status through multiple "registers of power" that allow them to "achieve bigness" (Lentz 1998, 48). In the case of the Dagomba new elite, the common avenue they have taken to "bigness" has been education, and their educated status, related as it is then to their economic and professional success, allows them to act as patrons to their network of clients in the north.

They are instrumental in the construction of a new Dagomba power structure. Perhaps most significantly, they wield their power and influence from a distance.. In some cases, their distance from Yendi and other Dagomba towns, in combination with their connections, is their power. Certainly for all, it is their education and mobility that provide cachet. They are what is known as opinion leaders. Their opinions vary: some are political, some about chieftaincy, some religious. Iliasu Adam, a former journalist, speaks of Tamale leadership as layered among the three areas, each of which is backed up by different constituencies/structures (November 9, 2005).

These patrons wield authority and enjoy favor and respect, and some have gone into politics. The reinvention or reworking of ethnic loyalties is part of the political mobilization of regional support to gain advantage in the state politics (Nyamnjoh and Rowlands 1998). In a country where the hometown figures large in the collective imagination, the members of this group also maintain strong ties to the people of and the place from which they hail. National politics has also made the hometown or region of origin an important power base for urban politicians (Gugler 2002), possibly altering its significance through privileges accruing from the patronage. The extent to which such urban elites (patrons) play a significant role in defining a regional identity for their home area depends on the resources they bring with them and their ability to mobilize followers (clients). The home region of Dagbon houses some of the poorest of the poor, and while this northern elite cohort has not contributed much to the transformation of their respective hometowns, they are patrons to their deprived brothers and sisters. Their patronage is largely that of the "social capital of loyalties" (Daloz 2003, 280) at the kinship/individual-based level. Some people come to them who they do not know but who have been referred to them by someone in the network. They are big-men in a region where patron-client relations are core to social organization. They accrue status while dispensing favors within personal networks.

Throughout West Africa urban-rural connections are ongoing: the rural pole provides social security for urbanites, while the urbanites function as a bridgehead for the village to the outside world (Geschiere and Gugler 1998; Lentz 1994). The patrons use symbols, rituals and rhetoric (sometimes customary, sometimes newly invented) to coordinate action beyond the local level, while also connecting with the central government (Kertzer 1988). Their attachment to the hometown area, as is the case elsewhere in West Africa, is reinforced by continuing urban–rural connections (Geschiere and Gugler 1998). As with transnational networks, links between the North and South are not fixed but are reworked from place to place through practice (Carter 2003). All of these individuals still have family homes in the Northern Region, and most have built a separate home in the north as well (or at least have a plot to build on in the future). Most travel periodically to the north; some say they will return there in retirement.

The relation between urban elites and their home areas can be marked by a mixture of sentimentality and jealousy, given the blatant inequality that exists (Geschiere and Nyamnjoh 1998). But for the Dagomba new elite the sentimental attachment is often paramount. Dr. Ramatu Alhassan is an agricultural economist, who was chair of her department at The University of Ghana when I met her. Professor Alhassan's family is still in Dagbon. She maintained (enacted) her ties by taking her children to visit during vacations. Some discharge their commitment to their hometown community through work. Lawyer Mohammed Mumuni, the previous Minister of Foreign Affairs, went back to Tamale after law school and opened a practice there. Huudu Yahaya, a prominent NDC politician, fulfilled his commitment, initially as the NDC (National Democratic Congress) regional minister for the north. Others travel between Accra and the north for business, for marriages and funerals, and for holidays. Some vote in the hometown rather than in Accra. Networks constitute and sustain diasporas generally, and this is true of the diaspora between Dagbon and Accra. When family members or close friends in Dagbon celebrate life cycle events, individuals travel from Accra to attend. The annual festivals—*Damba*, *Bugum*, and the two *Eid* celebrations—are special attractions. Damba commemorates the birthday of the Holy Prophet of Islam. Celebrants engage in prayers and fasting, and they process on horseback, amidst drumming and dancing. Bugum, or the Fire Festival, performed in commemoration of the dead, is observed on the tenth day of the lunar calendar. It is said to be a Remembrance Day, performed in commemoration of the deceased. In the evening, participants make their way to the Ya-Na's residence with bundles of grass. They are served some food, and then the elders light the bundles of grass. Amidst drumming and dancing, people go to the village outskirts and throw away their bundles of fire (Seyire 1968). Each of these festivals is a celebration that draws the diasporans back to their hometown, to share in the very celebrations that most identify the Dagomba in the north. Damba had also been performed annually in Accra, but after the Ya Na's murder, the community fell apart and the celebration was put on hold.

Life-cycle events (births, weddings, and funerals), which also brought the members of the small Dagomba diaspora together, were celebrated separately by members of the two gates during the seventeen-year interval. One obvious form of connection among and between the Dagomba is marriage. Most Dagomba I spent time with are married to other Dagomba. Both spouses are members of the 20 percent minority of literate people in Dagbon, and an intricate network of other marital links connects their two families. Examples of intramarriage among these Dagomba proliferate (see Chapter Five). To some extent, the Abudu–Andani schism caused by the Ya-Na's murder had for some, resulted in divorces, but even this schism further highlights the importance of Dagomba identity among those in the diaspora, as its very real effect on their social reality is a clear sign of their attachment to the clan division in the north. The basic pattern of the connection has been that of the rural pole providing social security for urbanites and the urbanites functioning as a bridge to the outside world for the village, a mutually reinforcing pattern (Geschiere and Gugler 1998; see also Lentz 2000 on Upper West elite local interests). This pattern is consistent with norms and values of the big man and relationships of reciprocal obligation prominent throughout West Africa.

In these networks, the elite play the very specific role of patron and have very clear responsibilities in that role. They play their part within the moral matrix of authority, into which their relatively new avenue to power, Western education, has been incorporated. In this way, even as educated and cosmopolitan professionals living in Ghana, they are constrained by what Mikael Karlstrom calls "a social matrix of substantive reciprocities" (2003, 68) or what Michael G. Schatzberg (1993, 452) describes as the failure of the father to provide.

As much as these elite form a diaspora community in the south, they also form one node of a translocal Dagomba community, spanning the distance and difference between the north and the south. As successful professionals, with a new kind of symbolic capital, they have become a new kind of patron to those in the north. All of my informants still have family in their hometowns, and as the hometown children mature, more and more are tapping into the Dagomba diaspora to help with schooling. The elite therefore support various people from Dagbon and act as a bridge to later success. Dr. Yahuza Gomda, the nuclear veterinarian, cares for the son of a friend as well as the boy's orphaned friend. His elder brother's son is also currently living with him while going to school. The house of Dr. Iddrisu, the neurosurgeon originally from Yendi, is often the first stop for young Dagomba men who come to Accra from the north in search of opportunity. He has educated all of the children of his assistant, who is a tailor but spends Mondays at the hospital running interference for the doctor when his countrymen come for help and advice.

Their pattern of patronage is consistent with understood social norms and expectations in Ghana, where "success or failure does not just depend on whom you know but also on notions such as what positions are held and with whom there is a connection" (Hanson 2005, 1292). The patrons themselves have new linkages and they have also created new rules for themselves. In Accra, they and their connections in the professional community in the south assist Dagomba newcomers in their attempts to move toward future goals, demonstrating that social relations and networks are essential assets.

The Study Schematic

This study follows the creation and evolution of a new elite in Ghana, a bridge generation, through their multi-sited experience as they have relocated: across space, time, levels of education, cultural openness, economic development and society. I've organized this book to follow the developmental life-cycle of the central characters in this study, applying the theoretical approach(es) that fit as I set out to delineate their remarkable routes.

Chapter 1 lays out the context within which these men and women were raised, particularly the inequities of socioeconomic development that they experienced. I begin with a narration of the Kingdom of Dagbon, its founding, and the core institutions of chieftaincy and custodianship of the land. Since gate identity has become so paramount to the Dagomba, I then lay out the history of how it has become embroiled in Ghanaian State politics. The British Colonial Administration set the path for the north and thus its peoples into the post-colonial period, and I deal with both, in terms of physical and social development. Chapter Two depicts the childhood home—the immediate locale, institutions of Dagomba life, the compound and family and kinship. Here we hear echoes of the nostalgia for a time and place past. The focus of Chapter Three is education—where individuals went to school, the trajectory of getting there and how family on the one hand and national politics on the other impacted their efforts and successes. This chapter in particular illustrates the role of serendipity in the lives of individuals that led to their (accidental) success. Chapter Four considers the careers chosen, examining them in terms of domains of specialty and musing about the transfer from traditional status to modern success. The in-betweenness of this generation is the focus of Chapter Five, in terms of their provenance and the new place, the difference in spaces they have created and behaviors they have adapted. Whether Abudu or Andani, they hail from the same towns and experience attachment to home. They are patrons to family and friends of family. And Chapter Six spells out the primal home attachment and how the chieftaincy solidifies that attachment—why it matters and what happens when it shatters, what happens to the community of dislocated patrons, who no longer share a communal bond, even as they are all invested in the hometown, albeit from afar. The Epilogue draws the tale together, through the royal funerals of the two former Ya-Nas and the installment of Ya-Na Mahama Abukari II.

NOTES

1. This contrast between British and African construction of space is significant throughout Africa.
2. It is no less true of other groups relocating and changing. My focus, however, is on members of the relocated Dagomba.
3. I spoke at some length with Henry Kaleem (March 13, 2013) and Iliasu Adam (March 18, 2013) about the Dagomba power brokers. While Ibrahim Mahama is Andani, he is a very controversial figure even among members of that gate.

CHAPTER 1

Dagbon in Context

> At the overlord's place [in Yendi], we all come from a single cousin, who was Gbewa . . . Naa Gbewa's father was called Kpogonumbo. Kpogonumbo's father was called Tohadzie, The Red Hunter. Kpogonumbo took a wife called Soyini and gave birth to Gbewa. Then Gbewa too gave birth to his sons. Gbewa gave birth to Sitobu. Sitobu also gave birth to Naa Nyagsi.
>
> —Da Tchwuma Baba Fuseini Lu Na, September 26, 2005

More than half of the population of northern Ghana live in Dagbon, the region. The Dagomba (originally Dagbamba) people speak Dagbani. The origins of the Dagomba people and their chieftaincy are collectively held memories told in the "drum history"—recitations, like that above, are done to the accompaniment of drumming by the chiefs' praise-singers. It is through the drum chant, "solemnly and liturgically recited from time to time" (Agyekum 2002, 567) that the history is preserved. Some were recited to me by Baba Fuseini, the Dagomba chief genealogist (*lu na*) of Tamale in northern Ghana. It is he, and his genealogist colleagues, who are the keepers of the flame. They help provide the anchor to place that keeps the Dagomba people, especially those who live afar, attached to Dagbon the place, its history and customs. The place is inhabited, in memory and attachment, providing collective identity for the Dagomba at home as well as those who live afar.

The tales told, the memories elicited, and the practices maintained, sustain and reinforce patrons' attachment to the hometown areas. They may be remembered differently, understood differently, by different people. Even if they all remember an event or its telling, they may not interpret it in the same way. Social meaning is relational. Meaning is generated by communality—it is tied to believing others. Thus, it is never fixed or settled—it can be ambiguous or undone in another circumstance (Gergen 1994). As we consider Dagomba society, the mutability of peoples' interpretation of its customs and practices, what matters, who is eligible for what, criteria for advancement, and such, is critical. Clearly the positionality of an Andani man versus an Abudu man can influence his interpretation of Ya-Na Mahamadu's de-skinment or the Gbonlana's decision to hold his own Fire Festival. Was either based on historical precedent (see Comaroff and Comaroff 1993) or is it a function of how we read history and its basis for ritual? Or again, is it an invention of tradition? As Hobsbawm so memorably wrote (1983, 1) "'traditions' which appear or claim to be old are often quite recent in origin and sometimes invented." They instill values and norms, implying continuity with the past. The invention itself "is essentially a process of formalization and ritualization, characterized by reference to the past . . ." (Hobsbawm 1983, 4). The routine enactment of traditions or rituals may constitute "the totalizing moments when kings or chiefs, presidents or priests, may (re)make history by their actions" (Comaroff and Comaroff 1993, xviii). These are enabled by communality, read by the community(ies) in particular ways. Indeed, the tale of the Red Hunter can be said to be "sustained by nostalgia for an idealized past that is symbolically dissociated from a troubled present" (Kaspin 1993, 34). As I write in Chapter Six, the chieftaincy or kingship no longer carries the sway it once did. And yet to most of those I spoke with, the office (and its traditions) matters greatly—it is an anchor, a symbol, and it validates the coherence of the group.

The Dagomba also, like groups throughout the colonial empire in Africa, were subject to the invention of new tradition by the British. For example, William Jones, Chief Commissioner of the Northern Territories, and the British administration, regarded chieftaincy as "the only truly legitimate 'tribal institution' and made it the principal element of indirect rule in the Northern Territories" (Talton 2003, 196). Because the Konkomba, a northern group, are acephalous and have no chiefs, they were subjugated to the Dagomba *nas*, enforceable by colonial law. H. A. Blair, appointed District Commissioner to Western Dagomba in 1929, spoke fluent Dagbani and was very knowledgeable about Dagomba culture and history. Blair, "particularly intent on restoring the authority of the Ya-Na" (Staniland 1975, 86), convened a conference of elders and youth in Yendi in November 1930, which produced the Dagomba Constitution. The 1930 Constitution empowered a four-man Selection Committee to select a new Ya-Na and tied the selection to soothsaying as a central event. One of the provisions made clear that election to Dagomba chieftainship does not exist. The selection was made by consensus. Then, in 1948, some of the first educated elite Dagomba agitated to change the actual ritual for selecting a new king and chiefs. A group of them, who were Abudu, "pushed through the State Council of Dagbon on May 12, 1948 a change in the rules of succession to the throne, the 'skin' of Yendi, to make it a matter of election by a committee of chiefs and elders rather than, as in the past, a choice by specially consulted oracles" (MacGaffey 2006, 82). The Committee added on seven divisional chiefs and expanded the four-man traditional Selection Committee—which the 1930 Constitution endorsed—to an eleven-man committee. This produced a mutually rewarding interaction between the British administration and some Dagomba elite, the expanded membership made up of divisional chiefs, who were on the payroll of the British government. And now, if consensus was not reached, the decision was to be made through election (Bolaji 2016). The 1948 succession was critical—"creating confusion that has lasted up to today" (Issa Naseri September 28, 2005)—in that it was a radical change in the selection process (for a very conservative-minded society), Different groups interpret these actions differently. As the Ya-Na traditionally elected sub-Divisional Chiefs, the Andani felt the 1948 change took away this right (Staniland 1975, 122). Abudu, on the other hand, interpreted this as just formalizing consultation with senior chiefs which formerly was done in private.

In this chapter, I lay out in a scalar manner the cultural and political elements that historically disadvantaged the Dagomba I spent time with, their families and friends and the locale itself. I orient the reader by beginning with the uneven development that was set in place by the British during the colonial period. Much of this determined the opportunity structure and its correlation with place, and how authority, also spatialized, came to be recognized, ignoring old structures and creating new ones. One of the oldest, land custodianship, continues to matter even as chieftaincy was given precedence. The kingdom of Dagbon and its political traditions include chieftaincy, but they are also complicated by the clan (gate) structuring of succession. I conclude with Dagbon's resultant post-colonial lag. The chapter delineates some of the forces at work that thwarted the possibilities of social, economic, professional success for the Dagomba but that the new elite in fact overcame.

Uneven Development, the North

Saaka (2001, 1) argues that while one can describe Northern Ghana, and specifically Dagbon, in terms of its geography and climate, the way in which "Northern Ghanaians perceive themselves and are often perceived by other Ghanaians has very little to do with geography, common ethnicity, or even shared cultural norms." Rather, the actuality of northern Ghana as Ghana's problem area is largely due to its lag in economic development (Dickson 1968). In Ghana "[t]here is unevenness to the geography of wellbeing and access to basic services" and, indeed, it has been estimated that as much as 90 percent of the Upper West and Upper East regions live in poverty (Grant and Nijman 2003, 475–476). The southern region, largely Accra, has been the beneficiary of developmental projects and increased investment (Grant and Nijman 2003, 477–78). As a result, Accra has grown extensively (Yeboah 2001) and is today a cosmopolitan administrative center, with an international airport, an increasing number of four-star hotels, an outward-looking Western ethos that is welcoming to foreign companies, a teaching hospital, the country's first university, highly reputed secondary schools, law offices, and architectural firms.

The Greater Accra Region, which incorporates the city of Accra, is today the most economically comfortable region in the country: in 1998 per capita income in Greater Accra was 932,000 Ghanaian cedi ($396.59). By comparison, the Northern Region was less than one quarter of that, or 210,000 Ghanaian cedi ($89.36) (GSS 2000; Osei-Fosu 2008). Between 1987–88 and 1998 this kind of income inequality increased massively in Ghana (Cogneau and Mesple-Somps 2008, 11, 14).

This resulted from the British administration's pursuit of a deliberate policy of neglect that has been the bane of the region ever since. Some have argued that this in part was due to lack of resources. But in fact, "prior to colonial conquest, the North had been at the heart of 19th century trade routes and food production" (Plange 1979, 4). Dagomba, like the other territorially defined states of Gonja and Mamprussi, was drawn into the orbit of the great Asante Empire between 1700 and 1750 when Asante expanded northwards to capture the trade in slaves and gold to the coast and kola nuts to the Sokoto Caliphate. Much has been written about the rise and fall of the Asante Empire (Claridge 1915; Agbodeka 1971; McCaskie 1972; Wilks 1975). I include a brief reprise, as it affected the Dagomba.

By the beginning of the eighteenth century, Asante pre-eminence over the Gold Coast was exemplified by the unitary state, presided over by the Asantehene. Access to European traders on the coast and Denkyira gold enabled them to buy guns and slaves. The first invasion of the Dagomba occurred in 1744–45, leading to Dagomba acknowledgment of Asante overlordship (Wilks 1975). In the early 1770s, the Asante imposed tribute upon them. While much of the eighteenth century was characterized by expansionist wars, by the end, commerce replaced warfare. The Asante state became increasingly complex, and its command over and mediation of access to wealth gave it authority (McCaskie 1983). Bowdich's map of greater Asante published in 1819 shows an empire that stretches from Yendi in the north (Dagomba and its trade links) all the way to the coast in the south, with Kumase as the pivot point (Wilks 1975, 45).

In his characterization of Asante overrule in Dagomba, Capt A. H. C. Kenney-Herbert writes ". . . Yendi was a vassal kingdom, and, moreover, the Ashantis were able to keep their vassal states in very real subjection..." (quoted in Wilks 1975, 64). When the Asante invaded southern Fante country on the coast in 1807, it brought the Asante into conflict with the British, which played out in a series of political and military encounters (Claridge 1915; Agbodeka 1971).

British political influence and economic power grew, undermining Asante stability. In 1876, an important European trade developed between Dagomba, Eastern Gonja and Accra, outside Asante control. British fear of an alliance between the Asante and the forces of Samori, a Muslim leader occupying Bonduku to the west in Ivory Coast and expanding eastward, led them to invade Kumase mid-January 1896. Three days later the Asante surrendered (Wilks 1975; Grischow 2006). The Asantehene Agyeman Prempe I was taken captive by the British, ending 150 years of Asante domination.

Asante's defeat translated into Dagbon political structures losing much of their strength and Yendi losing much of its authority (see Ferguson and Wilks 1970). The British felt compelled to secure its sphere of interest in the Gold Coast's north following the Berlin Conference of 1884, when Britain had negotiated a neutral zone with Germany, which included all of Dagbon and parts of Eastern Gonja (Salaga, Yapei and Daboya) (Cammaert 2016; Grischow 2006). In 1897, the British renamed the "Asante Hinterland" as "The Northern Territories of the Gold Coast." They divided this Protectorate into "three districts for convenience of military command"[1] (Bening 1983, 326). Then in 1898, The British Colonial Administration delineated the Protectorate of Northern Territories as the Northern Territories, having finally secured the region through separate agreements with the French and the Germans. An Anglo-German Agreement (1899) ended the neutral zone, leading to the division of Dagomba, Germans occupied eastern Dagomba, including its capital Yendi, while the British occupied western Dagomba. This marked the beginning of European overlordship in Dagomba.

The first Chief Commissioner of the Northern Territories, Lt. Col. Northcott, had to develop strategies to incorporate territory into the Gold Coast Colony. He pushed for development in the Northern Territories (NT), which included using the land in the NT as a way of raising revenue. In Ashanti and the Gold Coast Colony, concessions were granted by chiefs who received rents, but because the administration assumed large tracts of land in the NT were uninhabited or occupied by people without chiefs, the government appropriated that right. The Governor F. M. Hodgson perceived the NT as unproductive (Bening 1977, 1983), for example declaring that "the trade value of the Northern Territories are not favourable as to their future . . ." (quoted in Bening 1975, 72). Communicating with Joseph Chamberlain, Secretary of State for the Colonies, Governor Hodgson wrote in 1899, "I would not at present spend upon the Northern Territories . . . a single penny more than is absolutely necessary for their suitable administration and the encouragement of the transit trade" (Brukum 1998, 117).

What this meant is that the north and south of what would become Ghana were constituted as two regions with different policies (Bening 1975). In the south, the investment of money and attention paid off; in contrast, "the colonial takeover of the north of Ghana prepared the way for several decades of neglect and stagnation . . ." (Eades 1993, 26). The London Chamber of Commerce also believed that the north was commercially unimportant (Eades 1993)—this despite the potential, for example, of a nascent shea nut industry.

This also meant little investment in infrastructure. There was no good system of transport and m any areas of the north were not accessible. At the turn of the century, the system was human porterage, which was slow and costly. Construction of the Kumase-Tamale road, connecting the south and the north, had begun in 1898. Work stopped for financial reasons after only 96 of the 378 km were completed. In 1919, when F. G. Guggisberg became Governor of the Gold Coast, he recognized the economic potential of the north, and the fact that the Northern Territories were being starved. But the government believed the railroad would never be profitable, whether for transporting people, crops, or animals (Dickson 1968). Because the British government abandoned the construction of the railroad, Guggisberg dropped his support for the NT (Bening 1975).

Soeters makes the interesting argument that the long-term colonial officers in the north developed hostility toward the southern administration because the latter was not interested in spending any resources to develop the north (2012, 95). "A dim view was taken of the feeling that the 'northern interest' had become, as a group isolated from the central administration in Accra" (Soeters 2012, 96). Some have argued that the north lacked the exploitable resources that had attracted private enterprise in the British Gold Coast Colony and Ashanti (Kimble 1963). Because the British were interested in exportable crops, such as the cocoa, oil palm, kola nuts and precious minerals found in Ashanti, they neglected staple crops found in the north. Little training was provided in improved farming techniques.. The distance and transport to the coast was difficult

(Saaka 2001). The British may have promoted cotton growing (instructing the locals and installing a cotton gin and press in Tamale), but they discouraged its commercialization, along with groundnuts and rice, by providing no markets for producers "and conscripting the male into labour gangs for the south" (Plange 1979, 9).

In late 1901, as a result of Colonial Secretary Chamberlain's decree that the British were obliged to develop their colonial possessions, Britain annexed the Northern Territories as a Protectorate of the Gold Coast Colony. While the Dagomba capital of Yendi lost significance, Tamale, which had had little significance in the pre-colonial era, gained worth due to the arrival of colonial rule (the establishment of colonial headquarters there) and the city's linkage to Kumase through the Great North Road (Soeters 2012). By moving their headquarters to Tamale in the early 1900s, the British felt that they were in the "most advanced" part of the Protectorate (Soeters 2012, 21).

Thus, between 1904 and 1929, the only real development was in service of the Administration, not the local people; the economic stagnation of the Northern Territories was a casualty of the economizing of the colonial office—they were averse to putting any money into the area—and the ignorance of the Accra officials (Bening 1977). It is not an exaggeration to say that much of the deprivation in the north resulted from the colonial system of organization on the landscape, with the social, economic, and political hierarchy centralized in the south, complemented by inequalities between the regions in terms of population density, modernization, and residential amenities. British economic policy starved the protectorate of investment. Officials were encouraged to regard the protectorate "as a 'hinterland' rather than as a component part of the Gold Coast in its own right" (Kimble 1963, 533). Local revenues grew slowly in the north, leading the British to limit expenditure to the minimum to maintain rights there (Saaka 2001, 18). Instead, the north became a source of cheap migrant labor and a supplier of food to the south (Antoine 1985; Bening 1972; Kimble 1963; van Hear 1982). In the run-up to independence and later, "the educated elite of the North; and Marxist-inspired authors spoke not only of neglect, but of a deliberate policy of protracted 'under-development', pursued by the colonial government for the express purpose of sustaining in the North a reservoir of labour" (Lentz 2006, 57).

To facilitate the engagement of migrant laborers and public works employees, where chieftaincy did not exist the colonial administration built a system of chiefdoms and established the chiefs as labor contractors. Young northern men were attracted to work in the gold mines and cocoa farms in Ashanti and farther south. The push for the labor flow south meant that the north was robbed of a critical mass of productive laborers, that there was less interest in investing in the north and to keep the northerners working in the south, wages were kept low (Abdulai 2012). By 1917, the administration established an annual supply of about 15,000 northern laborers to the south (Kimble 1963, 42). Initially, the colonial administration feared that permanent migration might arise out of the yearly departure south. It became clear that this would not occur, though some district commissioners did not welcome the new consumer goods that migrants brought home.

As early as 1921, Gov. Guggisberg favored introducing to northern Ghana Indirect Rule, as employed in northern Nigeria. He asserted that Dagomba, Gonja and Mamprussi would become "strong native states." In the Ghanaian version, the Native Authority would consist of a paramount chief or group of chiefs in a confederation. The Native Authority powers came from the government, with chiefs on salary. There would be Native Authority courts. The functioning of the Native Authority would be scrutinized by British officers, so that chiefs would learn to exercise political authority in the context of modern government. This position was fiercely resisted by the British administrators in the north, and the plan did not advance.

On January 3, 1929, the British administrators held a political conference at Tamale to again discuss the advisability of introducing Indirect Rule. They concluded that the Northern Territories were not ready for Native Administration for at least a decade for many reasons, including the lack of educated local staff, insufficient funding for infrastructure, and the preference of people to go south to work for money rather than staying. Despite this, the British introduced Indirect Rule to the Northern Territories later that year. Retirements of British officers in the north in 1930 opened the door to change.

The change in administrative staff included H. A. Blair, the new District Commissioner. Blair was the son of a missionary, an Oxford graduate and spent about ten years in Dagbon. Unlike any of his predecessors, he was fluent in Dagbani and knowledgeable in Dagomba culture and history (Staniland 1975). Blair wanted the authority of the Ya-Na restored, which led him to convene a conference of chiefs and elders at Yendi in November 1930. The acting chief commissioner of the Northern Territories announced that

> it was intended to give "a more particular acknowledgement than... heretofore, to the standing and authority of Chiefs over people; and to clothe them with powers, enforceable by law, which they have not previously exercised." (quoted in Staniland 1975, 86)

They drew up a "constitution" of Dagbon. In 1932, Eastern and Western Dagomba were amalgamated with British headquarters established at Tamale and the Na-ship at Yendi. The Native Authority Ordinance enabled the constitution of Native Authority areas and "'to appoint any chief or other native or any group of natives to be a Native Authority for any area'" (Staniland 1975, 86). But how independent were the chiefs? According to A. W. Cardinall, "the chiefs are practically powerless; they have neither revenue nor authority; they have tended to become mere sergeant-majors through whom the Administration can address the rank and file" (quoted in Ladouceur 1979, 44). Indeed, the chiefs were closely supervised by British officers while political officers treated them as subordinates, and their power could be curtailed by the government (the Crown) "simply by withdrawing recognition from him, as an approved Native Authority" (Staniland 1975, 88).

During the years that Dagbon was split between the east and the west (German and British, respectively), the Dakpema, Tamale's *tindamba* claimed the mantle of Chief of Tamale. Unwilling to relinquish his title (which the British had acknowledged during the English-German split), it was only after he had a stroke that the Gulkpe-Na was reinstated as chief of Gulpekpeogu, a division of Tamale. But his authority never replaced that of the Dakpema. With Dagbon's re-unification in 1920 under Ya-Na Abdulai II, the Ya-Na's authority was reinstated at the peak of authority over all of Dagbon, The Dakpema was subject to the Ya-Na and the Gulkpe-Na, who when traveling with the district commissioner issued instructions in the Ya-Na's name (MacGaffey 2013).

Protectorate lands were declared public land in 1927, so that the government could undertake development projects such as the building of schools and hospitals and foreigners and traders from the south would be prevented from acquiring large plots. Local people, dispossessed of their land, were settled without reference to the traditional custodians, the *tindanas*. Meanwhile, a change in agricultural policy in 1932 meant that the focus would be on improving local farming methods rather than cultivating export crops.

Early nationalists in the south waged a campaign against the north-south division. Northern public servants were afraid to get politically involved, lest they have problems with the government. The United Gold Coast Convention (UGCC), formed in 1947, was the first political movement to bring the north into national politics and a regional branch was opened in Tamale. The UGCC gave way to the Convention Peoples' Party (CPP) under Kwame Nkrumah, but the CPP failed to win over the chiefs because the British convinced them that Nkrumah was hostile to chieftaincy. "But however difficult the CPP must have found it to operate in the North, there is no doubt that it was responsible for the introduction of party politics into the region, and in this way it helped raise the political consciousness of the otherwise dormant population" (Saaka 2001, 146).

It was in national politics, however, that the north's isolation under the colonial administration was most evident. A small educated group formed the Northern Territorial Council (NTC) in 1936. Initially, "the N.T.C. was a 'chiefs' Council which was in line with the long-held British view that if political power in West Africa was to devolve at all, it should devolve to the 'natural rulers of the people', who were the chiefs" (Brukum 1998, 19). Realizing they could not cope with elections, political parties and a legislature, the chiefs gave way to the non-chiefs without a struggle.

After World War II, the colonial authorities saw the desirability of integrating Northern Ghana into national politics. The northerners were hesitant about the time-table for independence and the creation of a unified nation. Their charge was carried by a small, educated elite, mostly Achimota-trained teachers,[2] who were dissatisfied with education in the north. When he became Prime Minister, Kwame Nkrumah did a tour of the whole country and realized that the north-south division could only be dissolved by bettering education in the north, which he spearheaded (see Chapter Three). In late 1949, a constitutional committee, headed by the jurist Mr. Justice Henley Coussey of the Gold Coast High Court, presented its report on the institutionalization of various mechanisms that would help lead the country to self-rule. The Gold Coast Legislative Council asked the NTC to advise it on the Coussey Committee's report on local government as it affected the Northern Territories. They advocated a slower approach to local government reforms than had been recommended by the Coussey Committee, reflecting the policy of isolation, i.e.

> the lack of political consciousness among people of the Protectorate, paucity of educational facilities in the area which accounted for the lack of an educated class and their reliance and satisfaction with chieftaincy as the pivot of Northern administration which the reforms wanted to undermine. (Brukum 1998, 20)

But the reality of the socio-economic neglect of the area had already begun to dawn on the northern elites, which they understood from the attitude of southern clerks and teachers posted to the north. They also figured out that they had little bargaining power and a tenuous identity vis-à-vis the south. Because the northerners had no say in the amalgamation of the Protectorate with the Colony and Ashanti, they wanted their views on independence to be heard. As articulated by the NTC, they felt that independence "should be delayed until such time as the region was on a footing of equality socially and economically with the South" (Brukum 1998, 21). Thus they did not oppose independence, but they wanted the north better developed first so that it would have equal footing with the south. This was underlined by their formation of the Northern Peoples' Party (NPP) in April 1954 to contest the elections.

A Dagomba District Council was set up as part of the Local Government Ordinance of 1951; the British system of Indirect Rule ended in 1952, and the British left Tamale. Upon Independence five years later in 1957, the Protectorate of the Northern Territories of the Gold Coast became Northern Ghana (Staniland 1975).

Custodianship

No matter where one is from in northern Ghana, no matter the ethnic group, the *tindana/tindamba* (referred to in the Introduction) are the custodians of the land and of the earth shrines. They exercise ritual control over the land in every town or village, which also has its god, and it is the *tindana* who knows the ways of the god. They are responsible for passifying the god and engaging in the required sacrifices (Mohammed Tijani, DCE Yendi September 25, 2005). According to A W Cardinall writing in 1920, in addition to other ritual relating to the land, the *tindana* also selects and marks out sites of new compounds (p. 25).

When the Dagombas and Gonjas claim that they are the "landowners," or that "the land on which they reside belongs to 'them,'" the word for "land" may be translated as *"nam"*, that is chieftaincy, or sometimes by *"tindana"* (Manboah-Rockson 2007). The office of *tindana* was the highest office held by the autochthones, the original inhabitants, particularly the Konkombas of Northern Ghana. This office was exercised through a religious role as their authority was ultimately vested in their ancestors; each had authority over a particular area of land and he was often attached to a shrine (Manboah-Rockson 2007). "The *tindana* was the original owner of the land" (Cardinall 1920, 16). Before the chiefs, "We were here," the Dakpema, *tindana* and leader of Tamale,[3] said to me (May 12, 2006).

According to MacGaffey (2012), there are two types of tindanas—those who see themselves as chiefs in their own right and those subordinate to the Ya-Na in Yendi. There is a "primacy" in the office of tindana as relating to farming matters and day-to-day living and management of land matters. "The chiefs, they fear us the Tindanas. They don't know how the lands are performed for long life and prosperity." So declared the Tamale Dakpema (Richard Alhassan May 12, 2006). Moreover, he continued, the whole of Tamale land belongs to me. Nobody dare come to Tamale to play nonsense. They fear me. [And yet, in playing politics] they abuse me—who is the Dakpema, the landowner? And I laugh at them—those particular people die.

Because the Dakpema was not well when I met him—he was elderly and confined to a wheelchair—he rarely left the palace and his activities were abbreviated. In September 2007, he died. One month later his son, Richard Alhassan Iddrisu, was installed as Regent. A much younger man, he was in his occupational prime. He worked as an Extension Cotton Officer, teaching people farming techniques, but he also took seriously the responsibilities attached to his Regency. The Regent elaborated on his father point that while "some people take [the *tindana*] as someone with no value" (June 23, 2008), a *tindana* is like a chief. Thus on Mondays and Fridays he remained at home to hear cases—relating to land, personal and family problems and quarrels.

> I have elders, same as with my father. They help me in judgments—fathers and then elders. Some of my uncles and their brothers, they help—when a case is brought I call them—we sit to judge/solve problems. If it is beyond our abilities [theft, murder] I forward it to the authorities [state]. If from two different jurisdictions, you solve the problem amicably, send a message to their chiefs. Or can bring a case not in your land—you can solve it—you can inform the other chief how you've settled the case for him. (June 23, 2008)

In the north, the office of ritual headship (what had been *tindana*) was assumed by the invaders, the Dagombas, the Gonjas, and the Nanumbas, who brought in chieftaincy, initially in the fifteenth century in western Dagbon, The final conquest of eastern Dagbon was later, in the seventeenth century. In western Dagbon particularly, the invaders killed off the original *tindanas* and usurped their functions. The distinction between, and importance attached to, a *tindana* and a chief evolved as the chief developed into a political head, accelerated by the advent of colonialism (Manboah-Rockson 2007). While in principle the right to dispose of land went to the Ya-Na who passed it on to his divisional and village chiefs, "a complementary relationship seems to have grown up in many places between the old *tindamba* and the new rulers" (Staniland 1975, 15). There was also an attempt to combine the offices of chief and *tindana* because of the support and indulgence of the British and Germans. As I discuss in Chapter Two, the *tindana* have continued to perform as fetish priests and in many places outside of Yendi to oversee land allocation. Before 1957, in northern Ghana, chiefs did not traditionally allocate land. This is no longer the case. The primacy of the *tindana* in the distribution of land to farmers only applies far in the bush, away from the district and regional centers where through government manipulation, chiefs claim this lucrative right.

The Kingdom

As briefly abstracted at the beginning of this chapter, the story of the Dagomba kingdom begins with the mythical Red Hunter, whose great grandson Gbewa founded a kingdom, later divided up by his sons into Mamprugu (Mamprussi), Dagbon (Dagomba) and Nanun (Nanumba). Thus the Mamprusi and Nanumba, together with the Dagomba, are all descended from the same man and constitute the three main Mole-Dagbani states. The Wala, now resident in the Upper West, are thought to be descended from Dagomba and Mamprusi cavalrymen. In his recitation, the *lu na* intoned (September 26, 2005) that it was Naa Nyagsi, son of Sitobu, grandson of Gbewa, who vanquished the local people and their leaders, the *tindanas* (custodian of the land).

Naa Nyagsi replaced the *tindanas* with his own relatives, "turning Dagbon into a single political unit with himself as Ya-Na, king of Dagbon" (MacGaffey 2010, 432). The kingdom of Dagbon itself was established sometime in the late fifteenth century (Staniland 1975; Tamakloe 1931). There have been two kingdoms: sixteen rulers in the first, twenty-two in the second. The sovereignty of the state is vested in the person of the Ya-Na, the king, who is resident in Yendi.[4]

The Ya-Na is commander of the army, is the highest judicial authority and appoints chiefs and elders (Staniland 1975). Before Ghana's independence and the existence of a central government, the Ya-Na had considerable significance. In a conversation with Abdulai Yakubu, a lawyer and businessman, who has written on the Dagomba chieftaincy crisis (2005) and was himself installed as Chief of Vteng in 2015, he said the Ya-Na

> was the very embodiment of Dagbon, such that in the Dagbon state, if you did not agree with him, you had to leave the place, you could not stay in Dagbon and fight the Ya-Na. But as soon as we had a central government, then the politician became the center of power and no longer the Ya-Na. So you could sit in Dagon, disagree with the Ya-Na, fight him . . . even slaughter him, and there would be no problem . . . That tells you how important the place of the Ya-Na is now for them. (November 23, 2005)

Around the year 1700, Ya-Na Zangina converted to Islam. Muslim officials were ensconced in the court at Yendi as well as lesser courts; yet, the political structure was highly evolved before Islam made any substantial impact (Ferguson and Wilks 1970). Thus "the whole has been strangely blended with that of paganism which is still frankly professed by the Ya-Na and the majority of his people" (J. N. D. Anderson quoted in Levtzion 1968, 108). This is apparent in practices such as marriage. So even though the chiefs are at least nominally Muslim, and Islam dictates that a man may have four wives at a time, tradition exceeds religion. When Ya-Na Yakubu Andani II died, he left behind twenty-six wives. Even lesser chiefs have more than four wives at any given time. Salamatu Abdulai claims that her father Yo-Na Abdulai II, chief of Savelugu, had thirty-three wives at one time. Alhassan Andani, Managing Director (CEO) of Stanbic Bank is the son of an important village chief who had eight wives. Alhassan's explanation is culturally based,

> It's been tradition that has held Dagbon together as a unified community for a very long time. If a chief is nominated, various clans and sub-villages will pick their best matings and send them to the chief so the matings can produce an heir to the throne. So in that way, every village was represented in the chief's house. So some of the women [wives] the chief had never seen with his eyes, but once you agree to be chief, it means that if a clan wants you to take their mating, you have to accept it, you cannot reject it. And the only object of that woman is not to come to be a wife but is also representing a clan, is there to reproduce and to represent their interests in the palace. (June 13, 2008)

For the sake of form, when Kampakuya-Na became the Regent of Yendi in 2006, he switched over to practicing Islam, after having been raised in the Catholic Church.

Chiefs and King

In Dagbon, the Ya-Na is the most paramount of chiefs. It is his throne (known as a skin in the north) to which the ambitious royals aspire. Throughout Ghana, the politics, economics and cultures cannot be adequately understood unless traditional authority is taken into account. By the same token, as throughout Africa, difficulties have arisen due to differences between traditional standards of conduct and standards of conduct as regulated by modern law. Moreover, representatives of the new social order have their own ideas "about who should rule the country" (Arhin 1985, 117). In Ghana, hereditary systems of leadership persist, and chieftaincy as established by customary law and usage is guaranteed under the Constitution. The Act of 1971 that defined chief or traditional leader was reaffirmed in the 1992 Constitution, Ch XXII, 270, "The institution of chieftaincy, together with its traditional councils as established by customary law and usage, is hereby guaranteed." And according to Ch XXII, 277, "'chief' means a person, who, hailing from the appropriate family and lineage, has been validly nominated, elected or selected and enstooled, enskinned or installed as a chief or queenmother in accordance with the relevant customary law and usage."

One way of understanding chieftaincy, and why it matters, is to think of it as an institution that constitutes the totality of social life. Given the different groups with interests in that institution, it may be *"differently manipulated according to specific group interests"* (Kuper 1972, 421, my emphasis). Chieftaincy in the Gold Coast (Ghana) goes back hundreds of years, and before contact with the Western world in the nineteenth century and the establishment of the British colonial rule in Ghana and Nigeria, traditional rulers were semi-gods. Chieftaincy is symbolized in southern Ghana by the right to sit on the stool, in northern Ghana on the (sheep) skin. It is an inalienable proprietorship that follows the line of genealogy, as well as other culturally specific criteria. Chiefs have authority over the stool/skin land but are supposed to remain in power only as long as they have the people's support. Even as the *tindana* are the spiritual custodians, the chiefs are also supposed to act as caretakers of "the people's" land, not alienating it from families and groups, the traditional landholders. Politically, the chiefs were over the people, not the place. Yet, land is a factor in social change in the north. The Dagomba and Gonja (as chiefly peoples) claim to be the "landowners" or that "the land is for us". In the past, neither "ever meant 'ownership', in the Western sense, over private property. But this is what is being meant by the chiefly peoples today" (Kirby 2006–07, 99). Traditionally chiefs did not allocate land—they might have overseen boundary disputes but not dispersed land. Today, where land in the urban and peri-urban areas is sought for development, the chiefs of the locales under question must sign off, "and very large sums can pass hands. None of this is done by the force of law but of custom—and . . . even that is without historical precedent" (Kirby 2006–07, 101). But this has meant that chieftaincy, and its resources in the modern world, matters in a new and significant way.

In the north of Ghana, sitting on a "skin" is the concrete symbol of traditional political office (Arhin 1985) and contests for royal "skins"—as potent political symbols (Kertzer 1988)—have been passionate. Chiefly installations and chieftaincy itself have often been the source of conflict. The chieftaincy conflicts in northern Ghana are embedded in and produced by historical and cultural baggage, including complex patterns of religion (Christian, Muslim, animist), local political organization (centralized and acephalous), exogenous political factors such as colonial administrations appointing chiefs where none had existed (Crook 1986; Grischow 1998) and ethnicity (there are over thirty ethnic groups).

A history of ethnic violence throughout the region has defied control by the state (Akwetey 1996, 102). The conflict has included fighting between the Dagomba and the nearby acephalous Konkomba and again with the invading Gonja in the seventeenth century (Saaka 2001; Staniland 1975), and within the Mamprusi (Drucker-Brown 1988–89, 101). In February 1994, a war pitting Konkomba against Nanumba, Dagomba, and Gonja resulted in 1,000 dead and 150,000 displaced (Akwetey 1996). For the past thirty years, inter-ethnic violence has increased, "defying the control of central government," and in 1994, the inter-ethnic fighting in the entire Northern Region resulted in "a full blown inter-ethnic war" (Akwetey 1996, 102). Chiefly installations and chieftaincy itself have often been the source of conflict. For example, chieftaincy may be contested because one group is subordinated to another. And once colonial administrators entered the scene, they too caused problems by appointing chiefs where none had existed before (Crook 1986; Grischow 1998). The Dagomba ya-na succession begins with Ya-Na Yakubu I (1829–1849). He had more than 30 sons, but it was Abdulai (Abudu) and Andani who took over the throne upon their father's death. Since 1856, the rivalry to become Ya-Na and thus sit on the skin, has been between the two gates, Abudu and Andani.

The Ya-Na, the King of the Dagomba, is described as a "lion" (Ferguson and Wilks 1970, 326–69). The sovereignty of the Dagomba state has been vested in the Ya-Na, who oversees a hierarchy of chiefs and appoints chiefs and elders. He is the head of the Dagomba state and the highest judicial authority; he is also "a figure surrounded by rituals of avoidance and deference" (Staniland 1975, 16). Under the Ya-Na are the three provincial chiefs (Karaga, Savelugu and Mion) whose "skins" are the gateway to election to Ya-Na. Below them are twelve divisions of chiefs, and each division consists of villages with their respective chiefs. Thus, everyone living in Dagbon has a local chief. And, like the Ya-Na, they too are involved in Dagomba institutions and rituals.

Dagomba chieftaincy is characterized by conservatism—concern for the past, for hierarchy and for protocol. Seniority, rank and appropriate behavior with respect to rank matter greatly, as does interest in promotion or advance. The skins (chieftaincies) are ranked and chiefly progression is channeled more and more narrowly until one reaches the *nam* (skin) of Yendi. Thus, succession to the Yendi skin is progressive and follows the promotional principle (Ferguson and Wilks 1970), that is, the ambitious man seeks to move through the hierarchically structured chieftaincies. He starts out on minor skins, miles away from whatever and wherever his

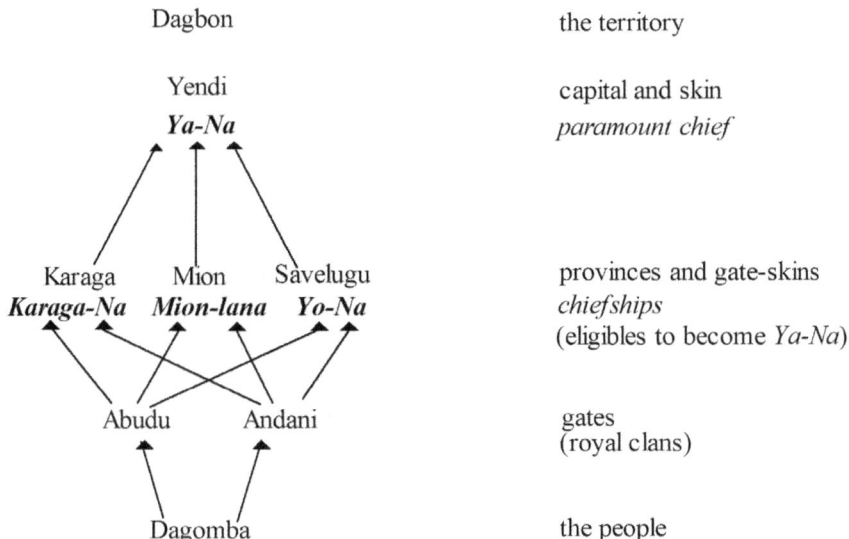

Figure 1.1. The route of succession to Ya-Na (created by Deborah Pellow).

hometown is, and he has no particular loyalty or connection there. Then he moves on (Iliasu Adam June 8, 2004). His goal is one of the three "gate skins," which channel the candidate to the Yendi skin (see Figure 1.1).

The elevation of a new Ya-Na is normally set off by the death of the sitting king,[5] for whom numerous rituals and events must be stage-managed. At the level of the king, the Dagomba distinguish between the funeral and the burial. For a new Ya-Na to be enskinned, the deceased king must be buried. While rituals accompany all funerals, the king's funeral has *royal* elements as well. Both Rattray (1932) and Cardinall (1921) have described the funeral/burial of the Dagomba king, and as the two events normally go together, they do not distinguish between them. So the deceased is bathed with cold water, the body laid on a mat and covered with a cloth. Initially the king's death is kept secret among the elders and ministers of Yendi. Drums are beaten and messengers are sent to inform the important chiefs.

The corpse is carried from the Ya-Na's living quarters; the grave is in the king's compound in a separate room, *yiri kpane*, and in a special hut which he may not enter during his lifetime. The body is carried on a cow that has been slaughtered. "All who have been faithful to the king, or have had no sexual intercourse with any of his wives, touch the animal's blood and rub it on their forehead, or dip a Kola nut in it and chew it. The meat is cooked and eaten" (Cardinall 1921, 90).

The king is buried. His wives gather at the grave, lamenting his death, which they continue each time a chief arrives to pay his respects. There is a day of shaving, when the heads of the wives and the heads of the king's children are shaved. There are other rituals of cooking and eating, of chiefs coming to mark the king's passing. The house over the grave is then knocked down, the ruins are left as is for a year, and it is finally marked by a stone.

These are some of the conditions or criteria that conform to "rules" of tradition—formulae that limit competition but are sufficiently flexible that they leave an element of uncertainty and can be differently interpreted by the two sides to the gate conflict. (While I am abbreviating this considerably, I want to provide context for the most recent chieftaincy conflict in Dagbon but without burying the reader in detail.) The transition from the death of one Ya-Na to the installation of the next has always been stormy and Staniland (1975) ties this to two basic issues of succession: constitutional (who is eligible and who has the authority to decide this) and dynastic (the rotation between the two royal gates). Both of these issues are inscribed in Dagomba protocol. On the selection side, there is the issue of who chooses the king. The customary selection body is composed of four elders of Yendi, 1) Kuga-Na, who is referred to as the kingmaker and whose name means literally "'Chief of the Stool'" (Rattray 1932, v. 2, 570). Kuga-Na is Vice President of the Dagbon Traditional Council and does not belong to any gate—he plays the role of custodian (Kuga-Na September 25, 2005). 2) Tuguru Nam, Kuga-Na's vice; 3) Kpati-Na and 4) Gomli.

The traditional selection involves divination. By custom, only the elders took part in the divination, which involved sacrifice to the spirits of former kings. In principle, it was the latter who chose the new king, although in practice many diviners might be consulted, the elders sometimes shopping around until they could be sure of obtaining an oracular declaration favorable to the candidate they actually preferred. Certainly they were seen as responsible for finding a chief with appropriate qualities (Staniland 1975, 23).

In 1947, not long before the death of Ya-Na Mahama II, an Andani, the British Chief Commissioner received a petition signed by an anonymous Dagomba citizen. He requested changes to the Dagomba Constitution, "so as to give more scope to educated royals, and particularly to royal grandsons" (Staniland 1975, 121), because "Dagomba was suffering from the incompetence of its senior chiefs, a condition made worse, he said, by Ya-Na Mahama's tendency to appoint only members of the Andani gate" (Ibid.). A State Council, on March 2, 1948, composed of Sub-Divisional Chiefs), agreed that eligible candidates should stand for election with the head of each family casting a secret vote. The State Council in 1947 in effect abolished a major rule of the 1930 Constitution, "the rule that kings were chosen, after divination, by a small committee of elders" (Staniland 1975, 122). This threw the decision-making into the hands of the educated few. Thus there are two roads to the king's selection. In the question of who is empowered to make the selection of a new Ya-Na, the Andani insist it is the Kuga-Na, his elders and the soothsayers, Abudu claim it is the Selection Committee (of 1948).

Both the traditional and new system of finding a good candidate is complicated by various stipulations, only direct sons of previous Ya-Nas can attain that office (thus, a son cannot rise further than his father). In an interesting way, place matters, eligibility for the kingship is based upon having sat on one of three "gate" skins (the skin of the town that is the "gate" to the kingship), each of which is in a town by that name. Karaga is fifty-three miles to the north and west of Yendi, Savelugu seventy-eight miles west and north of Yendi, and Mion just nine miles west on the Yendi-Tamale Road. According to "drum history," it was Na-Yiri, the Mamprussi king as the ultimate arbiter, who determined that to prevent quarrelling, the Dagomba limit the range of eligibles to the Yendi skin to those occupying the three divisional chieftaincies or so-called gate skins (see Figure 1.1). The Regent, the Gbonlana, applies as a matter of formality, "even though he is entitle [sic] only to the skin of the one who, out of the three mentioned first becomes the Ya-Naa" (personal papers, J. S. Kaleem, Zobogu-Na, the late Nyankpa-Lana). In other words, the regent, who has not sat on a gate skin, is not necessarily eligible for elevation to Ya-Na, but is also not ineligible.

While the alternation between gates is said to be the rule, it has not always been practiced. Mahama III, an Abudu who was Ya-Na between 1948 and 1953, was succeeded by Abdulai III, also an Abudu. There is also a question as to whether a Ya-Na can be de-stooled. Darimani, a Ya-Na in the late nineteenth century, was both promoted and deposed in 1899 (Staniland 1975). At the constitutional conference in 1930, when the Dagomba chiefs in attendance were asked what would happen in the event of the abdication or deposition of a Ya-Na, they responded that both are "Tabu" (Duncan-Johnstone and Blair 1930, 32, quoted in Bolaji 2016, 283). Thus, there was no accommodation for a Ya-Na's removal. Yet Ya-Na Mahamadu was de-skinned in 1974.

There is also the fact of performing the funeral, which is separate from the burial. Neither Mahamadu, who died in 1988, fourteen years after he was de-skinned, nor Na Yakubu, who was murdered in 2002, had a royal funeral at the respective time of interment. When Mahamadu died, he was buried in the Katin-duu, the royal crypt. The then Ya-Na, Yakubu Andani, the Kuga-Na and elders had asserted that Mahamadu's funeral, not a royal funeral because he was no longer king at time of death, should be performed in his own house where he died, not as "according to Dagbon custom" at the Palace. For the Andani, this was fitting to his non-royal status, for the Abudu it was another insult to them and their king and fed the chieftaincy conflict up to the time of its explosion and Na Yakubu's death.

Mahamadu's predecessor Ya-Na Andani III, who had been the Mion chief, was installed in 1968 after the death of Abdulai III. But Andani died three months later. There was noise from the pro-Abudu Busia Administration that Ya-Na Andani III had not been properly nominated and enskinned, that his successor Mahamadu Abdulai was properly nominated (by the Selection Committee, an entity which the Andani royal family feel marginalized them), and thus properly enskinned. After Ya-Na Mahamadu died, his son Mahamadu Abdulai was nominated by the Selection Committee to succeed him as regent. The Abudu wanted the Andani family to vacate the palace. Armed personnel went round the neighborhood of the palace and locked them up. Mahamadu Abdulai was escorted to the Katini-duu (hut for enskinment) to be installed by the New Selection Committee. Some days later he was appointed a Member of the Council of State. A January 1972 coup d'etat toppled Busia; the Andani family petitioned the National Redemption Council (NRC, the military government) for a commission of enquiry. The result: the Ollennu Committee deliberated and "called for the recognition of (the deceased) Andani III as the rightfully enskinned Ya-Na and the deskinment of Mahamadu Abdulai IV" (Ahorsu and Gebe 2011, 15). The Supreme Court affirmed the findings of the Ollenu Committee. The third issue that has been interwoven throughout this discussion is that of political interference, internal and exogenous. After 1899, British Indirect rule made clear that colonial officers were to "'act through the native chiefs as far as possible . . .'" (quoted in Soeters 2012, 20). If chiefs were not part of the structure, the British invented them. For example, once the British began their administration in the Northern Territories of the Gold Coast, among the stateless societies they "appointed 'native chiefs' who were to assist them in their newly acquired protectorate . . . and set up a hierarchy of village headmen, sub-chiefs and at the top echelon head chiefs (later called paramount chiefs)" (Lentz 2020, 91). Well after the end of colonial rule and into modern national politics, the north in general and the Dagomba in particular have maintained a strong pro-chieftaincy sensibility (Grischow 2006; Ladouceur 1979).

In the 1969 Yendi chieftaincy conflict that led to deaths and arrests, the Abudu faction did not recognize Ya-Na Andani and his regent son Yakubu

Andani, who were chosen by the traditional elders; at the same time, as just noted, the Andani did not recognize Mahadmadu Abdulai because he was chosen by the selection committee. It was only in 2001 that a new NPP (National Political Party, heir to Busia's Progress Party) national government came into office. It is said that the Abudu Gate Family felt supported by the Kufuor administration.

A major figure in national politics, gate and chiefly politics and selection for the last forty years is Ibrahim Mahama, whom I wrote about in the Introduction. He has gained considerable influence, which enabled him to influence chiefly promotions. Each side in the Yendi dispute has had its educated and articulate spokesmen—for the most recent chieftaincy conflict, that would be members of the 1.5 group. Like Ibrahim Mahama, these men are well-connected in both chiefly and state circles. They are patrons to their Dagomba client brothers back home. By all accounts, like the tiny but influential number of Dagomba literates from the 1940s, the contemporary bridge generation have inflamed the situation, possibly even incubating it (see Chapter Six).

Modern politicians have also created problems, making adjustments just as the Europeans did. As throughout Africa, difficulties have arisen due to differences between traditional standards of conduct and standards of conduct as regulated by modern law. Thus, when there is a change of government, many Dagomba think the succession to the Yendi skin should change as well. How have all of these factors impacted internal Dagomba politics?[6] Those northern Dagomba with little or no Western education are swayed by the urban-dwelling Western-educated who have re-invented tradition and the criteria of leadership (see Hobsbawm 1983; Jok and Hutchinson 1999). I suggest that the latter are engaging in leadership by remote control, engaging leadership from afar. And they are successful because they are big men, patrons, who those back home esteem, and listen to.

The relation of the Dagomba urban elite to their home area 400 miles distant is not neutral. Over the years they have developed an affective link that goes back to their growing-up years, to places and people through relationships and activities anchored there, which impact their identity (Bernardo Hernández et al. 2007). Their attachment can be marked by an explosive mixture of ostentatious emotional attachment and intimacy with the blatant inequality that holds between the two areas (Geschiere and Nyamnjoh 1998). It can play out in various kinds of support from afar, money, help, political involvement. But the connection is mutually reinforcing, while the rural pole provides social security for urbanites, the urbanites function as a bridgehead to the outside world for the village (Geschiere and Gugler 1998). Ethnic ties uniting those in town with kin and affines in regions of origin have helped to reinforce and transform traditional identities in the village. "Inventing tradition" (Hobsbawm 1983) in the village is a means of taking advantage of the political driving force emanating from the town by elites (Nyamnjoh and Rowlands 1998), who do not necessarily see things from the same perspective.

Gate Politics

The word "gate," used by the Dagomba to connote succession (MacGaffey 2013, 83), actually carries two meanings to which I referred above, first, that of Abudu and Andani branches or clans. As I observed, the gate skins are emplaced. The clans, however, are not. In Dagbon, Abudu and Andani members are intermixed spatially. Abudu-Andani constitute one family, even as the division is palpable. In Dagbon, spatially, their homes are intermingled. In the aftermath of Ya-Na Yakubu's death, this was quite clear in the neighborhood of Yendi around the palace (see Chapter Six).

Secondly, "gate" also refers to the three royal skins whose occupants may compete for the kingship (see Figure 1.1). The rotational principle, initiated in the late nineteenth century, followed the death of Ya-Na Yakubu I (Tsikata and Seini 2004; Staniland 1975). On his death, his son Abdullahi succeeded him, followed by his other son Andani. A third son, Darimani, succeeded to the kingship after Andani, but after seven weeks was deposed by the Germans, who controlled Eastern Dagbon during the nineteenth century. The third gate was then eliminated and the problem that arose over future successions to the position has only involved Andani and Abudu. "Clearly then, prior to the death of Ya-Na Andani there was nothing like a lineage gate system. The idea of Andani and Abudu gates that should rotate concretised after the deposition of Darimani" (Awedoba 2009, 205).

Prior to 1896, in the case of a problematic succession, the elders appealed to the Nayeri, chief of Mamprogu (Mamprussi), who would recommend a way out—delimiting who are royals, who qualify and instituting the rotational/promotional system; he would bring order. The disputants were not pegged as Abudus or Andanis but as eligible Dagomba royals. Over the years, that system fell away. The rotation between the two gates became unstable; at times it was subverted by inexact memory or representation, the consequent tensions threatening the stability of the region and the state. Thus while the rotational principle is accepted in theory by all, it has not always worked. It created conflict when the Na-ship was vacant in 1938, 1948, 1953 and 1967 (Ferguson and Wilks 1970).[7] At Christmas 1986 the problem was between supporters of the sitting Ya-Na

Andani Yakubu II and of the supporters of Ya-Na Mahamadu Abdulai IV, who had been deposed in 1974, culminating in deaths and rioting. This was the irritant that set off the 2002 chaos and murder.

The Dagbon chieftaincy crises have been complicated by outside politics. When Germans still controlled part of Dagbon before WWI, they killed an Andani and installed an Abudu (Staniland 1975). Post-Versailles, when the Germans lost ownership of the territory, the British Chief Commissioner of the Northern Territories chose a new king. Through the policy of indirect rule, the British colonial government removed chiefs that they considered not pliable (Mustapha Abdul-Hamid 2011). The British Colonial Administration also ignored historical divisions and strengthened the power of Dagomba chiefs over the neighboring Konkomba while appointing Konkomba sub-chiefs within Dagbon (Akwetey 1996).

Modern state politics, intertwined with internal Dagomba politics, have complicated the picture and muddied the waters. Since 1946, Dagomba politics have been closely aligned with national and regional politics. J. H. Allasani, an early Dagomba patron involved in national politics, sought to depose the sitting Ya-Na Abdulai (an Abudu, who failed to meet a variety of the basic selection criteria, including blindness in one eye), claiming the need to return to the rotational principle.[8] In 1959, the Government appointed the Afari Committee to deal with the issue, and while their decision was not published, it was known to reject Ya-Na Abdulai (because of his physical defect) and recommend he be deposed (Staniland 1975). In the meantime, the CPP (Convention Peoples Party) had become much stronger in Dagbon. The prominent Abudu partisan and patron Tolon-Na Yakubu Tali moved over from the NPP (Northern People's Party, of which he was a founding member) to the CPP. In turn, Nkrumah's government pulled back from deposing Ya-Na Abdulai. The Mion-Lana accepted the situation but as this meant that the Mion-Lana's children would not be eligible for the Yendi skin (since he was not an enskinned Ya-Na), he wrote to Nkrumah asking for help. This led to Nkrumah's promulgation of LI (Legislative Instrument) 59 in 1960, which laid down an order of succession to the Yendi skin. It reaffirmed the eligibility of Karaga, Mion and Savelugu, insisted the skin should rotate between the two gates of Andani and Abudu, and that there should always be a member of each on at least one of the gate skins. Moreover, as the Abdulais had reigned twice in a row, it was time to return the Andanis to equal footing with them (Ladouceur 1972; Staniland 1975).

This kind of adjustment mattered to the Dagomba because, with the change of the state regime, it is commonly expected that the royal Dagomba faction affiliated with that government's party will somehow be put on the paramount skin (Antoine 1985; Van Hear 1982).

Moreover, according to community opinion, prosperity in Dagbon correlated with gate, i.e. when their gate was in power, that gate prospered. And by the same token, following the classic rule of patron-clientage, by supporting the central government, the ruling gate gave supporters access to resources. This was the "social, economic and political importance of the Dagbon chieftaincy" and how groups aligned with the ruling gate derived huge benefits from that gate's political alliance with the ruling regime (Antoine 1985, 202).

In 1966, Nkrumah was overthrown by a coup d'etat. The Dagbon State Council through its Electoral Committee petitioned the NLC to repeal LI 59, which protected Ya-Na Abdulai III; this succeeded on a technicality (Ladouceur 1972).[9] Meanwhile, the following year, the Ya-Na died. His eldest son, Mahamadu, was installed as Regent and also became a candidate for Ya-Na. This side had political support. The Andanis' nomination of the aged Mion-Lana was supported by the soothsayers, some chiefs and the head of the military Government, Lt. General Ankrah. The Mion-Lana Mahama Andani was enskinned in November 1968 and the Abudus complained, so another commission was seated.[10] Ya-Na Andani IV died after less than four months on the skin. His son, Andani Yakubu, was made regent.

The country returned to civilian rule in 1969 and in Dagbon during the campaign for Prime Minster, "a vote for the Progress Party was equated with support for the Abdulai [Abudu], and a vote for the National Alliance of Liberals [replacing the CPP] with support for the Andani" (Ladouceur 1972, 111). Meanwhile, the Mate Kole Commission[11] reversed the Andani enskinment.[12] The findings were accepted by the newly elected Dr. Kofi Busia, the Progress Party (PP) candidate.

The Mate Kole Commission also repudiated the 1930 Dagomba Constitution (see Rattray 1969[1932] V. II), seeing it as a *record of*, not *formulation of*, customary law as it existed at the time and that it was superseded by the 1948 resolution instating a selection committee. It also found in favor of a regent's right to apply to become Ya-Na. Mahamadu Abdulai IV, son of Na Abdulai III, was enskinned in the midst of tensions and fighting in Yendi.

Prime Minister Busia was overthrown in early 1972. Perhaps not surprisingly, with the change in state government, some on the Andani took the case of Ya-Na Mahammadu Abdulai IV to the National Redemption Council, the military government in power. The NRC set up yet another commission, the Ollennu Commission. Their investigation led to Mahamadu being de-skinned and an Andani, Na Yakubu Andani II, being enskinned in 1974.

During the 2000 presidential campaign, with Na Yakubu on the skin, one of my informants heard a spokesperson for the New People's Party (NPP), a successor to Busia's Progress Party, say on the radio station Joy FM that if NPP won the Presidential elections, they would ensure a proper funeral for Ya-Na Mahamadu. Mahamadu had received a royal *burial* but not a kingly *funeral* (as he had been de-skinned before dying). NPP won the election. According to Emmanuel Bombande, founder and head of WANEP (West Africa Network for Peacebuilding), it was an open secret that Vice President Aliu, a Dagomba from Yendi, and an Abudu, had promised that the government would complete the Tamale-Yendi Road, and that the Abudu would gain the Ya-Naship (Bombande June 19, 2004). The Bishop of Yendi, Vincent Boi-Nai, told me more or less the same thing, although again there is no document to that effect. Malik Yakubu, the Minister of the Interior, an Abudu in the NPP government, had promised that if NPP were elected, Ya-Na Yakubu Andani would be removed (Boi-Nai June 24, 2008).

When members of the Abudu gate brutally murdered and beheaded Andani king Yakubu II on March 28, 2002 in the twenty-eighth year he was on the skin, people found particularly shocking that it occurred inside the palace—not in the field or on a campaign but *in his home.*

> You have two sides. Both want to kill the other. They both amassed arms ... A person holds up the chief's head. Does that mean he killed him? (Jake Obetsebi-Lamptey, an NPP official, September 9, 2005)

Five years later, fourteen Abudu men were remitted to the Adjabeng Magistrate Court in Accra to determine whether they would stand trial at the High Court. I accompanied Dr. Mohammed Mahama (Dr. M. M.), an Abudu activist, to the courtroom. Dr M. M. said, "if only justice is served." I responded, "A king was brutally murdered." And he replied, "It was a war and he started it" (June 28, 2010). This was also the position of the Abudu gate and their political party, the NPP (successor to Busia's PP). This was the position of Jake Obekyebi-Lamptey, an NPP activist and then-Minister of Tourism, who also characterized to me what had happened as "a war" (September 9, 2005). In response to this position, a number of Andani people said to me, if it were a war, would he have been in his house?

While Yendi skin affairs are nothing new, concern about the post-2002 tension between the two royal gates was editorialized in the *Accra Daily Mail* the day before the Ya-Na's murder. The particular brand of violence is like the February 1994 fighting of Konkomba versus Nanumba, Dagomba, and Gonja, when more than 1,000 persons were killed and 150,000 others displaced in the northeastern part of Ghana. It was disturbing and unnerved the entire country. Aggravating the Dagbon conflict has been the widespread presence of firearms. Guns have been a part of traditional northern life, as most men are socialized to hunt, but the guns were muzzle-loaded long guns. In the last few decades, the numbers of guns have become excessive and the kinds military-style, as the military has become an illicit source of weapons. This has become common at border crossings (Drucker-Brown 1988–89, 101), and the proliferation of small arms and light weapons "is part of the conflict system that has engulfed West Africa since the Liberian civil war began in 1989" (www.iansa.org, p. 5).

Through all these years, the Dagomba have lived as a whole, that is, members of the two gates have not occupied different spatial locations based upon gate identity. But the polarization of the two gates has periodically inflamed relations between the two. The murder of the Ya-Na in 2002 disrupted the Dagomba community in Accra. They no longer gathered as a whole to celebrate festivals or the birthday of the Prophet. Abudu gathered with Abudu, Andani with Andani. The killing also disrupted the northern pull for many of the Dagomba elite living in Accra. They feared being directly caught up in the conflict that erupted episodically in Dagbon. One man who is Abudu told me he would not drive to Dagbon because he feared someone would set fire to his car. Consequently, for the four years until the Ya-Na was buried and the regent enskinned, they got their knowledge of Yendi affairs indirectly, its accuracy often questionable.

This increased the politicization of the Naship, with national politics further manipulating and exploiting factions for political gain, and with those patrons who were particularly media savvy arguing for their side.

(Post-) Coloniality and Urbanizing the North

In West Africa, as elsewhere, the city was developed by foreigners to promote their own interests. In the Gold Coast (pre-Independence Ghana), it was the British colonial presence that initiated what became a culturally and spatially complex setting (King 1990). When the British decided to establish their northern headquarters in Tamale in 1906, it was just a village with a population of 1,435. Tamale market was the terminus of cattle trails from various other villages. The settling in of the British, bringing in military and government people, created a demand for goods and services. Yoruba from Nigeria sold manufactured goods. The Europeans created a quarter for themselves, with the requirements that it be built "away from bush or swampy land, have a good water supply and not be near native buildings" (MacGaffey 2006–07, 110). By 1909, Tamale had grown and diversified, its indigenous population joined by Yorubas, the British administrators and southerners working for the Europeans. The first primary school opened in Tamale in 1909. By the 1920s, there were nearly forty Europeans, and by 1932, the town was divided into eight wards, including so-called stranger quarters (*zongos*) for the Hausa and the Moshi. Post-World War II, Tamale expanded rapidly. The important Dagomba chiefs owned homes there, marking the town's political importance (MacGaffey 2006–07). In 1950, when it was approved as a Planning Area, its population was under 40,000.

It was in the 1950s and 1960s that the first Dagomba to attend secondary school in the north were growing up in Tamale and elsewhere in Dagbon. With time, Tamale became the "urban gateway to the north"; until Independence in 1957, it was the capital of the Northern Territories, which enlarged its economic role. In 1960, the Northern Region was separated out from the rest of the north, with Tamale as its capital as it has so remained. In 1988, Tamale became a district, called West Dagomba District Assembly and in 1994, it was promoted to West Dagomba Municipal Assembly, and finally to Metropolitan Assembly in 2004. With a population of around 400 thousand, Tamale is the third-largest city in Ghana and, and because of its physical spread and population growth since 2007, it is said to be the fastest growing city in West Africa.

Yendi is the seat of Dagbon but has largely lost its primacy to Tamale, Dagbon's political center. Today, Yendi has a population of about 31,000. It has gone from occupying a pivotal position in the important pre-colonial trade, to being a run-down town that seems bypassed by modern times. There is electricity in Yendi in the last decade—the state put up electric poles along the Tamale–Yendi Road—and water is not a problem as it is in Tamale, and a few of the roads have been tarred. Since around 2010, money has been coming into Yendi, as evidenced in new construction of private homes in an area considered for rich people because one can only build there with "blocks" (cement) and a guesthouse on the way east out of town.

Despite the improvements, including paving the road between Yendi and Tamale before the 2000 national elections, the infrastructure is dilapidated and buildings run-down. In Yendi, one sees "the same old buildings. Some houses have been razed down and people cannot even rebuild. Schools that are new and good are so deteriorated" (Dr. Y. Gomda September 15, 2005). People keep the same mud houses, because "those who live around those areas cannot afford any serious economic activity" (Dr. M. Iddrisu September 12, 2005). The opinion of Fuseini Baba, the head administrator in Ghana's Ministry of Finance, considered the condition of Yendi and responded that in fact despite some changes, infrastructure had worsened. "What is convenient, basic, for a person is water, shelter. We're still living in the same old houses. The water situation is even worse off. Sanitation is the same thing (April 28, 2006)." When he, a "child of Yendi," visits his hometown, he has to use the public toilet system. Such conditions, in the view of the professional Dagomba from afar, make it seem the town is going backwards, and as a result many people have left. If a relocated Dagomba decides to build up north, he is more likely to build in Tamale, rather than his hometown, be it Yendi, Kunbungu or elsewhere (Alhaji Sule October 21, 2005).

Many believe that the development that has occurred has been concentrated in Tamale alone. "Tamale was the nerve center of the colonial administration" (Osumanu 2008, 104) and today is a more cosmopolitan place, with a diverse population. It has modernized, some say, with better houses and facilities and a better road network. Electricity is regular. But it is situated in a region considered peripheral to the national enterprise. The discourse of Tamale as a marginal place in a marginal space has impacted conceptions of what it is, what its people are, and of their reality. This discourse has fashioned an imaginary geography, one that has tainted the place and its people. Thus the city has suffered from both partial and incomplete planning or attention for more than a century.

The infrastructure has suffered; indeed, some would say things have regressed. Tamale does have sixty-eight junior secondary schools, eleven senior secondary schools, two vocational/technical and one polytechnic, yet illiteracy is still high (UN Habitat 2009). Sanitation is bad and has overwhelmed the authorities. And the accessibility of water has reached crisis levels. Late in the day, one sees women and children all over town with containers on their heads looking for water. In Tamale, Adisa Munka'ila bought a tanker truck to fill with water and supply her pure water business. When she does not need the water, she sells to people who do.

Tamale is a friendly city, where people know one another and the locations of their homes. Much of Tamale's housing is composed of circular mud and thatch compound houses, with rectangular concretes structures composing all new housing and government/commercial buildings. Tamale is also well laid out, main roads are designed to accommodate bicycles, the concrete gutters engineered to contain the downpours during the rainy season. There is considerable street trade across from the local market; Burkinabe traders come from Burkina Faso to hawk bootlegged CDs and DVDs, and local weavers and tailors specialize in producing the iconic Dagomba striped smock. Tamale's commercial importance to the region is highlighted by the fact that some southern Ghanaian shops have established branches here, and there are a number of two-story buildings and traffic lights.

Economic activities center on farming and trading. Indeed, most Dagomba today are still subsistence farmers who engage in shifting cultivation and produce food largely for the home (Dickson 1968; Oppong 1973). Cultivation, the traditional means of support, has been insufficient as a source of wealth. In 1969, General I. K. Acheampong overthrew Prime Minister Busia. During the 1970s, when General Acheampong[13] was head of state, official economic policy was agricultural improvement and especially rice. The rice revolution and investments in cotton production positively impacted the region. While Acheampong was vilified in the south for his ruinous economic course of action and he was overthrown in a palace coup in 1978, he was praised in the north for investing in the region. His administration, the National Redemption Council (NRC), was the last post-Independence government with

> a positive vision for the development of the north. It promoted the development of state-subsidized large-scale capitalist agriculture in the north, taking advantage of the still-nationalized status of northern land to create a back of cheap land, as well as subsidized machinery and other agricultural inputs and state institutional investments in financial institutions and related processing operations. (Shepherd et al. 2004, 13)

From 1973 to 1978, rice farming increased from 19,000 to 130,000 acres. Most Dagomba farmers who participated in rice farming were part of the state-sponsored rice boom. It was the success or perceived success of rice cultivation in the 1970s that led people I spoke with to credit Acheampong for economic progress in Dagbon and indeed the whole of northern Ghana. This is particularly interesting, given that rice was viable only for big farmers with connections and that the successful rice-farmers "derived certain benefits through their connections with the ruling [Dagomba clan]" (Antoine 1985, 238). The prominent rice farmers in the north were important in winning local support for the regime. Indeed, government commissioners were encouraged by Acheampong to participate in rice farming.

Many Dagomba living in Dagbon today told me that what matters is that there was work for everyone. Dagomba found casual labor in villages next to farms, and the government's development policy encouraged small-scale rice farming as an alternative (van Hear 1982). Some told Antoine (1985, 309) in the 1980s that the program "represented an important contribution to the general development of the North," which would have continued had Acheampong remained in office. Sadly, by the late 1970s it was clear that the country's agricultural program, and especially rice production, initiated in 1972 "had failed in its major objective of making the country self-sufficient in food" (Antoine 1985, 337).[14]

Related to the ability to work and make a living is access to schooling. The north has been historically deprived in its educational infrastructure,[15] while the stratification system introduced by the British was education-based, incorporating role definitions grounded in achievement rather than ancestral privilege. They seeded a new elite that reflected African perceptions of European society. While custom continued to matter, the British formed the influential elite, their lifestyle and conceptions of social status and self-respect replacing those of the aspiring locals. "Convinced of their own superiority and hence of their civilizing mission [the British] attacked any African custom they considered immoral, unhealthy or primitive and compelled Africans to change in particular ways" (Wipper 1972, 331). Their values became a new reference point for modernity, and they filtered down through the new elite and percolated throughout society.

The Gold Coast modern elite was disposed to understand the new class conditions for the good life and to reproduce them through "practice-unifying" principles, i.e. class habitus (Bourdieu 1984). In effect, the group was unified by each actor producing and reproducing meaning through practice. They adopted styles of behavior that carried economic and cultural capital, while the accoutrements of their everyday existence objectified social relations (Bourdieu 1984, 77). This was true in the houses they built, the clothing they wore, the events they launched. And it was the symbolic space that marked out these structured practices, which constituted their version of modernity.

A new spatial ordering set up by colonial designers destroyed or overlaid traditional or indigenous architectural forms through urban planning (see also Boyd 1962 for Imperial China; Winter 1977 for Timbuktu). Accra exemplifies the impact of these concerns on the urban spatial landscape. The British moved their administrative headquarters there in 1877 and imposed European-style town planning. In 1908, the plague hit downtown Accra. The government decided that sanitary improvements were essential. They condemned much of the housing in the old quarter to relieve population density and laid out new town sites to relocate those affected (Pellow 2002). They transformed this relatively homogeneous small-scale community "into a heterogeneous large-scale community" (Acquah 1972, 28). When the British built a European quarter, they designed bungalows for the European population, which became a symbol of status. These built environments represented new habitats of meaning, their layouts expressing European systems of social organization.

At the same time, the north of Ghana suffers from poverty, a consequence of the British development of northern underdevelopment. In the GLSS (Ghanaian Living Standards Survey survey) from 2005/06, the poverty rate in the three northern regions—the Northern, Upper West and Upper East—was more than twice the national average. What one sees is that in the southern regions, including Accra, less than 10 percent of the population is listed as extremely poor. Looking at the Upper East and Upper West, the percentage was about seven times as much—that is, the majority of the population in the two regions are poor (Abdulai 2012, 23, 24). The north continues to account for a disproportionate amount of Ghana's poor and even got worse between 1992 and 2006 (Abdulai 2012). Thus, as little as an illiterate young woman might earn carrying loads in one of the southern markets, it is more than she can access up north. "Because there's nothing at home to do. When there was a rice boom, nobody wanted to come [to Accra]. Now—to make a tiny amount of money is a problem. She comes here and can make something—she prefers that. She sends it home" (Alh. Mahdi September 16, 2005).

According to Wayo Seini, an economist and a former MP of Tamale, "the north was seen as a labor reserve—for the mines, the farms down south. They [the British] didn't want to join The Colony and Ashanti as one. The argument was straightforward—because they were different and the standards were too wide. The south had education for more than a century while the north has had education for less than half a century. So there's no guarantee that we will ever catch up. And this is what has happened" (October 14, 2005). Even today, he goes on, "resources are not fairly dispersed [by the state]. If you don't have people in positions, you don't get resources. In the north it wouldn't take a lot of capital to carry out—don't have mountains, for infrastructure, and yet little has been done. And things are getting worse . . ." (October 14, 2005). According to Abdulai and Hulme (2015), this is the fault of southern-based elites who "publicly side-lined the GPRS [Ghana Poverty Reduction Strategy] formula and disbursed HIPC [Highly Indebted Poor Country] expenditures in ways that they believed would maintain their political power," thereby marginalizing the poorer northern regions in the actual distribution of HIPC resources (p. 548).

Abdul Majid, an economist and former state minister says, "Go to Burkina Faso and talk to the Minister of Agriculture and ask them how come irrigation is successful there and not in Ghana, and they will tell you none have been done lately without participation of the chiefs" (Abdul Majid October 22, 2005). In Ghana today there are some activist chiefs who lobby the government. According to Mohammed Mumuni, former Minister of Foreign Affairs, in the north, there are a few "who are concerned about development in their own communities but many also are illiterate and don't have capacities" (Mumuni May 1, 2006). In the town of Sunson, about 12 km north of Yendi, the Chief Na Mahama Shani Hamidu (who died in March 2021) exhibited real progressivism. "My people were suffering guinea worm. I said no. The water we drink that gives us guinea worm. So I quickly asked NORIP (Northern Region Integrated Programme, an NGO) to come and give me bore holes—four, for the community" (June 25, 2008). And with that, he eliminated guinea worm. More recently, in 2011, he initiated a dam project to irrigate 100 hectares of land. In 2013, it was complete. He did this with the help of World Bank funding and no state involvement. But others believe the chiefs are losing their hold on society—hence "the *zakyi* phenomenon." The *zakyi* are the youth, who are mobilized by their leader, the *Nachin Na*. When I met them, the zakyi—all in their thirties and forties—were without work, presumably because of the chieftaincy crisis in Dagbon. They would sit around complaining. And they undermined the chiefs (Janet Mohammed September 23, 2005)

Is it up to whoever is administering the region to develop it? During the colonial period, it would have been the British. Today, given the fact that the citizenry is paying taxes, "it's the duty of the State to provide certain facilities" (Dr. Y. Gomda September 15, 2005). "The State holds resources . . . Here, everything in infrastructure is government. So can't run away from State involvement" (Aminu Ahmadu December 5, 2005). The state has done things for the region, but in terms of what is needed, clearly not enough. The extreme water shortage was indicative of a crisis (Dr. Nasser April 30, 2006). The pumps, originally installed by the British during their administration some 15 km from town, need to be replaced, but it has not been a priority of the government. "We have elected politicians who should make it a political issue . . . . [The political parties] had enough time to do something about the water crisis. And within the context of Tamale local politics, all the political opinion, of MPs, since the switch to constitutional government has come from the NDC [National Democratic Congress, the majority party in the north]. So they should have used their political position to put pressure on government to do something about the water situation. But it is not happening" (Dr. Nasser April 30, 2006).

The Millennium Development Goals (MDGs) first agreed on by almost all world leaders at the United Nations in 2000, were set up to tackle growing inequalities in poor countries. The main policy instrument through which such countries sought to achieve MDGs is Poverty Reduction Strategy Papers (PRSPs). "A country's PRSP was required to set out a comprehensive national poverty reduction plan showing how donor funding (especially Enhanced Highly Indebted Poor Country (HIPC) debt relief) would be used to reduce poverty" (Abdulai and Hulme 2015, 529), targeting public resources at excluded regions. While Africa looks like it has done worse than it has (Easterly 2009), some areas have in fact done worse than others. This is true for the north of Ghana relative to the south of the country.

In 2004 the United States committed to the Millennium Goals, Congress establishing the Millennium Challenge Corporation, a bilateral United States foreign aid agency to fight poverty in developing countries. Ghana was one of sixteen beneficiary countries worldwide, on August 1, 2006 signing on for the award of $547 million. Haruna Iddrisu, one of Tamale's three MPs, questioned the criteria used in the distribution of the millennium account in Ghana,

> The minority has raised certain concerns about the exclusion of the Upper East and Upper West regions of Ghana from the beneficiary districts and regions. In our view those two regions has the highest incidence of poverty in Ghana. Therefore if the selection process was based on the incidence of poverty or the goals were to ameliorate poverty then they ought to have been included in order for us to achieve balance development on our achievement. We are also aware that no single district of the twenty-three districts emanated from the western region of Ghana. And we raised these concerns in parliament and in the national debate. (June 13, 2006; VOA http, //quickstart .clari.net/voa/art/ch/2006–06–13-voa44.html)

Conclusion

The Dagomba Kingdom makes up the largest of the ethnic groups in northern Ghana. Chieftaincy, important throughout the country as testified to by its inclusion in the Constitution of the State and also the sheer number of chieftaincy conflicts ongoing at any time, is especially significant in Dagbon. Here, chieftaincy is both conservative and progressive—conservative in that it holds onto traditions, progressive in the manner of succession to ever-higher skins. Moreover, chieftaincy is the heart of governance in this part of the country where through history the state has been largely absent. It is also a chiefly system that is complicated and prone to problems, because of differing interpretations of rules internal to the system as well as interference from outside.

In many respects, state government and traditional leadership have failed the area, just as the colonial administration before. The postcolonial state has given the north short shrift, enabling political parties and candidates for office to meddle with traditional affairs when it is to their advantage. Chiefs, regents and anyone else with a skin and control over land have engaged in monetization of land, corrupting many of the skins and not serving their people well. While one can't place blame, says Abdulai Yakubu, now himself a local chief, "whatever few resources are available, each village needs one school—primary. The land is not that expensive. They could use that to set up schools for the people, to send the children to school. If they could use their resources to put up some schools, that would be good. Because they are not sharing resources with the people—what are you doing with all that money?" (November 23, 2005).

The new Dagomba elite grew up within the bosom of the kingdom. Many of them experienced first-hand the deprivation fashioned by the colonial administration and its remnants countenanced by the postcolonial state. They were also among the first to benefit from the visionary first president of the new country Ghana, as higher education was introduced. But they were first and foremost children of Dagbon, who have maintained a social and transcendent relationship to Dagbon, even as they are not resident there (and may not visit often). Their attachment to the place is in part evidenced in their attachment to its king, who in his very being represents the place. At heart, an enduring issue is who has rights to the Naship. Any solution must consider the constitutional rules specifying who is eligible, the dynastic rule of rotation, who has the authority to select the Ya-Na, interference from the Dagomba new elite patrons, and the intersection of traditional authority and state authority, of state interference with traditional authority, indeed, of state authority trumping traditional authority.

One hopes that with the murdered Ya-Na buried and a new Ya-Na on the skin, life can normalize for the sons (and daughters) of Dagbon. This is the context for the changed circumstance of the new Dagomba elite, who largely live in the Accra capital district. The next chapter takes us back to their childhood environment in far more experiential terms—which helps explain why they care about the place, its people, its chiefs and king.

NOTES

1. Gambaga in what is now the Upper East, Wa in what is now the Upper West and Kintampo to the south of Dagbon.
2. Achimota is a private co-educational boarding secondary school founded in 1927 on the outskirts of Accra.
3. The word *dakpema* is literally a market elder, "one who collects tithes from the market on behalf of a tindana" (MacGaffey 2012 74).
4. The seat of the Dagomba court until the early eighteenth century was Yendi Dabari, about twenty miles north of Tamale, which was abandoned as a result of a Gonja invasion.

5. The predecessor to Na Yakubu Andani II, Mahammadu, was de-skinned in 1978. The aggrieved Abudu claimed this had never before happened and was a violation of ritual law, and it set in motion the conflict that eventuated in Na Yakubu's murder.
6. Staniland (1975) and MacGaffey (2006) both provide details (see also Sibidow 1969; Mumuni 1975; Yakubu 2006).
7. After Na Mahama III died in 1953, there were four candidates to succeed him. The regent, his eldest son, was chosen because the Savelugu chief was too old, the Karaga chief was a grandson and the Mion chief had angered the selection committee. The choice surprised many, because the Regent had physical defects that normally rule out one's eligibility (Yakubu 2006). Moreover, his succession confused the rotational order, as an Abudu was following an Abudu as Ya-Na.
8. J. H. Allasani was a ministerial secretary in 1954 in President Kwame Nkrumah's government and was an important Andani backer in Dagbon chieftaincy politics. 1954 was an election year, and the Northern People's Party, the strongest political force in the north, was founded the year before. Ya-Na Abdulai III had also been enskinned the year before, in 1953.
9. Dagomba men politically active at the time included the Tolon-Na Yakubu Tali and Bawa A Yakubu a spokesman for the Abudu side, who later became Inspector General of Police.
10. The NLC set up the Mate Kole Commission to ascertain customary enskinning procedure.
11. Nene Azzu Mate Kole, was paramount chief of Manya Krobo, as well as being a distinguished statesman. He was the first chief to be appointed to the Volta River Authority (VRA) Board.
12. finding that
    the alleged enskinment of Mion Lana was repugnant to Dagomba custom and that therefore the so-called enskinment of Mion Lana is null and void; . . . that the Gbon Lana [Regent] Mahamadu Abdulai was properly selected and directed that the ceremony of installation as Ya Na should be performed . . . . (Ladouceur 1972, 112)
13. The other being Kwame Nkrumah for his role in bringing education to the north.
14. Not all observers see the "feed-yourself" schemes in glowing terms. According to Jon Kirby (personal communication), the program ultimately failed abysmally due to the fact that the royals/politicians/elites commandeered the labor, land and product, sold it to Burkina Faso instead of plowing it back into the system and finally the commoners revolted by burning the crops. After three years of successive burnings (1977, 1978, 1979) the project crashed.
15. Chapter Three deals extensively with the development of education in the north as it relates to the Dagomba new elite.

CHAPTER 2

Childhood Home

We were in the family house. Eventually my father had four wives and they were all quite interesting women—such interesting women, we were all staying together. One would cook two days, the other would cook two days, the other would cook two days, and we never noticed any difference between our mothers. So we were there with them and it was the most interesting thing that happened. We were in the home and everybody was somebody else's child. We had common mothers. You didn't feel that you missed your own mother. We were there in the community. And our father was the father of the house.

—Adisa Munka'ila, November 10, 2005

When we were boys "Yendi was a very lovely place," that is, before the problems of chieftaincy; education was more careful; schools were clean; at the end of term would come to see family. I miss the customs. Because in Dagbon, we have split in loyalty to the two gates; this has divided people.

—Dr. Abubakari Alhassan, November 17, 2005

These two takes on childhood reflect on Dagbon, the place and its connections—the joys of everyone living together, the customs that held everyone together but have now divided people. Most of the members of the Dagomba bridge group I spoke with spent their childhood in Dagbon, in the Northern Region. They grew up in family houses in various towns including Yendi, Savelugu, Mion and Karaga, as well as the "big city" of Tamale. They made friends there, went to primary and middle school there. Some went to secondary school there, some elsewhere in the north. They developed the place attachment that has been described for the 1.5 generation, an attachment that has carried through the years as they took up professions and relocated hundreds of miles away. While they have become, in their adult and professional lives, cosmopolitans, open to new tastes, practices and values, they are also very much creatures of their upbringings. This is core to their attachment to "home."

What is it about home that has continued to matter so much to them, to the extent that they have been drawn into local politics? "There is no question that phenomenologically, certain places evoke a special feeling of attachment and/or protectiveness for the user" (Pellow 1991, 189). Ties to this place derive from the meanings it holds. Environmental psychologists would argue that this sector of human experience is represented by affect—feelings, moods, emotions, etc.—which people experience with reference to the places where they were born, live and act (Prato 2016). In Johannesburg South Africa, after the end of apartheid in the mid-1990s, poor families from the overcrowded townships were able to move into town to Canaansland. There were all sorts of hardships—there was only one water tap, no municipal services, so people used the toilets in the nearby train station. "Despite these problems, most of the children spoke of their shacks in Canaansland as safe and happy places" (Swart-Kruger 2001, 119). Families created areas of temporary stability which children remembered as livable and comfortable. They found places of conviviality, places of solidarity.

In this chapter, I consider some of the places, events, social activities and interactions that the Dagomba patrons were involved in, exposed to, socialized into, during childhood, in (this) particular locale(s) to explain in part the Dagomba patrons' attachment to their northern home areas. This chapter aims to flesh out this sense of attachment that I posit underlies behavior of the new Dagomba elite, in their dealings with one another, with their hometowns, and with their new environment as they have adapted and modernized. Their connectedness, I suggest, is anchored in their childhood years spent in their natal homes—the particular forms and layouts of the spaces, of activities engaged in in those spaces, the people they engaged with there, their primal associations. These flavor their "entangled modernities," in some measure producing their cultural hybridity. By the same token, these people export elements of their spaces and activities north—whether it is house shape, appliances and other consumer items not readily available in Dagbon, or values such as monogamy in place of the polygyny ideal. Individual patronage, through family and friendship networks, helps disseminate ideas from the south, along with the resources needed.

People in general develop a visceral connection to the materiality of home itself. My interlocutors in this particular case are tied to the soil, the mud-and-wattle construction, the dimensionality of the interior spaces, the geometry of the interior and how one interior (mud hut) connects both physically and socially with the others within the compound. Physically, the individual huts in Dagbon, each in effect a room inhabited by a family member and his/her dependents, are linked to those on either side by a connecting wall and to the round whole as one of the structures contained within. Socially, the inhabitants are connected to one another through descent and marriage, the dailiness of life, of chores, recreation, rituals.

The world of the Dagomba has not been secure, they have experienced periodic flare ups of violence both within the group and between them and others; as peasants who work the land, they saw a prosperous rice economy fall to politics. They cannot depend upon the state. But they can depend upon the patterns that have always been. At its core, Dagomba culture is conservative. Their lives at home look remarkably like those of their fathers. The king or chief is reliable; he epitomizes the pattern, and he in turn looks to them for support. The chief is a solid element in the midst of life's fluctuations. He dispenses justice, allocates land, enables community prosperity. The chiefly architecture is predictable. After the 2002 tragedy and the destruction of the king's palace, a new (aka "temporary") palace was built in Yendi. In style and layout, it was virtually no different than the old.

Physical space carries great social significance. Certain events and activities, roles and relationships, are rooted in certain places. In this case, Dagbon's sites play a symbolic role within the system of social relations, and they have pull for those who grew up here and now live in Accra. This passion is akin to that I described in Chapter One for chieftaincy.

> There is a condensation of values in particular sites, and transactions that constitute the totality of social life may be spatially mapped with specific sites expressing relatively durable structured interests and related values. (Kuper 1972, 421)

Thus, it represents the historical side to the social production of space. Since there is a mental blueprint that guides the structure's layout, "a traditional model can, therefore, incorporate into its timelessness, structures from different times" (Kuper 1972, 421).

Today the elite Dagomba diaspora dwellers live in very different circumstances in their Accra suburban homes; even those members of this elite who have returned to Dagbon in retirement inhabit houses quite different from the chiefly pattern, the circular pattern of the past. Their neighborhoods in the north now also contain square and rectangular houses. Yet, the Dagomba northern residents and the visitors from the south of this generation all feel a palpable sense of attachment to the hometown's socio-physical elements. Dr. Iddrisu, the neurosurgeon, is originally from Yendi. He has said for years that in retirement he would return to Dagbon to a home of his own. While he is not yet retired, he has built a house on the outskirts of Tamale. It incorporates elements of modernity that he enjoys in Accra—a full indoor kitchen, dining room, separate bedrooms. It is a contemporary structure, with a contemporary feel, but it also enables traditional practices such as cooking outside on a coalpot and it is "at home," in Dagbon. Just as rectangular structures are replacing the round iconic house shape in the north, carried back by those working down south, so the bungalow idea is becoming common, carried by the new elite, as it did in the south when the then-new elite were influenced by British values and their translation into material forms (see Chapter Five for greater discussion of this point).

The Childhood Locale

The Northern Region is very different in light, climate, vegetation and cultural traditions and groups from the south where diasporic Dagomba have relocated. Crossing north across the Black Volta into the Northern Region from the region of Brong Ahafo, one sees the graduated difference in landscape and terrain from the coastal plain and Ashanti with its forests. As the government anthropologist R. S. Rattray recounted, the north consists

> for the most part of open orchard country or treeless plains where an occasional baobab-tree breaks the otherwise flat monotony. The climate is hotter and less humid than the coastal region. (1932, vii)

The dryland savannah that constitutes the Northern Region is 40 percent of the country and is referred to by geographers as the Northern Guinea Zone (Prussin 1969). Sub-humid to semi-arid, it is fairly flat and has a relatively low population density. Lying in the southern savannah climatic belt, northern Ghana has two distinct seasons, wet and dry; the hottest and driest period is December to March. "During January the desiccating harmattan winds from the Sahara blow in from the northeast, bringing with them a sheet of fine dust which increases the heat and aridity of the area" (Prussin 1969, 9). The wet season has two periods, early summer and late, during which there are periodic at times torrential rains.

The area is characterized by tall tussocky grasses, which are used for roof thatching. The landscape is punctuated by short, deciduous and widely spaced trees, locust, baobab and shea nut. All are resistant to the common bush fires. The trees provide materials for building and food products. Circular compounds are scattered on the landscape in a dispersed settlement pattern, in some cases composing villages. There are kitchen gardens close by, where residents grow okra, melons, gourds and sweet potatoes. Cereal crops—sorghum, millet and guinea corn—are grown in fields that extend beyond the compound kitchen gardens. Those are the basic food staples, thus home compounds contain a granary. Rainy months are devoted to cultivation activities, while during the early months of the dry season crops are harvested. Land ownership continues to be communal, with use rights deriving from the *tindana*,[1] although the chiefs have also involved themselves in the allocation of land. Animals wander about, primarily sheep and goats and the occasional cow; herds of cattle, primarily N'Dama (which are resistant to the tsetse fly) are steered by children of the family or Fulani hired hands. This area produces a significant proportion of Ghana's beef, lamb, and goat meat.

When Fati Isaaka was a child in the 1950s, she said even around Tamale "it was all bush . . ." From the mosque to the hospital, it was scrubland. The stalls at the market were made of grass collected from the surrounding area. "Walking to Gbagagbaga to go to school, you pass through the bush and sometimes this forest was there. I remember one day, I don't remember if it was a hyena or a wolf . . . there were a lot of bushes around—and people were scared, because he was making a lot of noise . . . . Near the . . . market—we used to go and draw water there. There was a stream. Very clear water. Nobody thought that area would be built" (Fati November 14, 2005). There were wild fruit trees; they bore mangos and shea nuts, which the children would pick and eat. As one entered Yendi, there were two rows of cotton trees. "When I was a kid, it would take a long time to see more than one vehicle on the road" (Dr. David Abdulai March 14, 2013). The sparrows flew in and out of the family houses.

As detailed in Chapter One, the physical landscape and infrastructure in the Northern Region have been far less developed than in the south of the country. Tamale in the north is the third largest city in Ghana, with a population of about 400,000. It emerged as a growth center after Independence in 1957 (Fuseini et al. 2017). Accra in the south is the largest city in Ghana, its population in 2021 projected at 2,556,972 (worldpopulationreview.com/world-cities/accra-population). While the physical distance between the two cities is not that great—about 400 miles—by public road transportation it is a thirteen-hour journey. MP Haruna Iddrisu remembers that years ago, "it took three days to travel from Tamale by road. [One] slept in Kintampo, then in Kumase, en route to Accra" (October 26, 2005). A flight today is about fifty minutes. In addition to spatial difference and distance, the Northern Region is also socially distinct from the capital region on the coast. One could argue, as I have (Pellow 2011), that residents of the two areas operate in social environments that are *qualitatively* worlds apart.

The Dagomba bridge generation grew up during a significant period in Dagbon. Modernization was being introduced—new crops, land tenure systems, fertilizers, productivity, commerce—and outsiders were also coming in and adding heterogeneity to the community. Before 1969, there was a Yoruba community in Tamale and migrant workers, such as teachers and artisans, came up from southern Ghana. Tamale became more urban and relatively prosperous as a result of the arrival of mechanized agriculture and the cash crop farming of rice. These factors influenced the upbringing of the prospective new elite. At the same time, local language (Dagbani) and religion (Islam) were valued and maintained. There was a "customary community" with a given way of life, family system, values and attitudes, but there was also the diminishing role of the family, which weakened one's sense of responsibility to the family. This caused an interesting tension, wanting to hold onto old family life even as the region was becoming more modern and urban (Issa Naseri September 28, 2005).

Hometown Sites

As one Tamale-born man asserted to me, the hometown area, in its sociophysical elements, represents "our roots" (Abdulai Yakubu March 25, 2013). During childhood, those living in the various towns and villages could roam about. Even for those who grew up in Tamale, the city was compact, with little traffic and everyone knew everyone. Huudu Yahaya mused about this, "What is it about Tamale? What does one miss? Everything. I always tell people I'm here [in Accra] only to do a job. When I finish, I will return to Tamale. I can never leave Tamale. The people. [There], I feel like I've been released from prison. I can get so free—I can drive anywhere, stop in the middle of nowhere, call anybody, visit any house . . . I have internalized it" (November 28, 2005).

Like Huudu, the others remember childhood up north with fondness and nostalgia; they carry with them memories of family and community closeness and caring. "When I think of the hometown . . . I begin to feel something I have lost that is the closeness . . .

> When we were young we were very happy. Life was difficult but we were very happy. My school is just down there and we used to walk between school and home—my peers and I would walk around, visiting. Sometimes would go and cut firewood. Father wasn't here,

> so was living with relations and would have to work "for keep." In night, passing by central mosque—used to be market area—and opposite was lorry park and a lot of shops. Most owned by people from the south. In the night a lot of life—after lamps lit. Very lively. Walk around. Peace and security. (Former Deputy Speaker of Parliament Malik Yakubu, October 1, 2005)

As children, they developed ties to local places and specific elements. Dr. Iddrisu and his friends liked to touch a particular tree in Yendi. "When I go to Yendi, that tree is still standing there. And I go and look at that tree, and it reminds me of [my childhood]" (September 2, 2005). Some report that when as children they would play around on the way to school, they were warned of evil spirits, and they were fearful. That is not a fear that anyone reported to me as an adult. The place is no longer larger than life. "Now it looks so small. [But] when I go to Yendi, I always drive around it" (Aminu Ahmadu December 5, 2005). The father of Dr. Nasser and Iliasu Adam was a butcher, but he farmed rice and corn as well. Nasser loved the farm. "We'd always go there, although it was very hard work, but then . . . the atmosphere on the farm, those from other villages would all congregate there, crack jokes, have fun while working" (Dr. Nasser April 30, 2006).

> As adolescents and young adults, their ties with the place continued. When in third form in secondary school, we had a very strong tie to Yendi. We'd walk places, have meetings, hang out, go to teach Middle School children who hadn't yet vacated . . . Some elders at time—like Chambas, who's head of ECOWAS [Economic Community of West African States]—they were our leaders at the time. [Once there was] a strong moon. Things like that you remember fondly—moonlight walks, traditional dances, things like that. And teaching of younger children which we did. We organized ourselves and would go to Middle Schools. (Abdul Majid October 22, 2005)

The natural environment stuck with many of these men and women, who say they miss it. "Now all over the place I look I see buildings. Of course there must be human progress—people should build out. People should build roads, and so on, but I do miss that" (Haruna Atta May 29, 2006).

And progress today, in the form of the cell phone and even email, enables maintaining the sense of rootedness, even if one cannot visit. The latter was especially the case during the four years following Ya-Na Yakubu Andani II's murder, when most of the Dagomba elite in Accra were apprehensive about travelling there. They took advantage of modern communication. "As we speak now I spoke to my sister in Tamale this morning. I'm almost always in constant touch with them. And the call I just had from my sibling—he's my brother actually, and he traveled to the north...So I have constant information from them" (Haruna Atta May 29, 2006). This attachment to and concern for the hometown would not be unfamiliar to southern Ghanaians, for whom the hometown area is the source of a primal identity, of kinship and community—whether one is living there or not (see Middleton 1979). Like the southerners, the northerners were brought up to respect their background, to keep taboos, to not ask why things happen the way they happen but just do as required (Issa Naseri September 28, 2005).

When these people were growing up, like today there were marriages and funerals, festivals and holidays. There was the Id holiday at the end of Ramadan, the *Bugum* Fire Festival and *Damba*, the celebration of the birth of the Prophet Mohammed. "*Damba* or *bugum*, the whole festival design is given a certain aura . . . so a week before you begin preparing. We use raffia, etc. It's very beautiful" (Siddique October 19, 2005)

While a handful of the Dagomba new elite grew up outside of the hometown in Dagbon—normally because the father's work took them elsewhere, such as Accra or Kumase—most were born and bred in one of the Dagomba towns or villages. They lived near one another and interacted daily. Some today push their children to connect with that hometown area. Fuseini Baba, Chief Economics Officer at the Ministry of Finance, asserts "you don't have any family apart from those at home, and your roots is your roots. You cannot deny that. I encourage the children—I sometimes send them home so they see what is there . . . Yendi was a close knitted society, families were interrelated" (April 28, 2006). Like other northerners, today the Dagomba elite living in the south return to the hometown area for the celebratory occasions.

Hometown Lore

Even before the onset of heterogeneity brought by modernity, the north of Ghana was a complex medley of ethnicity (thirty+ ethnic groups) and religion (Christian, Muslim, animist). In terms of structure, it has been a mosaic of centralized and acephalous organization, "of three large, geographically expansive tribes interspersed with several smaller, segmented ethnic groups, and a large number of smaller tribes contiguous to them" (Prussin 1969, 14). The three large ethnic groups, the Dagomba, Mamprusi and Gonja, have enclosed and adjoined smaller groups that are internally coherent and distinct in terms of tradition, language and built environment. The typical Dagomba town was composed of settlements in sections, tom-tom beaters, hunters (aka the Ashantis), subchiefs, the market. In the hunter section, very few went to school. A few from the chiefs went to school. Some from the tom-tom beaters did as well (Yakubu October 18, 2005).

Dagomba cultural cohesion is tied to its rich history and to the place, Dagbon. The new educated elite, the bridge generation that grew up in the north, remember with nostalgia the community based celebrations of festivals and how individual households connected with those celebrations and the lore behind them in different ways. The festivals project pride and strength in local custom. Damba is important, because it exhibits the respectability of chieftaincy custom and the importance of leadership. Dagomba's centuries-old tie to Islam is evident in the celebration of *Id il Fitr* and *Id al Adha*—the special prayers said and cows slaughtered. "If you're a typical Dagomba and an elder or chief dies and you enter the community, you don't need anyone to tell you that someone has died. From the beat of the drum you know. Also have those luntse who narrate" (Haruna Iddrisu October 26, 2005).

As children, they were also exposed to the history in different ways. Those few with a literate father might have had early exposure to the history of Dagbon through the father's books. Or they learned local stories in primary school. Or a grandparent who played a one-stringed instrument while telling stories about certain heroes. "You grew up wanting to be the warrior or successful innovator in your community" (Alhaji Mahdi September 16, 2005; Alhaji Siddique October 19, 2005).

And there is the music. Indeed, as John Chernoff observed (1979), the Dagomba are noted for their music and their love of music. And Tamale, a Dagomba town, displays the Dagomba prolific music-making. Certainly until the 2002 upheaval, it was particularly during the festival months and funeral celebrations that musical activity hits its zenith there.

> Dagomba funerals are spectacles. The final funeral of an important or well-loved man or woman can draw several thousand people as participants and spectators . . . Spread out over a large area, all types of musical groups form their circles. In several large circles, relatives and friends dance to the music of *dondons* and *gongons*.[2] (Chernoff 1979, 44)

It is primarily at night after 11 pm that the music and dancing explode, continuing till dawn.

Most commonly, people remember the tales recited, sung, and accompanied by drumming by the *luntse*, characterized by Phyllis Ferguson as drummer-historians. They engage in praise-singing and praise-drumming—as accompanied by the *dondon*. The *luntse* are sim-

CHILDHOOD HOME 71

Figure 2.1. Da Tchuma Luna, Baba Fuseini (photo by Deborah Pellow).

ilar to the griots of Western Sudan, responsible for maintaining annals of the rulers. They "present accounts of individuals, places, and events seemingly no longer in the realm of myth but having a strongly historical character" (Ferguson 1972). While this material does not have the evidential value of written annals, it provides cycles of traditions which well-reflect changing political configurations. The *luna* (sing.) sings the tale in Dagbani, accompanied by other drummers. There are two types of early historical material, the first "is concerned with beings possessed of extraordinary physical traits, belonging to towns which can no longer be identified with any assurance, and involved in events which seem but remotely linked to the mainstreams of Dagomba history" (Ferguson 1972). The second type presents accounts of individuals, places, and events, more historical than mythical. The latter serves as a mnemonic device for the history of Dagbon. During the annual festivals, chiefly funerals and installations, as well as other Dagomba state occasions, the *luntse* recite and drum excerpts from the annals.

Da Tchuma Luna, Baba Fuseini, Tamale's current chief *luna* (Figure 2.1), characterized his job in the following way (September 26, 2005),

> I am the king of possessors of traditions of Dagbon. I hold the traditions. Even the government has rewarded me [he has a trophy on his table, with a musical note on it]. I am the royal chief of tom-tom in the whole country [actually Tamale].

In his retelling of Dagomba history, he recited names and events without pause. He told the story of the creation of the *luntse,* of the creation of Dagbon; Dagomba encounters/fights with the Gonja; how the only *tindana* in Tamale not killed (the Da Tchuma), had died naturally the day before. He recited the genealogies of Ya-Nas. His recitation encoded rules and moral lessons, several referring to the 2002 murder of the Ya-Na and the question of how to choose his successor and who would be eligible, no tom-tom till chief buried; if you kill the Ya-Na, you cannot be enstooled; even when soothsayers came up with a choice, people rejected it; the Mamprussi are conflict resolvers; there is a problem of choosing a chief because the Dagomba are divided into factions. And his recitation contained colorful proverbs, "A man's tongue is what you use to enter men's stomach" and "The best guinea corn will gather chickens."

The *luntse* have work, says Da Tchuma Luna, because Dagomba like to hear about their ancestors. His two sons, including one who lives in the south in Takoradi, also trained as *luntse*. As individuals relocate to the south, out of the motherland, much of this gets lost. One man recounted the tale of a man's daughter going to a school play. The man was somehow concerned about the girl's safety and asked his sister (the Auntie) to give her some protection, some talisman (a traditional thing). The Auntie said,

> We *have* lost our culture. The things we saw and valued we haven't preserved or paid attention to. Our grandfathers could find herbs in the bush to cure malaria—I don't know the name of one tree in Dagbani except for a few trees like kapok or baobab. I don't know trees or plants. Some people bring in their own wisdom and then they mess up the whole society and a whole culture and the whole picture. (Abdul Majid October 22, 2005)

A Dagomba child in Accra may not know *Damba*, or *Bugum*. Bugum marks the end of one year and the beginning of the next. One purges the evils of the year ending by throwing flaming torches into the bush.

> In the old days it was a festival of vengeance and purging . . . All the people took their bundles of grass and set light to the bush, thereby ridding it of any lurking evil spirits . . . Thus the whole land, and its population, was freed from evil influences, and the ordinary work of the people could again proceed in peace. (quoted in Ferguson 1972, 123)

The southern dwellers do not celebrate these occasions consistently, but up north they do, which the *luntse* highlight.

And yet, many of those I spoke with, nostalgia aside, observed that because of the proverbs and not always accessible narrative, children really could not understand the *luntse*. In fact, according to one man, "no one understands. It's poetic . . . For example, a lot of people [in the West] will go watch "Midsummer Night's Dream" and the English is different, but they will catch pieces. Same for the drummers" (Abdul Majid October 22, 2005). So one needed an elderly person to interpret. But, he would agree, the *luntse* were and are the keepers of the lore, the touchstone to history. And they are public performers.

The Chiefly Presence

Much of what the *luntse* talk about is the history of Dagomba chieftaincy. At Damba, the "tom-tom beaters" come and call all the royals' names and the family names (Abdulai Yakubu November 23, 2005). This is as true today as in the past. The Sunson chief observed, "when the tom-tom beater is singing he praises me alone and tells that my father is a chief, my mother's family they are just ordinary people, this is what my tom-tom beater will say. He will never combine them, say your father king, your mother king. Never. He will allow people to know that I belong to my father's side, the chief" (Sunson Na June 25, 2008).

The chiefs perform traditional social, religious, political and judicial duties. The Dagomba I spent time with grew up appreciating the chiefs' importance. Many of them came from royal families—having a chief father, uncle, grandfather, and surrounded by princes galore. They also spent time around the chiefly compounds. Abdulai Yakubu remembers from his childhood that his playground was the compound of one of the Tamale chiefs. And whenever there was a function in the palace, he and the other children would attend. This included the traditional court, where the chief would adjudicate.

The chiefs are bound by rules and taboos. On Mondays and Fridays, in the past and today, the chiefs sit in state. As a child, Haruna Iddrisu, a Tamale Member of Parliament, would spend time at the Tamale chief's house. When my assistant Zibilila was a boy, he said you would "hardly see the Ya-Na moving outside, so we used to be his telephone line. 'There's a funeral in town, there's an outdooring in town, there's a wedding in town . . .' And the Ya-Na will then send an elder and kola" (May 11, 2006).

Alhassan Andani, the Stanbic Bank president who came from a chiefly house, said all chiefs have various encumbrances and responsibilities.

> [In the past] chiefs led from the front; chiefs chose the spot where the village settled. They apportioned rules and responsibilities. And the way the community was settled was a very communal community. So you have a chief who provides the leadership and all the counsel and all the judgement, then you have your elders who are all the repositories of the traditions and the wisdom of the people, and you have your drummers and traditional *luntse* who keep the history of the clan. Then you have the blacksmith who fashioned our tools for farming and war and everything, then you have your butchers, who looked after the animals and provided meat. And if you weren't a butcher, you couldn't go and do butchering. And if you're not a *luna*, you can't say you are a *luna*. And all of that was held together by the chief. (June 13, 2008)

When Henry Kaleem became a chief, he said his life changed, his freedom of movement was curtailed, he was no longer allowed to eat in public, he had to wear a smock, cap and carry a walking stick (March 13, 2013). Some months before the Regent of Dagbon, Kampakuya-Na was installed in April 2006, I asked him about his life as the Ya-Na's firstborn son when he was young. As a royal, he had to be circumspect, so no one would talk about him. During the day, he could go to school and work. It was only at night that he was free to see friends. Because of the rivalry with the Abudu gate, he needed ancestral protection from black spirits. He could not attend festivals, because people carried weapons and anyone could harm him. The restrictions applied to all of the Ya-Na's children, since one could not predict who would be chosen regent (November 12, 2005).

Yet according to Bishop Vincent Boi-Nai, Bishop of Yendi and a Ga man from the south, this has not dampened the aspirations of many Dagomba men to become a chief (March 17, 2013), and this is because "you can't talk about Dagbon without talking about chiefs—they are central in Dagomba life" (Issa Naseri September 27, 2005). B. A. Fuseini, who played roles in government, foreign service and education, was also a sub-chief in his village. ". . . when I come, they bend down. So it's an honor to me. So Dagombas, they respect chieftaincy. And our smocks and so on, it gives us some dignity" (September 30, 2005). And as the Tuya-Na, Former Regional Director of Culture, observed, "If I am a chief, I don't come and greet you, you come and greet me" (November 9, 2005).

Dagomba society accepts that chiefs exercise some powers in the collective interests of the community. In many villages, there might not be a police station. Yet crimes are committed there. And they must be resolved. That falls to the chief. Dr. A. E. Abdulai's father was the chief of Savelugu, one of the three chiefly gates that leads to the kingship. "In my father's time . . . they had the courts themselves. They settled disputes. They were very respected. They came out to durbar and you see that . . ." (A. E. September 18, 2005).

"When we were children, a lot of the cases that came were rape cases. [And a little bit of land] most of it having to do with the chief himself, since he owns most of the land." Many of the lands are held in trust by the chiefs on behalf of the people. This also gives them considerable economic and political influence. "Also a few cases of witchcraft . . . If a woman was accused of witchcraft, the chief was supposed to have some powers to exorcise her so that she would be free of it" (Abdulai Yakubu November 23, 2005).

Witchcraft accusations have been documented in Ghana for years, and David Tait wrote about witchcraft and sorcery among the Konkomba, neighbors to the Dagomba (Tait 1963), which tend to be leveled against someone with whom the accuser has some connection. Yakubu does not remember the chief banishing the accused to one of the witches camps, settlements that still operate in the Northern and Upper East Regions today, and indeed forced exile has not been "a general practice in the Northern Region, nor among the Dagomba, but places of refuge" (Richter et al. 2017, 5). In July 2017, I visited Kpatina, one of the five operating in the Northern Region; within the Gushiegu district, it is off of a dirt road in the middle of the bush. Forty-one women live there with a male caretaker. The caretaker insisted that no one stays forever, though "sometimes as long as they stay here, they become old" (July 20, 2017). When a particular woman's problem is resolved, he asks the kin to come and get her. The caretaker also makes sure that whoever does return home is not harmed. Like other such communities, while based on stigma, the women develop a community. The group, sitting around me, serenaded me with two songs, the first, life is like a pot and should be handled with care, and the second, men and children won't see me again. While on the one hand one might see the witches' camps as loci of discrimination, they can also be seen as places to safeguard the lives of those women at risk from accusation. The chiefs "touch the highpoints of our culture. [They] represent the sum total of our culture. Of the people. [You] see chiefs as representing culture and therefore also pay allegiance to them" (M. Mumuni, former Minister of Foreign Affairs, May 1, 2006). If the average Dagomba man in Dagbon were to wake up to hear that there is no chief, "he would be a lost man. Because he defines his own position in relation to the chief. Therefore without the chief, [there's] no reference. For some elderly, the chief affects his life more than government" (Mumuni May 1, 2006).

Figure 2.2. The warriors of one of the Dagomba chiefs, Yendi, April 2006 (photo by Deborah Pellow).

In the old days, to send a child to school, one had to pass through the chiefs to be selected (Dr. Alhassan May 14, 2006). Yakubu, the former MP of Mion, thinks back to his childhood, "When we were kids, the chief was more important than the central government. My grandfather could institute penalties. In those days, the chief had a farm and it was the job of the villages to take turns working the farm. The chief could mobilize labor" (May 7, 2006). When Dr. Andani, older brother to the Stanbic Bank president and himself a cardiologist who practiced in Kumase, was to be installed as the Sarnargu-Na (the Chief of Sarnargu), a number of his peers went to Kumase, "we wore our robes and we danced through the streets of Kumase to his in-laws' place. And it attracted a lot of attention" (Joshua Hamidu June 20, 2008).

Even today, every chief still has his warriors who carry their muskets to formal occasions (Figure 2.2). "When they start firing their muskets and all that . . ." The day before Kampakuya-Na was being installed as Regent of Dagbon, there was considerable joy, as there had been no one sitting on the Yendi skin since his father's murder four years earlier. The air in Yendi was full of gun powder from the continual discharging of front-loaded muskets. Despite the heat, men were wearing two and three heavy woven smocks as they danced and twirled to the drumming that was everywhere.

At even lesser occasions, such as when the chief is just sitting in state on Fridays and Mondays, he is surrounded by pomp. He is accompanied by his elders and lesser chiefs. He wears the hat and robes appropriate to his role and status. When he attends formal occasions such as funerals, he arrives with a retinue preceded by drummers and praise-singers. The chief and his attendants represent the greatness of Dagbon.

Shrines

The god of a town "resides" in the sacred grove, a patch of woody vegetation often cited as a feature of the northern Ghana landscape conserved by communities for ritual purposes and the *tindana* is caretaker of the sacred grove or earth shrine. "The *tindana* does not only own the land, but by reason of his ownership is the only one who knows or is known by the 'spirit of the land'. Since the tradition and worship of the 'earth-gods' is common throughout Ghana and amongst its people it is only the landowners (*tindamba*) that can pacify the gods of the earth" (Manboah-Rockson 2007, 10).

> When A. W. Cardinall was writing in the early 1900s, he reported that the *tindana* arranges for the annual sacrifices; introduces new Chiefs to the Earth-god; is the chief peacemaker when the wars break out; orders the sacrifices when blood is on the ground or vile offenses such as incest (i.e. adultery with a female of too close a consanguinity or marriage connection) pollute the soil; appoints the day when the new crops may be eaten generally by the community at large, since one is always free to cut an ear or two of grain to stave off starvation; in short, regulates all matters touching his deity. (1920, 25f.)

Earth shrines are "ancient cultural features of the West African savannah" (MacGaffey 2013, 77). "Almost all Dagomba villages have such groves or *bugele*, locally translated as 'fetish'. Such *bugele* usually consist of a clump of trees, generally containing more species than are found in the surrounding landscape, and often on a mound or tumulus" (Blench and Dendo 2004, 2; emphasis included). The *bugele* is distinguished from other places by an unusual feature, a mound of earth, spring, dense patch of forest (MacGaffey 2013) and what defines the place are the rituals performed. Sacred groves have a variety of features, including small size, greater diversity of flora than the surrounding bush, and frequently evidence of a former settlement on the site (Blench and Dendo 2004).

The further into the bush, the larger the groves. In the Dagomba area, groves are attached to the community as a whole and are the location of communal rituals, although they are more responsive to the needs of extended households. While most Dagomba are Muslim, they do not see this as contradictory to maintenance of the groves, and they preserve societal rules in relation to the groves. For example, firewood may not be cut nor plants collected. There are also places where one cannot build a house. In Tamale, the area of the Victory Cinema has many trees. It is considered a place of the gods, thus one cannot build there. People say that even if the local chief, the Gulkpe-Na, gives land in that area to someone to build, if the person builds a house and moves in, he will not live for another year.

Adults, even women for whom the shrines are rarely accessible, develop ties to sacred groves as salient local places. When the occasion warrants, the connection to them may be greater than to other local spots. An auto parts dealer friend of mine in Tamale who must be around fifty years old remembers from his childhood busloads of people (whom he identified as Gonja) making pilgrimages to the shrines (March 19, 2013). And Dr. Mohammed Mahama, another friend of mine, now a physician in Accra, remembers Jagbo, near the Dagomba town of Tolon, as a very powerful shrine. It has three animals associated with it—the lion, crocodile and snake. After Mohammed's father died, his mother moved back to her hometown area. Feeling the need, she went to the Jagbo shrine. She said she saw a lion and collapsed (March 10, 2013).

The shrines are a tie to the place for many who grew up in the north. They are still widely maintained for traditional spiritual reasons and people from near and far visit them for help—because one's business is obstructed, his welfare is not good, a woman's pregnancy is prevented by witchcraft. According to David Tait, Dagomba believe that most sorcerers (witches) are women and elderly. The latter were most commonly accused of witchcraft by a member of the household. In his analysis, Tait (1963) connects the outbreak with fear of societal change. Indeed, people may go to shrines rather than the chief when there is alleged witchcraft—for adjudication, arbitration, reconciliation (Henry Kaleem March 13, 2013). Men and women also go to the shrine to ask for a child; they "make a vow," that is, engage in a ritual accompanied by a future sacrifice (Tait 1963). Thus, the shrines have provided relief at times of change.

At the shrines, the *tindamba* pour libations and make sacrifices of a chicken, goat or cow, depending upon the circumstance. The sacrifice, which is a gift, is to the shrine or an elder. There is also a sacrifice in Dagbon that may be carried out on behalf of chiefs, "not to request a fa-

Figure 2.3. The caretaker of the shrine at Katariga with her elders (photo by Deborah Pellow).

vor but to ward off a possible punitive event occasioned by some offense to the royal ancestors and their acolytes" (MacGaffey 2013, 81). Groves have specific names, which refer to the grove's origin and to the sacrifice carried out there. They often have familial relationships, for example, one grove referred to as the "child" of another. In the Tamale area, there are seven, Yong Duuni, Katariga, Yong-Dakpemyilli, Kpalinga, Pong-Tamale and Nawuni. People go to these shrines for particular reasons. For example, Yong-Duuni, off of the Kunbungu Road, about thirty minutes from Tamale, is said to be the most powerful of the shrines. This shrine is important because Nyangse, son of Sitobu, the founder of the Dagomba, is said to be buried here.

> At the time of the *tindamba*, it was Nyangse who was going around killing them and enskinning his [customary] children. When he reached Yong-Duuni in the evening, he said that in the morning he would cut off the head of the *tindana*, go straight to Tamale and cut off the head of Dakpema [Tamale's *tindana*]. The moment he said that, in 30 minutes he sees he is paralyzed and told his elders, "this is the place I am going to die—I can't proceed on my journey again."

After his death, he left his smock, walking stick, red hat, small calabash, small pot and spoon. (Kpana-lana, chief linguist to the shrine's chief, March 14, 2013)

According to local lore, it is Nyangse's smock, walking stick, and hat that are used to enskin the shrine's chief, Duu-Na.

Yong-Duuni has two holy spots, the big shrine, a grove of trees, and hill of dirt, which I was only allowed to view from a considerable distance, because of its sacredness, and the little shrine, which is a stone's throw from the caretaker's *zong*, a large round ante-chamber. The little shrine has a diameter of about 6', a mud wall about 3' high, a pile of faggots leaning up against in front, and a low dead tree in middle with oval form nestled on it with feathers on top. It is men who come to the shrine if they feel it is necessary to sacrifice or if they have a problem. But near the *zong*, there is a nim tree where a woman can go to commune for help, and at the time of the annual sacrifice, women can come and sit outside. Yong Duuni's caretaker, Duu-Na Alhassan Adam, told me the shrine is important "because we inherited it from our ancestors" (March 14, 2013).

The shrines provide tangible rootedness for petitioners and other Dagomba. They are the grounding for Dagomba origin myths. The myths reflect the unique contexts of their inception, revelation, and later ritual, social, or political practice (Blier 2004). They are often subject to multiple and conflicting interpretations. Culturally based, they impact the way one sees the world.

Work

The predominant occupation was and is farming, on land worked by family members. Until recent years, farming was done through rotational fallow. Now there is more bush fallow with mixed cropping for root crops and cash crops, unlike the south, which was and is tree crops. The water supply is primarily provided by rainfall. To deal with its unpredictability, the Chief of Sunson had a dam built (see Chapter One). The work was begun in 2010 on the spot of a large watering hole. By 2013, the dam was complete, including a "sea wall" to prevent village flooding, and a valve system for irrigation. A structure was built where farmers can dry their produce. When I was there in March 2013, farmers had begun planting rice and other vegetables, such as okra. Women were using the public pipes to wash clothes, which they then laid out to dry on grass and shrubs. Two groups of cattle were being watered. Management of the dam was handed over to the Ministry of Agriculture. Farmers should be able to irrigate about 100 acres. This will make a huge difference to farming that has been totally dependent on the vagaries of the rains.

The farmers mainly grow maize, yam, cassava, sorghum, millet, cowpeas, groundnut, soybean and tomatoes. "When I was young, most of the people were farmers, even in Tamale—all these places that we are staying now were farms. When we were children, most of our father's relations were farmers" (Tuya-Na November 9, 2005). There was a sexual division of crop production. So for example, Tuya-Na's mother would take 100 guinea fowl eggs to sell every market day at Kunbungu. He believes that the women during his growing up years were richer than their husbands. While they were harvesting okra, the men hadn't yet harvested the yams. Yam was the man's crop. The men prepared the ground and made the yam mounds and on that first day, the women would prepare a sumptuous meal for the communal laborers, who gave the women big yams, as ingredients for the meals and as a product to sell. The farms were divided up into one-third acre lots, each demarcated with okra or spinach or whatever which were the women's crops. At Christmastime, as they were Muslims, they were in the bush harvesting rice.

All children of these farming families had their chores. It was expected of them, before they started their schooling, to carry out farming tasks. Once they were enrolled in school, this continued. When B. A. Fuseini was young, he looked after his father's horse. Then he was "promoted" to look after the sheep. Once in school, he would come home and take care of the sheep, and as he matured, the cattle. Dr. Alhassan, an architect who retired to Tamale, took care of the poultry on his father's farm. Dr. Nasser and his siblings would work on their father's farm. While he was primarily a butcher, he farmed rice and corn as well. It was hard work, but the children from the various villages would congregate there to help and have fun while working. And others remembered that during the Christmas break, "we were in the bush harvesting rice" (Mahdi September 16, 2005). Dr. David Abdulai, the pro-bono medical doctor in Tamale, was born into a poverty-stricken family. His contribution to the household economy as a child was expected.

> So I used to help my mother as a kid. I used to go around peoples' houses weeding for some money, like two shillings in those days would be 20 pesewas. They would give it to me and I'd give it to my mother who would then buy some ingredients or she'd go to the mill and buy the droppings of millet and maize. They would gather everything together with stones and re-grind it and then sell it out to us. That's how we lived and I did that most of my life as a kid. My classmates started calling me "Ali the Grasscutter" because they saw me going into the bush. (March 14, 2013)

In some cases, farm work, and for the girls, domestic work, could and did interfere with schooling; "that is our folly, long ago" said Tamale Dakpema (May 12, 2006), because it gave the family the excuse not to send the child to school. In the case of girls, this is ongoing, as many still practice the custom of sending the girls "to the aunties." This demands that a father who has a daughter gives her to his sisters or other female relatives to train her; and "that child is presumed to be the servant of the house" (MP Mary Boforo June 8, 2006). Unless that caretaker is pro-education, the situation often eradicates the girls' educational opportunities. I discuss this in great detail in the next chapter.

Compound Life

The homes the Dagomba grew up in were family compounds, *yili* (family or house). In northern Ghana, the socio-spatial template of the Dagomba house is the round hut. In most cases, the enclosed structures were mud-and-wattle, the round rooms giving the compound a circular appearance. The spaces between compounds vary from two meters to fifty, the distance correlating with closeness of kinship. Major settlements today consist of twelve to fifteen compounds, far smaller than the 120 compounds during the pre-colonial era. Ghanaian architect Al-Hassan (1980) cites an 1898 description of Dagomba nucleated settlements and asserts that this description still the true picture of a Dagomba village of today,

> The villages are composed of small blocks of swish huts with thatched conical roofs. These huts are circular and connected together with swish walls. All the huts open in the court yard, which has only one opening. The swish walls are about 5 feet high, and the blocks are easily put into a state of defence by removing the thatched roofs and notching the walls. The thatch can be piled up to form born fires about 100 yards off in case of a night attack. (p. 177)

The size of the compound, as well as oblong rooms and roofs with corrugated galvanized iron or aluminum sheets, are indicative of economic prosperity and social status. A fully developed compound has three courtyards—each surrounded by the huts of a particular sex group. The courtyards are separate for men and women.

Titled compound heads all have a *zong*, a very large round hall. There is a doorway at the back of the *zong* through which one may access the compound yard. The uses of the *zong* depend upon the household head's social standing and profession and include the receiving of guests, ceremonies, holding the chief's council, and as a sleeping room for six- to

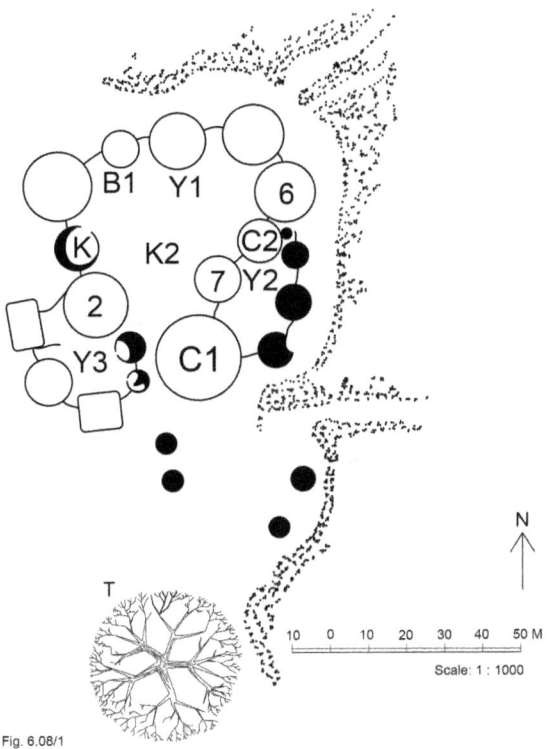

Figure 2.4. Drawing of a Dagomba compound (Al-Hassan 1980, 180b, redrawn by Liu Qi).

fourteen-year-old boys (Oppong 1973). "Once you [a boy] are weaned, you are past six years, you don't live with your mother again. You live in the *zong*—you stay there with [all of the male children]" (Alhassan Andani June 13, 2008). The owner/chief sits on a raised platform on the right of the inner entrance, while visitors sit between the horse and owner. A bicycle leans against the wall. The equestrian tradition rooted in the seventeenth-century migrant cavalrymen who are said to have created the Dagomba Kingdom is evident today in the chief's *zong*, where a horse is kept tethered.

The primary "room" in the compound (Figure 2.4) is the central yard Y1, the women's courtyard, with K2, the dry season kitchen, in the middle. The yard is entered through the *zong* (C1). Y2 is the compound head's courtyard and Y3 the male courtyard. The shower room is B1. The central

Figure 2.5. Courtyard of Sunson-Na's compound (photo by Deborah Pellow).

yard (Y1) is lively. This is where the women do many of their domestic chores, such as washing laundry and preparing food, and it is here that meals are eaten by all members of the household. The compound's cooking area (hearth, *daanga*), functionally the kitchen, is often demarcated by large rocks. Cooking is done on a coal pot. This kitchen is a communal facility, shared by all of the adult women. As illustrated in Figure 2.5, one sees various implements of domestic duties, mortars and pestles for pounding yam, fire places and coal pots for cooking. Cooking fuel may be wood but is more commonly charcoal. Cooking is labor intensive, ingredients are transported to the yard from the daily market, cupboards or (in some cases) refrigerators. Without a sink, water must be carried over in buckets from a compound spigot if there is one, or from a large drum when there isn't. When water is used for washing ingredients, it must be dumped somewhere—normally there is a channel from the shower room that leads outside of the compound wall, or the dirty water can be carried outside to be dumped.

All of the female members work in the courtyard. The senior wife is at the top of the women's hierarchy. The women squat or sit on low stools to peel vegetables, parboil tomatoes and eggplant, grind onions by hand on a stone, periodically washing off utensils with water in a bucket. Rice is picked through to remove stones. Once the yam has been boiled, it is pounded into a glutinous mass. Often, the women pound together, singing and throwing their pestles into the air in time with the rhythm of their work. Following the meal, bowls and pots are stacked nearby. More water is carried over in buckets, washing up is done in large basins and then stacked to dry. The washing water is then carried over in buckets and dumped.

Looking today at the spatiality of the circular houses where the new Dagomba elite were raised (Lawrence-Zuniga and Pellow 2008), it is hard to speak of individual "taste" or "style"—housing conformed to an ancestral template. Even today, very little in Yendi has changed. "They keep those same mud houses. In many places, I still see a lot of that. One or two areas people have put up houses, outskirts. The area I knew in Yendi town, is almost the same . . . the old area . . near the palace . . ." (Dr. M. Iddrisu September 2, 2005). Yet, material and lifestyle elements have changed throughout Dagbon over time, which has impacted the built environment. And local people make choices when deciding to build one shape rather than the other. While Prussin (1970) explains the diffusion of mud masonry building techniques—and thus rectangular shapes—through the movement of Muslim traders and Muslim building traditions across the Sahara to the southern savannah of the Western Sudan, Al-Hassan (1980) asserts that the introduction of rectangular forms into the Dagomba compound is evidence of carrying modernity from the south. When the British established their northern headquarters in Tamale in 1907, they introduced rectangular buildings. Over time, the circular huts in Tamale were engulfed by an expanding, European-designed town. As with the building choices that one sees in Accra today, shapes and contents represent a combination of personal taste and what the individual perceives as desirable. For example, as Moore (1986) pointed out for the Marakwet of Kenya, by making such alterations one enhances his/her status vis-à-vis others in the community. The ability to effect these changes, whether in the north or the south of Ghana, has been principally dependent on the cash incomes of the people but there is also a consciousness of distinction that provides the fuel for change.

Electricity came to some parts of Dagbon when these men and women were children, but it was from generators. "When I was young, there was no electricity. It was so dark [in Yendi]" (Aminu Ahmadu December 5, 2005). A. E. Abdulai, living in Savelugu in the chief's palace, also grew up without electricity, reading and studying by a candle (September 18, 2005). He used a fire to keep warm during the cool Harmattan nights. He also put grass on the floor under his sleeping mat, otherwise bugs would bite. Similarly, Ahminu Ahmadu remembers "sleeping *gbubgbala*," while sleeping on a mat, sometimes worms would get into your skin. And now his children have their own rooms with air conditioning, whereas he did not have even his own room till he was in sixth form of secondary school; he slept anywhere in the house like others (December 5, 2005).

Marriage and Children

The connection between the various generational members of a polygynous Dagomba household is enabled by the tradition of everyone eating from one cooking pot. Unlike in the south, the household head's wives cook by turns for the entire household during their respective rotation.

> The eldest of the wives who is the "paani" takes leadership of the women. So she actually rotates the cooking. So you do it for one week and you look after everybody—the kids and every member of the household is looked after by the woman who has the responsibility for the week. (Alhassan Andani June 13, 2008)

In Adisa Munka'ila's home, "one would cook two days, the other would cook two days, the other would cook two days, and we never noticed any difference between our mothers (November 10, 2005)." Only at the breakfast meal did the mothers cater for their own children (Ramatu Alhassan June 9, 2006). It was also not unusual for a child to walk into a neighbor's house when they are in the middle of a meal and to "jump right in" and eat (Yakubu Andani October 18, 2005). This was an extension of the polygynous household, where everyone was part of the same community.

In these polygynous households, there were a lot of wives and a lot of children. People told me that when they were growing up, there was no limit on family size. This was tied in part to the number of reproducing women. Only two of the Dagomba men and women in my study were born to men with only one wife. According to one of the two, his father just wasn't a very successful polygamist—"he had attempted a marriage here and there which didn't work" (Haruna Atta May 29, 2006). The majority of the fathers had between two and four wives while these men and women were growing up. For some men who had four wives at a time, given divorce and death, "it was difficult to say how many wives overall" (Fuseini Baba April 28, 2006). As former Vice President of Ghana Aliu observed to me, "there were shifts, some came, some went" (June 19, 2006).

Chiefs were (and are) in a different category. They often are married to more than the Muslim rule of four wives at any given time, "Tradition mixes with Islam. Tradition extended it beyond four—and they didn't marry them all at the same time. By the time you are marrying the fifth wife, the six wives have already had their children. After a while, another will come" (A. E Abdulai September 18, 2005).

The father of Lt General Joshua Hamidu and Mahama Shani Hamidu (the Sunson chief) was a chief and like all chiefs had multiple wives. Their mother started as Wife #5 and gradually became Wife #2, as some of the wives either died or left. The child who became Sunson-Na married a woman in Accra when he was in the military and stationed there. When he returned to Sunson and was made chief, he was forced to marry five more women. But why so many? "You met me in the farm. There are my wives. That's the reason. They are every day, anytime in the palace cooking for the visitors. One cannot handle that. Look at the size of the compound. One cannot handle it. So there's a reason for that . . . and tradition. [But] against my wish . . . They even wanted me to go further than that, I said no" (June 25, 2008).

Salamatu Abdulai confirms both tradition and farm needs. Her father (also the father of A. E. Abdulai and Mopson Abdulai) was a real player in Dagomba chieftaincy politics. When she was a child, he was the Chief of Banvim, on the edge of Tamale, and at that time he had thirty-three wives. By the time A. E. was a young boy, their father had progressed to Savelugu, where he had twenty-five wives.

> Because he was a chief, because of tradition, he could marry as many as he liked . . . You know the women . . . they were helping on the farm, and when it was time for millet, groundnut, instead of going to houses to bring people to come and do it . . . it's the women who do that.
>
> . . . you know, our mothers enjoyed more than these modern chiefs and their wives. At Banvim, when we were at Banvim, we get up dawn, during season like this, rainy season, we get up as early as 4 and go to the villages. Any farm we get, if it is okra, we just pluck everything. If it is pepper, we pluck everything. And sometimes I remember, on 2 or 3 occasions, the farmer would come and meet you. He'd say, Oh my mothers, good morning. Then my mothers would answer. Then the senior wife would tell the rest—Ok let's go, the farmer is now in. Then he'd say, oh you continue. Then we pluck everything and leave. Nobody will say anything. When it comes to dry season, you know after they are going to harvest the yam, before harvesting, the sticks—we'll go to one yam farm and remove all the sticks. When he comes to meet you, Oh let me give you yam. Then he will give you yam, and you carry the sticks [for the yam vines to climb] and the yam home. Now, you can't simply do that. (Salamatu Abdulai July 17, 2017)

Alhassan Andani, the Managing Director of Stanbic Bank whose father was a chief, understands the multiplicity of wives as a tradition that has held Dagbon together,

> If a chief is nominated various clans and sub-villages will pick their best matings and send them to the chief so the matings can produce an heir to the throne. So in that way every village was represented in the chief's house. So some of the women the chief had never seen with his eyes, but once you agree to be chief, it means that if a clan wants you to take their mating, you have to accept it, you cannot reject it. And the only object of that woman is not to come to be a wife but is also representing a clan, is there to reproduce and to represent their interests in the palace. (June 13, 2008)

Aminu Ahmadu grew up in Yendi. "We were in the family house. Eventually my father had four wives and they were all quite interesting women—such interesting women, we were all staying together" (December 5, 2005). A. A.'s father was an imam, his father's father was an imam, his father's father's father was an imam. "For people like that, don't get jealousy among wives. Even where mother is at home, not unusual to give you to another woman to raise" (Aminu Ahmadu December 5, 2005). He was the child of the senior wife, but she left when he was young. "I didn't grow up to even meet my mother in the house . . . I stayed with my father and stepmothers. That's normal. Stepmothers treated me like their own son" (December 5, 2005).

What is particularly telling is the household coherence even in households with many women. As A. E. Abdulai observed to me, "The thing about polygamy in the north is it is not like any other polygamy. We grow up mixed and it doesn't matter who is your mother" (September 18, 2005). In Adisa Munka'ila's home, "it was the most interesting thing that happened . . . everybody was somebody else's child. We had common mothers. You didn't feel that you missed your own mother. We were there in the community. And our father was the father of the house" (Adisa November 10, 2005). For some time, A. E. thought that his half-brother Mopson's mother was his mother, because she lived next door, like a sister in the very large chief's compound; "it's a culture for them" (A. E. Abdulai September 18, 2005).

Among the individuals I got to know, some households had as few as four, some as many as twenty-seven children. Joshua Hamidu observed that in his family "some wives had two, three, four, five, up to six . . . When my father died [1985], I didn't know how many siblings I had" (J. Hamidu June 20, 2008). While his father was still alive,

> whenever I went home, the first wife used to have a gourd and she would call me and pour out pebbles and say, "When you were away,

these were the children that were born," and tell me who their mothers were, so I was able to keep tap on how many children I could count as brothers and sisters. It was difficult to see them all but because we had this huge compound you saw everyone around, learned to know that is my sister, that is my brother. (J. Hamidu June 20, 2008)

Dr. Nasser, who teaches at University of Ghana, and his younger brother Iliasu, who worked as a journalist in Tamale, are both sons of their father's senior wife—who had ten children. Their father's second wife had seven children and the third had nine. Because of the way the family operated, as among so many others in the north, there was no rivalry among the children of the wives because of their seniority.

In some households, just as it was difficult to say how many wives there had been overall, it was difficult to tell how many children one's father had produced (Fuseini Baba April 28, 2006). When Ramatu was still young, living with her father in Yendi or later in Tamale, they lived all together in the compound house, all of the wives and all of the children. Things might have been difficult, "but you had each other" (Ramatu Alhassan June 9, 2006)—and that included full and half siblings. When A. E. Abdulai was a child, it was his half-brother Mopson, the older of the two, who took A. E. to school.

During the period this bridge generation was growing up, the children initially stayed with the mother in her hut. Children of three to four years of age slept in the senior wife's room on a mat. Unmarried women, such as daughters, grandchildren, and younger sisters, moved back into their mother's or grandmother's room, staying on until they married—unless they were loaned out to the aunties, in which case they relocated altogether. Once a boy reached six years of age, "you don't live with your mother again [any longer]" (Alhassan Andani June 13, 2008). The boy moved out to the "bigger house," that is the *zong*, along with all of the other boys of the compound (Oppong 1973).

The children eat/ate together by sex and age cohort, in the compound yard. "They will group you according to ages. You will sit around one bowl" (DCE Tijiani September 25, 2005). "Up till my sixth form, when I was in primary school, we were probably about 16 eating from one bowl. It's a very big calabash. With 16 sitting around it. If you run out of soup, you take it back and they put soup in it. [By] the time I finished Secondary Form 5, I remember we were about eight eating from the same bowl" (Aminu Ahmadu December 5, 2005).

While the children squatted or sat on their haunches, sharing in the common bowl, the wives (the mothers) and other adult women also ate together, elsewhere in the compound yard. The adult men of the household ate together outside of the compound walls. For many still living in the north today, this household cohesion is the same. One friend of mine is a successful small businessman in Tamale, selling automotive parts. He has two wives, two houses, nine children. He has blended the children of the two women in the two houses to make them jell as siblings.

Conclusion

The members of the Dagomba bridge generation grew up in Dagbon—or, if they had moved elsewhere with parents for the father's job, came back regularly. All spent considerable time there in their youth, until they went to their A levels in secondary school (Tamale Secondary only went through O levels), to university in the south or overseas, or to work. Through all of this, they developed attachment to their hometowns, pieces of physical space that carry great social significance. These places have facilitated relationships and activities and play a symbolic role within the system of social relations. They are tied to tales of chiefs and cultural heroes, to festivals and religious sites, to childhoods, work and play, marriages and households of multiple wives. Unlike polygynous households in the south, age cohorts of half-siblings all ate together from the same bowl cooked by the same person, as the wives of the patriarch rotated through their roles.

These ties have infiltrated not just their memories but their contemporary behavior. They return "home" for holidays (during the four years after the Ya-Na's murder, this was far less true), they support their kin, and they absorb those referred to them into their network in Accra. They have in turn subsidized households up north, primarily their own kin network. It is particularly the connection with chieftaincy and the kingship that has become entangled in their relocated lives. As I detail later in the book, the background I have laid out in this chapter, of people, places and things, has also particularly fed into the excitement of members of the 1.5 generation regarding who is sitting on the skin in Yendi. Many are highly placed, in government or business, their opinions matter, and they have resources to sink into evolving situations, indeed to fuel them.

NOTES

1. Although for the past few decades, chiefs have been enriching themselves by selling off land.
2. The dondon, the more common, is a tension drum, fitted under the arm. It is "carved in the shape of an hourglass, with two mouths; the two skins,

thinned almost to parchment and sewn onto rings of bound reeds, are laced together with leather string." A gongon is a drum that hangs from the shoulder. It is a large tom-tom with hide stretched across two large circular drumheads (Chernoff 1979, 43–44).

CHAPTER 3

Getting Educated

In those days, you had to put your arm over your head to try to touch the ear on the other side—if you could, you could go [to primary school] . . . If [you] couldn't reach, [you were] not up to age.

—Wayo Seini, October 14, 2005; Salamatu Abdulai, July 17, 2017; Fuseini Baba, April 28, 2006 (paraphrase)

Education was to be a major tool in the cultural conquest of Africa, and the colonial powers recognized that fact at an early date. The earliest Western schools set up by the British in Africa were in Sierra Leone, but throughout their African colonies, the British followed the missionaries. Christian groups such as the Church Mission Society (CMS), the African Inland Mission and the Church of Scotland are among the oldest European institutions in sub-Saharan Africa (White 1996). The missionaries "began with the idea that formal schools were essential to education, simply because education worked that way in Europe" (Curtin et al. 1978, 532). In the Gold Coast as elsewhere, the British allowed the missionary activity to relieve them of "educational administration and policy formation which the French assumed in their colonies before the turn of the century" (White 1996, 12). But the British also collaborated with the missions, a policy characteristic of British colonial education and different from the French system. There was great belief in a Christian-based system, as it would spread enlightenment. In the literature, the British express cultural sensitivity to values, practices and so on of the local people.

Like the system instituted by the French in their African colonies, the British colonial education system segregated schools and also distinguished between technical/vocational training and the purely academic. They emphasized academic rather than vocational training, retaining the latter for those they felt would not rise to high posts. The early vocational schools had an agricultural emphasis.

Following the establishment of primary education, the colonial government moved to establish teachers' training schools, secondary schools, seminaries, vocational schools, and lastly universities. Secondary schools were strong agents of European socialization and most were boarding schools. As in Britain, those who attended secondary school were a select minority, largely limited to men. They emphasized knowledge of English as necessary for civilization (Curtin et al. 1978, 533), as the British came to constitute a reference group for the aspiring cosmopolitans; this was true especially in the towns where their economic and political presence was most evident. The British brought with them a worldview that gave men primary access to the avenues of modernity and upward mobility, with education at its base.

In Chapter One, I touched on education as an element in the disadvantaging of the north of Ghana. The British colonial legacy is manifested in heavy investments in infrastructure, education and health in more endowed regions of the south (Senadza 2012), excluding the north. Girls were and are particularly adversely impacted. From a purely economics point of view, gender disparities in education may be attributed to poverty, as the poor tend to use their limited resources in educating boys rather than girls. In Dagbon, there are also cultural reasons, which I discuss later in this chapter. Apart from gender, there are significant spatial disparities in education in Ghana. This has been crucial in the (under) development of the north and its people, and in this chapter, I argue that the foundation to the success of the Dagomba 1.5ers was the fact of their gaining access to education. Clearly it was not the only factor and it was not a guarantee, but without it they could not have achieved their professional, social and economic success. Today the story is presumably different, as education is far more equitably distributed, far more northerners have been through secondary school and university, there are far more credentialed individuals throughout the country, and occupational positions are not plentiful. Even at the time that the 1.5ers were coming of age, many southerners with education finished higher education (secondary school) with no guarantees of a job. Perhaps most importantly, at the time that the 1.5 generation was coming of age, there was political will to better incorporate northerners into mainstream society. Kwame Nkrumah, Ghana's first president, is still beloved in Dagbon, because following his tour of the whole country in the early 1950s, he was persuaded that the regional inequalities dividing the north from the south could only be rectified by making education compulsory and, in the north, completely free. At that time, gaining professional education was generally far less common than today and thus gave the Dagomba who gained it a real advantage. During the initial sittings of the 1951–1954 parliament, while a majority of parliamentarians were southern regionalists, many from the south were sympathetic to northern problems.

> On education, for instance, one of the earliest demands for its improvement in the North in the 1951–1954 Assembly came from the Omanhene of Atandansu[1] when he asked the government for special considerations such as the award of Scholarships to northerners to study in South schools. (Saaka 2001, 148)

Well-known politicians, such as E. Ofori-Atta and Dr. K. E. Busia, also called on the government to do more to improve the educational system in the north.

Finally, because we are talking about a relatively small cohort of people, in a context of general illiteracy, I would assert that their educational and professional accomplishments have bestowed them with considerable status among the hometown people. This has facilitated their role as patrons.

They are very much a bridge generation: smart, academically gifted, and professionally accomplished, they left the old homesteads, occupations and insularity, and moved into modernity, in their home lives and work lives and in their openness to innovation. But they have not forgotten their roots. Nurtured by a culture of collectivity, they have blossomed into patrons for those they left behind. None of this would have been possible, if 1) the educational structures had not been put into place, 2) they (or an influential other) had not recognized the opportunity, and 3) they had not seized that opportunity. The last is particularly striking. The combination of poverty, uneducated elders, and basic unfamiliarity with the potential benefits of Western schooling presented major obstacles. As we shall see, they overcame them and flourished.

In this chapter, I briefly recite the educational context in Dagbon at the turn of the century starting with the place of *makaranta* (Quranic school), and missionary and colonial roles in setting up Western educational systems in the Northern Territories. The heart of the chapter is a series of conversations with various members of the Dagomba new educated elite to document the educational foundation of their journeys to becoming professionals. What many of this cohort emphasized to me was the role of serendipity in getting to secondary school and on to university. This is particularly the case with the (few) women members of this generation. A lot of the experience of going through the educational system was idiosyncratic, for both boys and girls. At the same time, those individuals who made it in and through did so because they were clearly smart enough, the facilities were there, the opportunities presented themselves, and families were supportive.

Gender bias in education is hardly confined to the north. Apart from whatever gender bias existed within Christian and colonial ideology, Dagomba culture then and to this day has discriminated against women. The imbalance is far worse in the north than in the south. But this is also true among the boys as well. And it makes the educational success of the 1.5ers all the more remarkable.

Foundations

The northern population generally has been characterized as unschooled, the new elite as the surprisingly literate. But to say that the populations in the north were illiterate prior to European occupation and the arrival of secular (Western) education is not completely correct, as Nigerian scholar S. A. S. Galadanci has written, "the introduction of colonial administration to Africans 'instantly made all previous scholarship burdensome'" (quoted in Owusu-Ansah, et al. 2013, 5).

Muslim children throughout the country have always been sent to *makaranta*, the basic traditional Islamic Quranic recitation school. Whether the education provided was limited or not, the socialization provided by the schools mattered greatly (Owusu-Ansah et al. 2013). *Makaranta* pupils learned the Arabic alphabets and words, learned to recite the Quran, to copy religious passages and were introduced to basic concepts and rituals of Islam (Skinner 1976).

In Ghana, the two main sources of Islamic learning were the Wangara, a Muslim merchant group from Mali, and Hausa traders, both of whom migrated into Ghana and after the sixteenth century spread throughout. They carried along Islam and Islamic education (Iddrisu 2005). The Quranic tradition of learning was firmly rooted by the mid-eighteenth century, as evidenced "by the fact that after the 1774/5 [sic] Asante invasion of Dagomba many plundered Arabic books were taken to Accra" (John Hunwick 2004, cited in Iddrisu 2005, 56).

Quranic learning has survived up to the present, "*every* [sic] child in the Muslim community is required to attend [some] form of Islamic learning institutions like the Qur'anic School or Makaranta" (Iddrisu 2005, 56, emphasis added). A child would begin this schooling by age six, with an Islamic teacher, a *mallam*, and progress to read the Quran. Talented students advance to studying the Islamic sciences.

While Dagbon never became a theocracy (Staniland 1975), the Dagomba are among the most highly Islamized of major Ghanaian groups (Ferguson 1972; Levtzion 1968).[2] A very important and powerful Muslim intellectual class developed after Ya-Na Muhammad Zangina (reign ca. 1692–1715) converted to Islam during his reign (Ferguson 1972, 15) and has existed since that time. What comes up in the histories of the Dagomba new elite is that *most* were sent to *makaranta*.

English-language literacy and secular education, core to the project of modernity as were those who gained access to both, came late to the north. As the northerners continue to lag, especially in comparison with the south, it is clear is that the colonial period created the footprint for development issues in northern Ghana, which "are not merely a matter of history; they persist into the present" (Kirby 2004, 36).

The north was deprived in its educational infrastructure, especially post-primary level education, until the last days of colonialism, because the British never considered that the Protectorate would ultimately become part of the national whole. British officials reinforced the region's backwardness, as they acted to prevent "progressive ideas from the south" from creeping in (Kimble 1963, 535; see also Grischow 2006). Throughout the British colonial period, the government kept a tight rein on educational development in the north. Government endeavored to maintain the power of traditional institutions, but colonial policy also set up the north as a source of cheap labor (Thomas 1974, 427).

"Colonial education policy in northern Ghana was initially inspired by administrative, and later by political, considerations arising from experiences in Ashanti and south Ghana" (Bening 1975, 66). There were three main phases to the development of education in the north. The first, during the first two decades of the twentieth century, had no policy to speak of; indeed, "the early history of education in the Gold Coast is largely the record of missionary enterprise" (Bening 1990, 21). While their work in southern Ghana (Gold Coast) was considered outstanding, in the north the missions were held back by the British Colonial Administration. The Society of Missionaries of Africa, known as the White Fathers, requested permission from the British to open a mission in Navrongo in 1905. The government was hostile to the White Fathers' educational establishments because they felt the missionaries were neglecting education in favor of proselytizing. By the same token, they preferred that the White Fathers be there as educators to lessen any native confusion regarding authority.

Thus, secular learning began with Christianity. In 1907, the White Fathers opened "the first school ever" in the north. One of the conditions was that English be the language of instruction. Another was that attendance was compulsory, though it quickly declined due to community or family agricultural needs, leading the White Fathers to convert the day school to boarding. The second class of twelve boys ten- to thirteen-years old were able to read one syllable words, write letters of alphabet and numbers, copy, answer simple questions (Bening 1990; Der 2001). The school lasted only six years, largely because it lacked adequate funding and teachers. In 1912, the Basel Mission came to Yendi, and in 1913 the Wesleyan Methodist Church Mission commenced work in Tamale (Der 2001). But British interference meant that by 1925, there were only five government and two mission primary schools (Bening 1990).

Meanwhile, some in the Colonial government suggested that they set up government schools in the administrative centers. The first, primary through Standard VII, opened at Tamale in March 1909 with fourteen pupils. Until 1912, when a school was established at Gambaga at the northernmost point of what is today the Northern Region, the Tamale school remained the only educational institution in the protectorate apart from that of the White Fathers. Its student body was largely local. The director of education suggested in 1915 that teachers be recruited from Standard VII boys at Tamale school, which the Acting Chief Commissioner commended, since he felt that the employment of indigenous teachers would encourage parents to send their children to school. Because of the variety of languages, teaching was done in English.

Initially parents were loath to send their children to school; they feared that the children might be alienated from their rural provenance; they did not want to lose the services of their children; the children would have to travel distances; and Muslims regarded the schools as Christian institutions (Bening 1990). According to Huudu Yahaya, whose father was a tailor and a Quranic teacher, it was the last that frightened his father as well as other northern parents. But Huudu Yahaya said in the 1950s Nkrumah came up with a clever trick, he introduced Islamic instruction, known as religious studies, alongside formal schooling. So during religious instruction, Christians would go to the Christian side, Muslims to the Muslim side. He enlisted Arabic teachers renowned in the community to instruct children, so parents would have confidence and send children to school (Huudu Yahaya November 28, 2005).

At the beginning, the British administration did push families to send children to secular school, leaning particularly on the chiefs, but they mandated only one child per family. Henry Kaleem, the son of J. S. Kaleem, one of the north's first and most renowned educators, told me,

> the chiefs did not trust the British, so they were sending [the] children of their subjects to school [rather than their own children], and that's how my father and others [from royalty] were not [educated] with [the] first generation. They were playing a wait and see game with the British, who quickly discovered the chiefs were not bringing their own children. They persuaded my grandfather to give them one of his sons to serve as an example that you really and truly welcome us to your land. (May 12, 2006)

By 1925, the British administration had only four schools in the north, with a total enrollment of 243 out of about 210,379 children of school-going age. But the 1920s saw a rising demand for education in the north. First of all, families regarded education as carrying prestige. Additionally, they began to understand that those educated were an economic asset (Der 2001). In 1927, the first middle school was built in the north: Tamale Government Middle Boarding School was a catchment for the entire north—what today constitutes the Northern, Upper West and Upper East Regions. In 1949, middle schools opened in Gambaga, now just outside of Tamale, and in Yendi (Gbadamosi May 27, 2006). But this response of the colonial government was insufficient.

The second phase in the development of education in the north was evidenced by Governor Guggisberg's support for education. The British administration did push families to send some children to secular school, but there were few schools, it was not a universal policy, and as noted above, the majority of the people were not receptive for cultural reasons.[3]

The opening of the Achimota School (secondary) in 1924 in Accra, the raising of teaching standards, and the increase in government grants are prime examples of Guggisberg's interest and efforts (Thomas 1974, 438). It was in fact Governor Guggisberg's policies for the development of education in the Gold Coast generally and the north more specifically after 1919 that really made a difference. He was concerned about the maintenance of traditional authority, believing that traditional institutions had to be protected from "'the advance of the semi-literate class of African'" (Guggisberg, quoted in Thomas 1974, 438). He set the policy of using northerners as teachers and emphasized the relationship of education to the rural economy. For the north, he wanted to build an educational system integrated with local life, in other words, one based on a restrictive policy. By 1919, in addition to Tamale and Gambaga, government primary schools were also operating at Lawra and Wa in the Upper West.

The deputy director of education suggested that Protectorate residents did not need a high academic standard—only enough to carry on business and trades—so he decided on a split system, Yendi as a center for training in trade and Tamale for academe. In 1922, a junior trade school for carpentry, bricklaying, and farming, opened in Yendi and in 1923 a primary school in Salaga. Guggisberg's focus on Achimota resulted in the school's founding various departments in stages, as follows, a training college, kindergarten and primary school, middle school, secondary school, and a department for university studies (Nketia 1953). Tight finances and Guggisberg's attention to Achimota rather than government primary schools in the north, meant that by 1925 the north was still side-lined. The governor created a separate Department of Education for the north, a Northern Territories Ordinance on Education and a Board of Education in Tamale.

Unfortunately, the new northern policy did not emphasize academic subjects. Government was concerned that northern education be practical, relating it to the rural economy. This meant that northerners only needed schooling through Standard III/Primary Six to make them "useful adults." Yet in 1927, they opened a middle school in Tamale, where students would "have their advanced education under better conditions, with instruction and supervision by Europeans . . ." (Bening 1975, 67). But as "the Standard VII certificate was seen as a high honor to be achieved only by a chosen few," this school was very restricted in the number accepted (Thomas 1974, 441). In 1924, out of 280 boy and fourteen girl students, five reached Standard VII.

The British sought to prevent the creation of a politically conscious and articulate political class in the north who were trained by southerners. Thus, the British followed Guggisberg's policy of employing teachers of northern origin whenever possible. In fact, the leading political voices in the north interested in education had themselves been educated only through Middle School, completing post-primary school training in the south. These included J. H. Allassani, one of the most important northern politicians in the CPP (Convention People's Party) who served as Minister of Education in Kwame Nkrumah's Cabinet; E. A. Mahama (Northern Regional Commissioner, Bole), Mumuni Bawumia (Northern Regional Commissioner, Mamprusi), J. A. Karbo (Northern Territories Council, Lawra-Na) and J. A. Braimah (Minister of Works/Communication and Works, Kabachewura of Gonja).

In the third period, Indirect Rule was introduced as a definite policy. Schools were to be associated with the new native administrations. Guggisberg elaborated his plans for linking education with the preservation of chiefly power, feeling strongly that it was the chiefs, and not the educated Africans, who represented the people (Agbodeka 1972). Guggisberg was influenced by the tenets of Indirect Rule and needed the chiefs to gain support for it, while the chiefs needed the colonial administration to shore up their authority. While Guggisberg believed that the course to African advancement and progress was through the gradual evolution of indigenous institutions, he accorded the state councils no authority and no funds so that traditional leaders and state councils "could never hope to become responsible institutions" (Agbodeka 1972, 61).

The Native Authorities took over existing (primary) schools in 1935, setting out to coach the chiefs on the value of sending children to school.

Reverend A. H. Candler, Superintendent of Education, proposed a three-part scheme, preparing rulers in their future duties, training chiefs' sons and heirs, and educating native administration officials (Thomas 1974).

> Chiefs were told to tell people to send children to school . . . When time of enlightenment comes, they will lead you. Colonial masters fought every chief to send their child to school. There was someone in chief's court who went monthly to the school to make sure all children of other sub-chiefs also there. So those chiefs and those who followed them knew that we the elite, the educated, would lead them. (Abdul Majid October 22, 2005)

The chiefs and people began to see the benefit of education for their children; Guggisberg felt that the experience of seasonal workers in the south encouraged a demand for education, that they brought north an appreciation of the material comforts typical of European lifestyle and opportunities attainable through education (Thomas 1974). In 1937, Ya-Na Abdulai felt that having enough potential students to open a Native Authorities school in Yendi was a sign of the Dagomba wanting to advance. But the administration also made efforts to guarantee that the supply of literates did not exceed the new job opportunities in education and in the expanding technical department (Thomas 1974).

In 1940, the object for the north was to provide education up to Standard II universally, up to Standard VII for those who were exceptional (Bening 1975). The idea was to make education relevant to local life. The British did not favor bringing in southern teachers, because they didn't trust them to instill civic responsibility. Until 1947, the Government Senior School in Tamale was the only one of its kind in the north. Here pupils could advance through exams, but only as far as Standard III-VII. "Tamale Central had been converted to a boarding school in 1927; it was well-equipped but was intended to produce 'not clerks but capable and self-reliant citizens, agriculturists and artisans'" (MacGaffey 2006–07, 119). The British, as observed for Guggisberg, sought to preserve the north from "disruptive outside influences" (Ladouceur 1979, 58). The nurturance of traditional institutions and values was epitomized by Indirect Rule.

On the other hand, northern schoolboys were not allowed to travel south during holidays, were required to wear their traditional smock while on school grounds (even though southerners could wear what they chose), and when the school term finished, they were prohibited from wandering around in Accra or Kumase. When J. S. Kaleem, the famous northern educator, was one of the pioneering students at Achimota, they used to walk from Tamale to Ejura in Ashanti [193 miles] and it took them four days. That's the first point where they could get a vehicle to take them to Kumase and then in Kumase get a vehicle to Accra. They were only allowed to wear a smock from Tamale. When they arrived at Achimota, they would go to the senior house mother, deposit their northern attire, and get shorts, shirts and blazers. The day Achimota finished, they'd deposit the clothing and get back into their northern attire. The British did not want the southern affluence to be imported up north and they were not allowed to carry anything from the south to the north, even sea water was forbidden. Also not allowed to stay down south during the school vacation, so even though his uncle was in Takoradi, my father could only visit him during the term. Once the term was over, he had to come back to the north—to Ejura and then walk home. [This was] because [the British] didn't want the Gold Coast influence on the northerners. (Henry Kaleem May 12, 2006)

Kaleem was not misspeaking or embellishing the truth. B. A. Fuseini tells a similar story. He was among the first generation to attend secondary school in the north. As a professional, he initially taught secondary school, going on to become head master at Ghana Secondary School, Regional Director of Education, a Member of Parliament, Regional Minister for the North and finally Ambassador to Libya. He said that when he was young (and there was no secondary education in the north),

it would be Achimota that people would go to, but the policy of the colonial government was not to let Northerners go to school. Only allowed a year or so after primary. Keep people as illiterates not to communicate. Didn't want us to be educated because concern about agitation for independence and that the northerners shouldn't be "contaminated." (September 30, 2005)

Thus, in clothing, in travel, in opportunities, the boys from the north were treated differently *because* they were from the north. This in turn was underpinned significantly by its educational exclusion. "Until the mid-1930s, when the primary schools were turned over to the Native Authorities, there was little encouragement to expand the education system significantly, and even Guggisberg restricted the growth of schools" (Ladouceur 1979, 58). The first secondary school for the *whole* of the north (today's Northern, Upper East and Upper West Regions) opened in Tamale in 1951, six years before Independence, whereas Mfantsipim, the first secondary school in the country, opened in Cape Coast in 1876, seventy-five years earlier. Eight of the country's top ten secondary schools opened before Tamale Secondary—including Adisadel in 1910,

Accra Academy in 1931, and even Wesley Girls, which opened initially as a primary school for girls in 1836.

Guggisberg's reforms in the north were clearly not designed to train northerners to participate fully in national life (Abdulai 2012). Rather, they resulted in a system of educational exclusion, which played a pivotal role in maintaining the north as a labor reserve, enabling "a protracted delay in the emergence of an indigenous educated *elite*" (Kimble 1963, 536) and a narrowing of horizons. There was a shortage of clerical workers in the region. To deal with the need, such workers were brought up to the north from the south, further underlining the north-south divide.

This meant that in the immediate post-colonial period, northerners were never in a position to assume the mantle of political leadership. But in the late 1930s and early 1940s, it had become clear to the British that educational standards among the locals had to be raised so that managers could be recruited locally, native administration personnel in the north trained and chiefs and their heirs function well within Indirect Rule.

"We've been victims of circumstance—formal education did not get to the north early and there are gaps between south and north and that has affected patterns of development in the north," says Hon. Haruna Iddrissu, one of Tamale's three members of parliament (October 26, 2005).

The Making of A Northern Elite

The emergence of the northern elite had a humble beginning. Islamic learning was common. Many adults in northern Ghana have been to *makaranta*, others have not, and still others have just enough knowledge of Arabic to read the Quran in Arabic or they read it in English.

Among the Dagomba new elite, the most typical pattern was to have attended *makaranta* from childhood. Indeed, in some cases, a parent or extended family member ran a *makaranta* in the house. But there was a gender imbalance. "There were always more boys than girls because when we came back from secular school to attend *makaranta* in evening, girls were still doing housework, so their progress was slower; so girls' chance at that time at being knowledgeable [was] very slim" (Abdul Majid October 22, 2005).

Then there were those whose families were not steadfast Muslims. Dr. David Abdulai, the "mad doctor,"[4] was born "a traditional worshipper in Tamale here. [I] went back and forth between Islam and Christianity" (March 14, 2013). Henry Kaleem was told that when his father returned from school at Achimota, "he was a Christian. He was converted to Islam when he went to Yendi, because he had to work with the chief and the

Muslims and found himself not being completely trusted by the community as a Christian" (Henry Kaleem May 12, 2006). Henry remembered men being brought to the house to teach the Quran, but Henry was never a Quranic pupil. When his father J. S. Kaleem became Director of Education in the Northern Region, he initiated the dual *makaranta*/Western education curriculum. It was first introduced on an experimental basis at Zogbele Primary in Tamale. This was done to generate interest in secular schools, although the idea of secular education within the Muslim communities was not terribly successful (Iddrisu 2002).

I was led to believe that a lot of royals never went to *makaranta*—some didn't read the Quran at all, some just learned how to pray. This was confirmed by a variety of people. "As chiefs, even though they thought of themselves as Muslims, they were more concerned with traditional religion. Chiefs don't participate as such in the prayers. Chiefs have accepted Islam as a state religion but don't really practice it themselves" (Abdulai Yakubu, aka Sabon Kudi November 23, 2005). Dr. A. E. Abdulai is from Abudu royalty. His father started out in Banvim, moved on to Sarnarigu, and ended his chiefly career in Savelugu, one of the three gate skins. A. E. did not attend *makaranta*.

> When coming from the chief's house, it was very liberal, Many wives, many children. We are free, roaming about . . . [My] father wasn't strict. Most of the verses I learned to pray. Learned them via transliteration. Can't read Arabic. I read the Quran in English. (September 18, 2005)

Wayo Seini, a University of Ghana faculty member and former Member of Parliament, had a similar response (October 14, 2005). Of all of his father's children, only a few went to makaranta. He thought that royal families never took Quranic study seriously on the one hand, and on the other, that the elders feared that those educated that way would forget tradition.[5]

> According to Dr. Abubakar Alhassan, the architect, the belief was that . . . the world here is for those who go to [secular] school, and then the world after is for those who go to *makaranta*. So my father said, "Son, I'll send you to school. Yeah, yeah, yeah, we're covered." So my brother, Mohamed and all them, they went to *makaranta*. (May 14, 2006)

A Dagomba lawyer told me that, whether you go to *makaranta* or not, because Islam is pervasive in the north, "you will learn Quran. You have imams and malams [teachers] in your house. Even if [you] don't go to *makaranta*" ("Lawyer" Inussa September 14, 2005). The former member of parliament from Tamale, Abukari Sumani, was not sent to *makaranta*.

But, as a result of staying with friends who were, he started learning verses of the Quran for his prayers. Mohammed Mumuni, a lawyer and former politician, has a similar story. He did not go to *makaranta*, but for one year he "lived with a cousin who lived in big *makaranta* house. For that period, I learned to read Quran, but not too far" (May 1, 2006).

And some were sent to *makaranta* late. Dr. Gomda, who has a doctorate in animal science from Germany, is a member of the Andani royal family. As I have already noted, children of the royals were less likely to be sent to secular school, but they were also less likely to be sent to Quranic school. Gomda in fact was sent to both. When he finished Primary 6, "my father decided I should go and stay with an uncle in Kumase, so I could learn Islamic—I could acquire knowledge in Islam. So I went to Kumase because of Islam" (September 15, 2005). Dr. Yakubu, the former MP from Mion, was raised by his uncle in the village of Sang near Yendi. When he finished primary, he joined his father in Yendi and that was when he started to attend *makaranta*.

Quranic learning was not viewed by the colonial administration as useful to their enterprise. By the same token, by distinguishing between the south and the north, the British could better ration their resources and control the population, differentiating them in terms of access to education, occupations and social status. They also determined which populations would be allowed access to these tools for social change. And they enforced this social delineation through spatial segregation—similar to the *cordon sanitaire* built in Accra and many other British colonies to separate the "natives" from the Europeans.

In 1914, the first batch of northerners entered the Accra Training College. As was true elsewhere in British Africa, the Teachers' Training Colleges recruited mainly from middle school leavers (Birmingham et al 1967). Before they completed their course, they informed the Chief Commissioner that,

> [w]e will try our best with your help to get ourselves experienced and properly trained to become good qualified teachers. We will honour and obey our masters in order that they may impart to us what they have in them. And we beg to promise faithfully to continue working hard after our course, to become a credit to our country, and to do the good that we can, to satisfy you and the Director of Education. (Brukum 1998, 18)

This group helped to chart the role of the elite, a role which subsequent northern teachers came to play in the political and social life of the region. The opening of the Achimota College (Accra) in 1927 saw an increase in the number of northerners trained in the south as teachers, such as J. S. Kaleem. These northern Achimota-trained teachers began to criticize the system of education and administration existing in the northern dependency. Yakubu Tali, one of the Achimota-trained teachers, was reported to have been critical of the British administration in the north. He made it clear that he was out of sympathy with Indirect Rule. Tali also criticized the educational system, which he thought was not sufficiently progressive. Politically, Yakubu Tali was regarded as a disturbing and disruptive element (Brukum 1998). By the late 1930s, British officials in the north began to raise objections about the training of northerners at Achimota because they noted signs of discontent among them. The chief complaints were that they adopted an independent attitude and outlook when they returned home (Brukum 2003).[6]

The British sent the bright boys south to school. But again, this was strategic. From Henry Kaleem (May 12, 2006),

> The purpose was to serve the British and they decided in what capacity they had to serve. And those who did not go to school, they recruited some into the police service, some into the military, some into going down south to help surveyors map out the roads. Also the education—those with academic bent, must be teachers. The second batch, had to be nursing. The third batch were trained as cooks, to serve the British. Majority of British didn't come with wives so needed personnel. Steward boys.

Thus, in the north progress in English-language literacy and secular education came late, because Ashanti and the Gold Coast Colony were the priority. Educational, economic and political policies in the north were subordinated to the interests of the two southern regions (Brukum 2003).

There was a remarkable growth in primary, middle, and secondary education in the country after 1950 (Birmingham et al. 1967), but despite cost-free primary and middle school, regional differences persisted. At a time when 67.6 percent of the school age population was attending school throughout the country, only 24.8 percent were attending in the Northern Region. This was far less than any other region in the country, except for the Upper Region, i.e. the Upper West and Upper East (30.7). In 1956, five years after secondary schooling came to the north, the Gold Coast Legislative Assembly had seventeen university graduates from the South and not one from the north (Ladouceur 1979, 87). Four years later, in 1960, the Northern Region enrolled only 3 percent in primary, 2 percent in middle and 3 percent in secondary school. At all levels throughout the country, there were fewer girls enrolled than boys—but in the north, the number of girls attending was far worse (as I discuss later in this chapter).

The post-colonial governments failed to close the north-south sociospatial distinction (Shepherd et al. 2004). Nkrumah's party the CPP (Convention People's Party) won election in 1951 (six years before Independence) and he was appointed prime minister by the colonial government. While campaigning he had recognized the regional imbalance between north and south due to the educational disparity; for example, in 1951 "in the Colony and Ashanti there [were] many thousand Standard Seven pupils coming out of the schools each year, in the Northern Territories there [were] only about 100" (Ibid. p. 198–9). Once in office, members of the Northern Territories lobbied their government to do something about the lack of educational facilities in the north (Bening 1990, 197).

The government accelerated the process of expanding primary education throughout the country, making it compulsory and tuition-free, and for the north, in recognition of the economic struggle as compared with the south, parents did not have to pay book fees (McWilliam 1962, 84). A collaboration was set up between Ghanaian community-based organization and a Danish development agency. Called School for Life, the goal was

> to enable the formal education system to achieve and sustain increases in functional literacy and in the quality and equitable access to relevant basic ed. This is seen as a means to address the problems of poverty, underdevelopment and gender inequality in northern Ghana. (Akyeampong 2006, 224)

School for Life is based on educating in the mother tongue and targets the eight- to fifteen-years age group. Its focus is on literacy, numeracy and writing. It is a nine-month program that runs during the dry season. It has a high-level community involvement in hiring teachers. In Ghana's Northern Region, between 1995–2001, it had coverage in eight districts, including much of Dagbon. While gender parity is a goal, that has been difficult to achieve.

From 1951 to 2005, enactment of basic, fee-free education has been a major item on all government agendas. But economic problems and mismanaged education policy led to a deterioration in educational infrastructure and a decline in enrollment in the 1980s. To address the paucity of teachers, unqualified people were hired to do the job. The 1987 Education Reforms were adopted to help address the educational decimation, with funding coming in from the World Bank and other outside donors. These led to increases in enrollment but not much improvement in quality. In the first decade of the new millennium, *"Ghana has seen huge gains in access to basic education in all regions, among the poor by gender and by urban and rural status"* (Darvas and Balwanz 2014, 39, emphasis in original). Enrollment in basic education nearly doubled, with progress even in the northern regions. A large share of government resources went toward education.

Despite the improvements, access to basic education at the national level is simply more accessible to the wealthier and those from urban areas. In Ghana, 25 percent of the poor come from the Northern Region; in combination with the Upper West and Upper East, the percentage is 30. In addition to the quantitative element of number of schools and thus, simple access, there has also been an issue with the deployment of trained teachers. In 2011–12, in Ashanti, Volta, Greater Accra and Eastern Regions, the trained teachers per student was at 70–90 percent. In the Western, Upper East, Brong-Ahafo and the Northern Regions, the percentage is only 40–50 percent (Darvas and Balwanz 2014).

In the north, English-language literacy is at abysmally low levels for the adult population. "Almost the entire population in the three regions in northern Ghana . . . is illiterate . . . over 80 percent of their people have never been to school" (Songsore et al. 2001, 228). Looking at Primary 6 English proficiency, in 2012 the percentage was only 20 percent in the Northern Region (only the Upper West was lower), whereas in Greater Accra, it was about 75 percent (Darvas and Balwanz 2014, 9).

Once secondary education was established in the north, like primary school, it was fee-free (Bening 1990, 101). The district assemblies helped, for example "providing us with uniforms, fares to school—and boarding was all paid for by Government" (Fuseini Baba April 28, 2006). In 2003, for all ten regions in Ghana, the average for boys attending primary school was 59 percent, and for girls 57.6 percent, with the highest in Accra at 72.3 percent and 71.1 percent, respectively. Focusing in on the Northern Region, the percentage was 47.4 for boys and 39.5 for girls—about 12 percent lower for both sexes at the national level, 25 percent as compared to the capital district. The only regions with lower numbers are the Upper West and Upper East, which along with the North constituted the colonial Northern Territories.

For all 10 regions, the average in 2003 for secondary (junior and senior) school was 32 for boys, 31.9 for girls. For the Northern Region it was 17.4 for boys,15.8 for girls. Curiously, the secondary numbers in the Upper West and Upper East were considerably higher for women—22.5 and 23.2, respectively. Both sets of statistics should be viewed alongside numbers from elsewhere in the country (Shepard et al. 2004, 61). Throughout the country, school enrollment drops in the higher grades. In Dagbon itself, looking at the numbers in 2002 for five districts of Gushiegu-Karaga, Savelugu-Nanton, Tamale, Tolon-Kunbungu and Yendi, the drop is severe, from 84,305 in primary school to 9,946 in senior secondary. In Dagbon's districts, there are 581 primary schools, yet only 12 secondary schools—eight in Tamale, two in Yendi, and two in Savelugu-Nanton—and Tamale Secondary, the first to be opened, was only established in 1951. If one takes into account gender, the numbers are even worse: only 39.6 percent of the primary enrollments are girls, and again this worsens as one advances up in grades: 31.4 percent of junior secondary school and 26.7 percent of senior secondary school students are women. But what this does not show are the low absolute numbers, that in Tamale where there were almost 48,000 primary school enrollees, only 4 percent of that total are girls attending senior secondary school.

At the university level, only 4 to 7 percent of total admission is of northerners. Even in 2003, the only regions with lower percentages than The Northern Region were the Upper West and Upper East (Shepard et al. 2004, 61). In Dagbon's districts, there are 581 primary schools, yet only fourteen secondary schools—seven in Tamale, two in Yendi, and two in Tolon-Kumbungu. Savelugu/Nanton, Zabzugu/Tatale and Gushegu-Karaga districts have one each.

A New Kind of Education

Given the ideology of both British policy and indigenous culture, that members of this new elite got to Western school at all was remarkable. Many of the Dagomba new elite I spoke with observed that they had gotten to Western school somewhat by accident. As I observe later in this chapter, most women did not attend, but for those who did, they confirm that serendipity played a large role. With education, they have been accorded considerable symbolic and political capital among their people. They have become patrons in the truest sense of the word.

The Men

Members of the Western-educated Dagomba elite are representative of Arhin's (1985, 117) "new social order." They are urban dwellers, resident primarily in Accra, some in Kumase, and some (largely retired) back in Tamale. They are among the first to be able to attend secondary school at a northern school—after Tamale Secondary, the first one, opened in 1951. Only four of the Dagomba cohort went to secondary school in the south, one went to Kumase—"The southern schools were more famous. Just look at the track record of the students who go to university from the southern schools" (Wayo Seini October 14, 2005). Dr. Mutawakil Iddrisu chose Accra Academy over Tamale Secondary School, because his father, who was exposed to the south, thought it would be an advantage. He also had an older brother in Accra who had been a member of Kwame Nkrumah's cabinet, S. I. Iddrisu (Dr. Iddrisu September 12, 2005). And one of the six women in my study went to Achimota in Accra, it was 1953, her parents were living in Accra where her father was a cook for a British couple, and she could spend holidays with them (Adisa Munka'ila November 10, 2005). Major Gomda was actually born in Accra, his father having migrated from Yendi first to Sekondi, then settling in Accra. But because his father was afraid that he would become completely assimilated, he took Major back to Yendi, where the six-year-old lived with his paternal grandmother and did three years of primary school. "Then my father realized his mother was over-pampering me and that I would not be able to attend school to the fullest. So he brought me back to Accra, under repair" (May 2, 2006). And there he remained throughout his years of schooling.

Parents who were both models and enablers for this bridge generation were unusual, as most of them had been denied the educational opportunity. But not all. There were a few literate parents: of forty-three cases, two went through teacher training, six had been to Middle School and could read and write, two went to adult literacy classes, and one had technical training.

The British pressed each chief to send at least one child from his respective household. "Some of the chiefs who were enlightened managed to send their children to school. Those not enlightened, sent nephews, not their direct children" (Mahdi September 16, 2005). So, for example, Alhaji Mahdi's father's brother was the Kunbun-Na, the Chief of Kunbun. Rather than send his own children, he sent Mahdi's father (his brother's son), the first in the family to be educated. He completed Standard 7.

This was true of M. P. Sumani's father as well. He was raised by his senior brother, who was a chief. As with Mahdi's father, when the British came calling, the chiefs (and the mothers) were reluctant to send their own sons to school, substituting other children who were in the palace. "My father did not have a mother in the palace—he [my father] would go find grass for the horses in the chief's palace. One day he had just brought the grass when the white people arrived. So my uncle decided, 'Sumani, why don't you take this [take the offer to attend school]?'" (M.P. Sumani June 2, 2006).

Similarly, with Henry Kaleem's, father J. S. Kaleem, the British would come to the house and play with the children. One day they returned, wanting a child from the household to be put in school. The women didn't trust the British, lest they steal the children. J. S. Kaleem's "direct" grandmother was not present—had she been there, she would have flatly refused. The old lady who was present agreed to let them take J. S. if they'd leave her one of the others. He was sent to school in Tamale. When he finished in 1923, the British decided he was intelligent enough so he was sent on to Achimota (Henry Kaleem May 12, 2006).

And again, the mother of Issifu Sumani's father's father "had left the house and there was no one to cry 'you can't go!' So his father's father [was sent to] the church school" (December 3, 2005). Later, when the British opened a trade school in Yendi, the young man was sent. His son, Issifu's father, was then sent to school in Yendi at the age of seven, then to middle school (Tamale Secondary), then to the teacher training college at Gbagabaga (Government Training College).

Abdulai II, last of Savelugu, perhaps of the same generation as educator J. S. Kaleem, was one of the important Dagomba chiefs, who was in line for the Yendi kingship. He was also one of the few northern chiefs who was educated—he had gone through Standard 7 (middle school), he had a typewriter and he took care of his own correspondence. He sent all of his sons to school but only one of his daughters, and she in particular to ensure that her mother was taken care of as she had no sons (Salamatu Abdulai May 13, 2013).

The southern influence was also significant. The father of Haruna Atta, publisher of the *Accra Daily Mail*, was born in southern Ghana, where education was far more the norm than in the north. Because of his education and the possibilities and the exuberance that independence brought, he decided to move his wife and children north. "He had that mentality of education, so he educated all of us, and then brought in the extended family, educated them, so his sister's children, brother's children, and other relations"—but because of Dagomba tradition, not the girls (Haruna Atta May 29, 2006).

What I find quite intriguing is the fathers who were not educated but had always been interested in going to school, like Iliasu and Nasser's butcher father, or Siddique's soldier father, both of whom took advantage of adult literacy programs, and became literate. But as already noted, the parents of the vast majority of the group were not literate in English and three-quarters of the fathers had never been to school. Then, in the 1950s, "our parents, especially the clergy, were not eager to send children to school because they were afraid they'd be turned into Christians and the clergy were most resistant" (Aminu Ahmadu December 5, 2005). Indeed, even though he went to local authority (not mission) schools, they sang hymns and made the children go to church. A lot of the children were given Christian names—like B. A. Fuseini. "The 'B' was Christian, though [I] changed it. Or Roland Alhassan, Ambassador to Germany . . .

I refused—there was no way I could add a Christian name to my name. But those from less religious houses had to—later they changed it back" (Aminu Ahmadu December 5, 2005).

Aminu Ahmadu's maternal grandfather felt Ahmadu's father was taking a risk by educating him. Indeed, when Ahmadu started school (at age ten), it was surprising to everybody. Why did his father send him? "I don't know —maybe by instincts." He was the oldest and all of his brothers were sent after him. The older girls were not, because of gender discrimination. Of course, the mothers were largely uneducated because it was not fashionable to educate women, and they were also not well-travelled, so they had somewhat insular views of the world.

Most of the fathers had customary jobs, as farmers, butchers, Quranic teachers, tailors; jobs with the colonial service, such as messengers and laborers; and the rare ones with a bit of education worked as teachers, in the police force, as surveyors. The mothers helped on the farm or sold prepared food.

> When we were children, you had to come from a privileged family to attend school. Those in villages, the father had to be enlightened to know the value of education. Need for all the children on the farm—in [my] house, my father was not a farmer to begin with, so no trouble about needing someone to farm. (Abdulai Yakubu November 23, 2005)

Yakubu's father was a trader, who owned a provision shop. He had twenty-three children. He himself was uneducated but, after spending time in the south of the country for several years, he decided his children had to go to school and he was passionate about it, sending every one of them.

Over and over, in my conversations with educated Dagomba in their fifties and older, Kwame Nkrumah was lauded for his educational policies to advance the North. "Lawyer" Inussa's father had the means to send him to school, but his resources were unnecessary because Nkrumah had set up free compulsory education because of the north-south disparity. And yet, "the inhibiting factor is still poverty" ("Lawyer" Inussa September 14, 2005).

Some fathers, even when dissuaded from doing so, sent their children to school. Fuseini Baba, the administrator in the Ministry of Finance, is the son of the chief butcher to the Ya-Na—in effect, the Ya-Na of the butchers. In Dagbon, the butchers are supposed to be the people who control funds in commercial activities. So they travel a lot, they see a lot, they are exposed to all sorts of places and ideas. "My father was exposed, he saw a lot of things, he mixed with the whites, and even against all odds in those days, Islam dominated and they saw anybody going to formal education as somebody going to hell. But he didn't care. They used to talk to him and say, why do you send your kids to school—let them go to farm, let them go on and do business. He said no" (Fuseini Baba April 28, 2006). The father of Dr. Nasser and Iliasu Adam, both members of my study, was a farmer and a butcher. He had three wives and twenty-six children. He was uneducated and regretted it, because he perceived that that situation prevented him from taking up certain responsibilities when he himself got involved in politics. During colonialism and the struggle for independence, he came into contact with a lot of literates. He decided all of his kids would have the opportunities denied him and he educated them all. When he died in 1994, he left no property for his children—he had given them all their inheritance in the form of education (Iliasu September 27, 2005).

The older brother of Ghana's former vice president, Mahama Aliu, had been sent to school, thereby fulfilling the British mandate that each family educate one child. As a consequence, Aliu's father initially decided against sending the younger son to secular school, leaving him in the hands of his itinerant Quranic teacher uncle. But because the man was often gone, Aliu's father figured he might as well have Aliu join the son already enrolled in school in Tamale. Thus, young Aliu too was lucky to attend school. The fact that he did ultimately go to secular school, culminating in a degree from University of Science and Technology in Kumase, underlines the combination of chance and luck for many of those northerners who were successful early on in gaining an education (June 19, 2006).

Dr. Yahuza Gomda's path is quite instructive, in terms of opportunity, serendipity, and sheer grit. Even though he is from the royal family—his mother's mother and Ya-Na Yakubu Andani II's father were siblings—he was sent to school. After he finished primary school, his father sent him to live with his mother's brother in Kumase to acquire knowledge in Islam and to attend middle school. He was known as "the one from the north who couldn't speak Twi," Kumase's language and the main language in southern Ghana. In completing middle school, he chose Navrongo Secondary School, 119 miles north of Tamale, because a brother had gone there. He finished his A levels in 1975.

After a year of teaching in Dagbon, he made his way south, landing in Accra. While buying a ticket at the bus station, his bag was stolen. "I started life in Accra with one shirt, one pair of trousers." A few days later, he saw an advertisement in the newspaper that a secondary school was looking for science teachers. He was hired. Then he saw an advertisement for Eastern European university scholarships. The then-Soviet Union and other communist countries sought to create an elite in Africa by training them at their universities and institutes, creating attitudes favorable to the Soviet Union and to communism. Many African students eagerly grabbed the opportunity for a free education (Kanet 1968).

Gomda applied. "I remember very well when I was called for the interview, one asked me a question, why are you in Accra? Why are you not in the north and in Accra? My answer was, because I wanted to get this scholarship. Because I thought if I were in the north I would not get it. [laughter] They all laughed and then I had the scholarship."

From 1978–84, he did veterinary medicine in Rumania, first having to learn the language. To continue his studies, he went to Germany—where again he had to learn a new language. In Hanover he moved from professor to professor looking for interest and opportunity, ending up in Bonn where he got his PhD in 1988. He spent three years in Berlin in tropical veterinary medicine and finally went home to Ghana in 1992. Fourteen years overseas, having to learn two new languages, and with no opportunity to return home to visit.

I met Dr. Gomda through Dr. Muta Iddrisu, the neurosurgeon. Their educational experiences were similar: after going to secondary school (although in Accra), Dr. Iddrisu was awarded a scholarship to read medicine in Germany. He did not return for thirteen years until he completed his training. Gomda laughingly mimicked what Mumuni had told me about being sent to school—that because he was a naughty child, his parents thought he would not fit in in the family, so they sent him to primary school—"I went 'by default'" (Dr. Gomda September 15, 2005). The parents either saw or were told of the benefits of education, motivating them to send their children. But not all of them. In any compound, there were many siblings and half-siblings. In some cases, all (at least the boys) were sent to school; in most cases, it was only one or two, and then it was by chance.

Chance also played a part in Dr. Nasser's higher education. He finished his BA at Legon in 1984. After the first degree, the department would pick its best students for training. Nasser ended up as the best student in the Russian language class. "At that time in the '80s, training within the university was still very rudimentary, so most of the students went outside . . . The University proposed that I join academia, so I was sent out" (April 30, 2006). He went to the Soviet Union on a government scholarship to do a PhD. There were many scholarships for students from Third World countries and a very large Ghanaian community, the aftereffect of Nkrumah and the Soviet policy for so-called Third World countries. "I was at Moscow. At Pushkin Institute of Languages. Used to be affiliated with Moscow State University. Sustenance there was provided by the Ghana Government. Stayed there for five years without coming home because I couldn't afford it . . . It made things worse than they would have been. If I could have come home every year, I would have looked forward to the next trip. But the community, the friendship . . ." (April 30, 2006). This may have been compounded by racism—"one of the major complaints of the Africans [was] that the Russians and other East Europeans are racists" (Kanet 1968, 172).

Before Dr. M. M. applied to secondary school, his father had died. He qualified for Tamale Secondary, but he did not have money for a uniform—"my friends helped (June 22, 2010)." When Dr. M. M. was ready for university, he went south to Kumase to go to KNUST (Kwame Nkrumah University of Science and Technology) and study biochemistry, but he did not qualify in English. So, he took some gap time and taught at the Northern School of Business for a few years. And then he was accepted to do medicine in Ukraine on a Friendship scholarship. He had to learn Russian and was there for seven years in the 1980s without returning to Ghana. For several years, he then took up various positions to make some money—he went to Britain, then back to Ghana to work at Korle Bu, Ghana's teaching hospital, and as a junior doctor at a private Accra hospital. In 2002, he went to Wuhan, China, to do a fellowship in surgery. Thus like Dr. Gomda and Dr. Nasser, Dr. M. M. could not return home until he had finished his education, because he simply did not have the money for a ticket.

Curiously enough, many of the mothers somehow understood the value of education for their children. In speaking of his father's generation, Henry Kaleem said it was the father who made the decision to send the child to school, but, "if the women opposed it, that was the end of it. The women distrusted the British and felt if they allowed their children to go for British formal education, the children would be left out of the chieftainship. So they didn't want to disadvantage their children (Henry Kaleem May 12, 2006)

I spoke with some of the mothers of the new elite group, but they demurred from taking credit or having influence. The thinking of Iliasu and Nasser's mother was on par with their father, when it came to educating the children. "Those days, their eyes were not opened to school—but she and her husband thought it important" (Iliasu May 17, 2006). Dr. Nasser observes that "in a male-dominated society like ours, our father took that decision to take us to school, he had that ultimate right, power, to take us to school. But then subsequently if our mother had not been involved, I don't think we would have been where we are today . . . A lot of the resources, the financial resources, the support . . . The moral support, the material support, and I think she had a better vision of what the future was in store for us if we attended school. Just now I remember all the things that she said—the questions that she was asking. She had a better picture. Of course, our father wanted us to go to school—just go and get an education. But it looks like our mother had a better vision of what education would go forward. [She wasn't literate, but] she's a very observant person" (April 30, 2006). She also did extra things for her children, like pounding extra fufu to sell in her restaurant to get some extra money to pay for their "chop" (food) money and petty things. Somehow she thought she was taking a risk in sending the children to school, as it was not the norm and she was not sure how it would turn out. But she refused any credit when I asked her about the significance of her support for her children's education.

When Mohammed Mumuni, a lawyer, vice-presidential candidate and Ghana's former Minister of Foreign Affairs, was in middle school in Kunbungu, his father went blind. While education was completely covered financially, the child needed money to travel, to buy small things. His father felt he should leave school. Yet, in his favor, his mother prevailed. Why, he said to me, is a mystery. "I don't know where the woman got her inspiration from—that the child must have education and he must have the best" (October 10, 2005). And it was just him, of her six children, he was the only one sent to school. For Yakubu Andani, an accountant born and bred in Savelugu, his father's side did not like education. He had to be taken from his father's house to his mother's mother to attend school. His mother's side was motivated because they had gone to school and insisted their children go to school.

Alhaji Mahdi, a contractor, felt that it was because his father was alive that he (Mahdi) was educated through secondary school. But he also says that his mother, his father's second wife, helped send him to school. The school fees were taken care of by the district assemblies, but his mother provided him with food. In the case of Alhaji Sule, a lecturer in religion at the University of Ghana, his mother had considerable impact. When I asked him what her motivation was for sending her children to school, he thought it was due to his mother's father's brother, who had been sent to school by Sule's grandmother. The latter was very interested in education so, presumably, she was the influence. Sule and his mother lived in the same village (Kunbungu) but in different houses. When his grandfather (father's father) wanted him to stop going to school, his mother disagreed and took financial responsibility for the boy. Since fees and boarding were covered, she paid for clothing and transport. And scientist Yahuza Gomda's mother saved him from humiliation within his school peer group. She had come to Kumase where he was in school and his uniform was torn. "My father was patching [it], and so you didn't see the original cloth. And I nearly left school because of that. Because my colleagues were mocking at me and I felt very bad. But I kept going and so I think my mother returned and bought me new school uniforms" (September 15, 2005). The primary school that Professor Sandoh went to was not a local authority school (public) therefore there were fees to be paid. "I always escaped from school and my mother always made sure I went back. So I don't know, how come? Anytime I came asking for anything, for books, she'd go and buy (May 29, 2006).

Such stories, of which there are many, speak to the obstacles, not the least of which was the degree of poverty that had to be negotiated. Abubakari Sumani became a lawyer, ambassador and a Member of Parliament. His father died when he was in lower sixth form. He was able to continue "with the help of aunties, uncles, cousins. It wasn't about money, right? There were no school fees. It was about pocket money, clothing, moral support, things like that. Uniforms" (June 2, 2006).

Others had it far worse. Dr. David Abdulai, who remained in Tamale to practice *pro bono* medicine, was one of twelve children. He alone survived childhood, his siblings all dying of malnutrition or hunger-related diseases. Dr. Abdulai's mother, an illiterate, was the last of six wives and the breadwinner for the house. He was sent to school because he was considered useless as a farmer. But when he was in fourth grade, his great uncle died so he left school. "I didn't go to school anymore because of financial difficulties" (May 4, 2013). But then a priest supported him to go to school. "While I was in school I depended upon my teachers' good will just to give me something to eat, and in the afternoons I would go to the dunghills in Tamale where people had left and I would pick for lunch." He could not go to school without a uniform, but he did not have the money to buy one. "I used to sell toffees, biscuits, mosquito coils just to get enough to get a school uniform and survive and when I didn't, I'd go to the dunghills and food vendors. Then I managed to get to P6 and I went to see the Canadian priest again and he gave me money to buy a school uniform." He got to know "an English lady"—he went "to help her every week-end and weekdays in her garden—she saw me through Middle School Form 1 and 2." When he was accepted at what is now called Ghana Secondary School, some South Asians "were kind enough to buy me the books and the exercise books." Things settled down once he started Tamale Secondary School, because all costs were covered. But then, when he went on to sixth form, "we were asked for the first time to buy some trousers." He had no money. "I was delayed from wearing those pants for one term—managed to get a little bit of money from friends and I was able to get a pair of trousers for two years."

The poverty that many experienced was anchored in the poverty of the region. Dr. Alhassan, the architect who received a PhD in Denmark, was almost thwarted at the primary school level when the head of the school told his father that the school was full,

> but if my father can manufacture a chair and a table, they would fit me, and this is what happened! My father saw a carpenter, bought wood, and they made me a table and chair. I carried it to school and they admitted me into the classroom. (May 14, 2006)

Other severe infrastructural limitations, caused by regional poverty, could also impede school admission. Mohammed Mumuni, who got to secondary school largely at the determination of his mother, was then hired by the Peace Corps to teach Dagbani. He then applied to the University of Ghana. His letter from the University would come to his hometown, Kunbungu. He travelled there. There was no letter, because someone who had taken it and read it secreted it away. Mumuni managed to verify that he had in fact been invited for a prospective student interview, but he was expected at the University of Ghana two days later at 8:30 am—a considerable distance in those days. He bicycled from Kunbungu to Savelugu (10 miles), and the following day got a bus from Savelugu to Accra (400 miles). Because of the state of the roads, he arrived Accra at dawn on the appointed day. He was lucky.

Mumuni's tale was not unique. Iliasu Adam was encouraged by a secondary school teacher to apply to the Institute of Journalism in Accra. He applied but heard nothing. At that time, it took two weeks for a letter posted in Accra to reach Tamale. Then a friend heard a radio message that he was granted an interview in Kumase—but it was the very day. If one could get transport, it took 10 hours to Kumase. He found a tractor trailer truck driver who was transporting cattle—jumped in around 6 pm—got to Kumase at 7 am the next morning. By that time, the Institute had finished interviewing but he went there anyway and explained to two of the interviewers what had happened; they were sympathetic. At that time (1986) Tamale was "dark"—the only electricity was accessible by generator (the city was only attached to the National Grid in 1992). He got home late—it was dark. Someone passing through Tamale to Navrongo had slipped the admission letter under the door. He did not see it and the envelope was swept away. Fortunately it was not thrown out, it was retrieved, and he matriculated at the Institute.

Iliasu's brother Dr. Nasser reflected on their father's insistence on their schooling. What did their former playmates, who did not have educational opportunity, think?

> Initially they didn't see the consequences or the future results. Now that the difference is very clear, I think that there's a certain level of envy that translates into bitterness, Not among all of them but some,

and it's very visible. Visible in the sense that it's contributed to my electoral misfortunes when I stood for political office, when I stood for election, especially in my area. Some of them, we even went to primary school together, but for one reason or another, somewhere along the line they fell out. Of course, with education, the quality of our lives, there's a marked difference, and we have tried to relate to them just as we used to. (April 30, 2006)

What matters is that this difference has enabled a route out of deprivation, and Nasser understands that. It has provided opportunities that simply would not exist otherwise. It is when Aminu Ahmadu thinks back to his childhood that he realizes that he grew up in poverty, and he wanted to get out of that poverty. He is conscious of how his education and the profession that made possible has elevated him. He has told his children "they belong to Nima [a poor Accra neighborhood] if not for my hard work" (Aminu Ahmadu December 5, 2005). "Savannah," a contractor who stayed in Tamale but whose second wife (and thus his second home) is in Accra, started primary school in the early 1950s.

They gave us clothing. We wore smocks to school. They would give us the smocks. You would wear your home clothing to school and you would come and change to smocks. On Fridays you would wash your smock—they would iron for you—and then you come home and then on Monday you start wearing it. We didn't have shoes. We didn't have anything. Nothing. In those days things were cheap but our parents couldn't afford them. We were too many in the family and one person alone couldn't have some. (May 14, 2006)

The schooling of another Tamale man, Issa Naseri (September 28, 2005), was adversely impacted by politics—his father supported the "wrong" political party, so the locals would not support Issa for school. As a result, he decided to leave the region to attend school in Lawra, miles away in the Upper West. Several boys were interviewed—only Issa did not receive a letter of admission. With the beginning of the school year, he decided to go in person. The bus from Tamale to Lawra via Wa took two days. He went to the school, told them he was from Tamale, and he was told he had been admitted—they had posted him a letter that was returned. A second letter had been sent. At the school he was told to go home and retrieve the letter. The next day, his uncle produced the letter, which he may have appropriated out of some jealousy. (Like Dr. Gomda, Issa was successful in obtaining a scholarship to Eastern Europe—in his case Bulgaria—where he subsequently did his university schooling. Unlike Gomda, upon graduating, he settled back in the north.)

Beyond poverty and petty grievances, this marginalized population was also oppressed by the chanciness of opportunity. "Just like apartheid everywhere. We have apartheid in Ghana too," reflected A. E. Abdulai (September 18, 2005). A. E. finished all of his secondary schooling in Tamale and wanted to go to medical school to do dentistry. At his interview, "they said, 'oh they've never heard of Abdulai, Dr. Abdulai . . . The people were all southerners and figured a northerner would do well with agriculture.'" There was a dentist in Tamale when he was in secondary school who had a Ford Mustang "and he was really painting the town red. I thought I would want to be like that." So he applied to do dentistry in Australia or Canada—there were scholarships for that. They had to go for an interview at the scholarship secretariat. But someone said, once they find out you're already at Legon they won't give you a scholarship.

A. E. was advised to go see the chairman of the Public Services Commission, a northerner by the name of Abayifaa Karbo. In 1947, as a student at the Government Training College in Tamale, Karbo had "protested against the rule which obliged Northerners, both pupils and teachers, to wear the smock at all times on school premises" (Ladouceur 1979, 80)—a means of differentiating between southerners, who could wear European clothing, and northerners who could not.

> His office was *so big*. A vast room. I walked in quietly. "Young man, what do you want?" he asked. I explained I had applied to do dentistry and someone said coming from the north you won't be taken . . . I said I went for the interview and they didn't take me. He said, "What were your grades?" I told him. He took his telephone and called the medical school at Korle Bu and asked what was the least grade they took this year for medicine. Don't know what answer he got but he banged the phone on the table—he was so angry. "So how come I have a guy here who has his grades and he wasn't taken?" he argued on the phone.

A. E. was sent to the medical school with a note from Karbo. But then they told Karbo A. E. did not appear for the interview! "Because they couldn't defend why they didn't take me." A. E. spent a term at the University of Ghana in agriculture, finally returning to Karbo's office. He asked A. E., "'Where have you been? Why didn't I go for interview, why did I lie to him?' I told him I hadn't lied. Then he said, this is what I've always been fighting against." This is how A. E. got to medical school (September 18, 2005).

But, Alhaji Mahdi muses (September 16, 2005), even today it's tough. "A northerner going to university may have qualification, but it will be difficult. The southerner stands more chance"—because he has a southern name.

> Except you find a lecturer who says, "let's try him." Some time ago, in an exam, a southerner gets aggregate 10 and a northerner 12, they pick the northerner because he has no facilities, no electricity,

no water, no better textbooks, and he was able to get 12. "Let's take him and try him." THAT's how some of our boys got in. [is that true today?] No, our boys have a real struggle—we have to go lobby—how many can you lobby for? (Mahdi September 18, 2005)

The Women

From the beginning, as I observed earlier, gender disparity in education in The Gold Coast/Ghana was great. Girls, not expected to take on such occupational roles, would not need the same level of education. As I have written elsewhere, "it is not surprising that the education of males was different from that of female students. Moreover, it could hardly be expected that the quantity and quality of schools for females in the colonies would be greater than that available for girls in England itself" (1977, 74). The inequality of schooling by gender in Africa was not simply a function of British attitudes, or even of missionaries; local populations themselves were resistant to educating girls.

Under Nkrumah, from 1952 (when he was prime minister) till 1966 (when his government was overthrown), education expanded greatly in Ghana. Fee-free compulsory education at the primary and middle school levels was established in 1961, regardless of sex. Throughout the years, educational facilities have expanded. At the same time, boys have outnumbered girls in enrollment, the imbalance increasing as one goes up the educational ladder.

Amongst the Dagomba, the story is worse. Hardly any girls in the bridge-group's age-group were sent to school. Female education was not popular until the arrival of the Native Authorities (although this was not unique to the Protectorate). After 1936, all Native Authority schools offered girls free schooling if their parents agreed to their employment by the Native Authorities after their completion. In 1942, the White Fathers established a private Senior Girls School at Navrongo, in 1947 the government opened a Senior Girls Boarding School in Tamale, and in 1956 a Girls Middle School in Bolgatanga. 1958, the Women's Training College opened in Tamale. In Tamale District, the enrollment rate for girls in primary school is 44.1 percent and Junior Secondary School 39 percent, as compared to 59 percent and 61 percent, respectively, for boys (Sutherland-Addy 2002).

Strong societal disincentives have continued even today to hinder girls' enrollment in primary school, and it is worse for secondary school—as community members worry, would they rebel against social norms? Early marriage and poverty are both problems adversely affecting the education of girls, as is the tradition of sending girls to the "auntie," to work in her home or business (Sutherland-Addy 2002). Basic to the problem is that if you were giving your child up to someone, whether girl or boy,

> it is assumed 100 percent that he or she would look after their interests. So it was not customary for you to interfere. So even if you wanted—like the old man, my dad, with a burning desire wanted all of his children to go to school, knew that his sisters who were taking his daughters away were not looking after them in school, he couldn't do anything. He could not interfere. It's not Dagomba custom. (Alhassan Andani June 13, 2008)

In the case of the girls, usually the receiving woman is a sister of one of the girl's parents, who either does not have any daughters or who needs more help in her enterprises. The practice is reminiscent of kinship fostering that Esther and Jack Goody wrote about for the Gonja also in northern Ghana.

> Great emphasis is placed on the institution of kinship fostering whereby from the age of about five, children are sent to be brought up by non-parental kin. Claims to a foster child are formally expressed as the rights held by a man in his sister's children (more particularly, in their sons) and by a woman in her brother's daughters. But in practice children are reared by a wide range of kin and girls in particular are often asked to go and stay with a grandparent. (Goody and Goody 1967, 231)

This circulation of children—fostering one another's offspring—is a way of strengthening the bonds between siblings that have been loosened by marriage (Goody and Goody 1967).

Hence the tradition in Dagbon: give any girl of age eight or nine to the auntie to cement ties to relatives. The auntie would teach her a trade and discipline her. Boys had a very different existence—boys stayed with parents and worked and had a chance; girls went to aunties and were socialized into female domesticity (Abdul Majid October 22, 2005). The custom even held in the case of an only child because "that's what tradition demands. You shouldn't bring up your own children, you should give them to your sisters and your brother. Especially since my auntie had no child of her own" (Fati Isaaka November 14, 2005).

Generally, the Dagomba aunties were not educated, which made many of them unsympathetic to the cause of education for the girls, especially those of the generation my study deals with. Seemingly as a result, they did not see to the education of the children in their care. One of bank president Alhassan Andani's sisters was not educated "because she had to be taken by an aunt, who was a trader" (June 13, 2008).

But a father could prevent a child from being sent away. Salamatu Abdulai is one of the few educated Dagomba women I spent time with. Her experience is both testament to the power of tradition and luck—the tradition of her aunt taking her away, her luck at being the daughter who her father chose to be schooled and the power of patriarchy—in this case positive.

The father of Salamatu and her much younger half-brother A. E. Abdulai was the Chief of Banvim, a small northern village, when Salamatu was still young. Following the classic Dagomba upward progression in chiefly succession, he then went on to be chief of Sarnarigu and finally of Savelugu, one of the three gate skins that can lead a man to the Yendi kingship. Salamatu's mother had no sons. One day, when she was almost nine years old, her father asked if she would like to go to school so that when her mother was old, she would be able to support her (Salamatu Abdulai July 17, 2017). She excitedly said "Oh yes, I will go, Chief," which was how all of his children addressed him. I am allowing Salamatu to tell her tale, with little commentary (Salamatu Abdulai July 17, 2017).

So Chief set about making arrangements for Salamatu and five others of his children to attend. Some months before she was to begin,

> one morning, we were at Banvim, my aunt was in Tamale here, when she came to the village. My father was away. And when she came in, she said, "Oh, today I'm sending [taking] this girl [Salamatu] to Tamale." (Salamatu Abdulai July 17, 2017)

Salamatu's father's sister Bamini brewed pito (corn beer). She had six girls working for her. "All the girls they would just be carrying water, washing the calabashes, and doing the odd jobs in the houses." Even though Bamini had the six, she wanted another worker.

> And my senior mother, who was my father's first wife said no, she wouldn't allow her to take me—she [Bamini, the sister] said no, she's taking me. So everybody intervened but she refused . . . (Salamatu Abdulai July 17, 2017)

What is extraordinary is that none of the chief's wives, including the most senior, had the power to intercede—such was the power of "the auntie."

> In those days, when you are given to an auntie, and especially your father's sister, you will be in hell, all the girls were in hell. They wouldn't eat and become satisfied. They would give them food, just a little in a bowl—maybe somebody who could not eat fast . . . —and that will be the end. Til in the evening. (Salamatu Abdulai July 17, 2017)

The women in the house finally said, "Let her take her away—by all means, once he's come, he'll go and bring her back."

> When they brought me to Tamale, we entered the house, and she said, "Go and put your things"—my things were wrapped in a cloth—"go and put your things in that room." I put my things in that room and came out. When I saw the other girls in the house—nobody was wearing pants. Only some beads and cloth. So I was saying to myself, am I going to take this kind of horrible treatment? Because I've never seen that. I was just sitting in the corner—I wasn't crying—I was just thinking how can I stay in this house. So, this is the sort of training I'm going to receive. (Salamatu Abdulai July 17, 2017)

As the daughter of a highly placed chief, Salamatu was accustomed to wearing proper clothing in the house.

Salamatu's father came home in the evening and she wasn't there. He called the first wife, "Where is this girl?" She said, "Ah, Auntie Bamini, she took her away." As the women thought, the chief immediately got on his horse to his sister's to retrieve the child.

> I heard my father. "Ba-mini, Ba-mini." And then my aunt. "Where is that girl?" And I said, "Chief I'm here." (We don't call our father "father"—because he was a chief—it was our senior father we used to call our father.) So I told him, "Chief I'm here." So he came down from the horse and entered. "Ba-min!" and my aunt answered and came out from the room. "I'm going to take this girl. You know her mother just has girls, no boy, so I'm sending her to school." So I just got up. So I just brought my things. "I will take her away and when I get another child and I'll bring her, but this one, she belongs to her mother." We just went out—my father sat on the horse and they lifted me on the horse, then we went home. [laughter]. (Salamatu Abdulai July 17, 2017)

After Salamatu recited this tale she said, "I was very lucky, very very lucky!" For one thing, given all of the children living in his compound, it is remarkable that he noticed her absence. And then, the fact that her father sidestepped tradition by taking on his sister. But even then, there was a glitch.

On the morning the six children were to go to school, their father told the mothers to get them ready.

> So he brought six of us. [were you the only girl?] No we were 2 girls. When we went and the woman [Miss Meron, the headmistress] saw us, she said, oh she would pick only the 3 or 4, leaving the 2 of us, myself and another brother. He was also 9 years. In those days, before they pick you for school, they like to put your hand this way [put

right or left arm over head to touch ear]—whether you could reach. Mine was over—and those who couldn't reach were the people she took. So she told my father, Oh Chief, unfortunately the boy and the girl they are over so you can take them home—I'll pick the rest.

We were coming back to the village when a bicycle rider came. "Chief, Chief. Miss Meron says you should come, you should come back." So we went back—I was always on his horse. He went back and the woman said, "Oh, where is the girl?" "She's outside." "Bring her here. We want girls. So for her, she's lucky—I'll pick her." When they brought me and said, "Good morning Lady." And I said, "Good morning Madam." "What's you name?" And I said . . . "What's your father's name?" And I said . . . "How old are you?" I said, "I'm nine, I'll be nine in September." And so, "Ok, I'm taking you. You are over [too old] but in the north we need girls now for education, so I will pick you. Will you go to school?" I said, "Madam, I will go." So I was picked. (Salamatu Abdulai July 17, 2017)

Salamatu was again lucky, while British educational policy did not favor girls, the headmistress of the local school saw it as beneficial to admit her, as the school was coeducational and she did not have enough girl students. Salamatu was at the right place at the right time. There was room for administrative discretion. As Miss Meron herself said, "she's lucky, I'll pick her." Salamatu did not go on to secondary school—Tamale Girls did not become a secondary school until the late 1950s, and she was not sent south. But she finished middle form in 1955 and was recruited to participate in mass education. She took courses that taught how to handle adults, teach them to read, to wash and keep the room clean, feed children good food, and so on. After about seven years, she was hired by the Ghana Broadcasting Corporation as an accountant. Salamatu was lucky on three counts: her father was a royal (and the British pushed the chiefs to send their children to school), her father was literate and understood from his own experience the importance of an education, and her mother had no boys.

Adisa Munka'ila, about the same age as Salamatu, was also born in Tamale. But unlike Salamatu, Adisa initially lived in the south with her parents. It was the colonial period, and Adisa's father was a cook to a British family in Accra. When her mother was very pregnant, she travelled home to Tamale to give birth. After the requisite time, she returned to Accra with infant Adisa. They lived at Korle Bu, near the teaching hospital. Adisa was sent to primary school. Not far from Korle Bu there was a fishing beach at Korle Gonno. Adisa would go to school, and then like many of her schoolmates, she would skip class and go and help pull in the nets. One day, the wife of her father's employer saw Adisa there. When

Figure 3.1. Salamatu Abdulai (photo by Deborah Pellow).

she got home, she told the father that if he was to educate his daughter, he should send her north. Neither her father nor any of his wives was educated, but he was interested because he had been working with "white people" and through them learned the value of education—he was self-educated, spoke and wrote very good English.

He took Adisa back to Tamale to stay with her mother's mother. She went to primary and middle school in Tamale, with girls from all over the north. When she completed the fourth form, in 1952, she sat for the Common Entrance for Secondary School—the first year allowing girls. She entered Achimota (in Accra) in 1953 for fifth form, and then two years of sixth form. By the time she and the five other girls got there, they were somewhat accepted, "they bullied us a lot—the other students—we were the first set of northern girls to come—they used to say, did we live in trees, did we wear any clothes?" Meanwhile, her father "was abused by others for sending his daughters to school—'sending your daughters to school???'" (Adisa November 10, 2005). Adisa's father, like Salamatu's, defied tradition by sending her to school. His decision came from his own exposure to education and its value-added benefits; he also had ballast from his employer.

A much younger woman Gifty Mahama was, like Adisa and Salamatu, also lucky. Gifty is at the lower age bracket of the 1.5ers and one of the few highly educated women in the group. In her case, it was her *father's* luck that particularly benefited her. After her father's father died, he was taken in by J. S. Kaleem and schooled by the north's first educator. As a result, her father then pushed Gifty's schooling—she did sixth form in Navrongo and then attended University of Cape Coast. Like Salamatu and Adisa, it was her father who made her education a reality. In the three cases, the reasoning was different—to support the mother, to take advantage of the benefits and to be better able to navigate modern society.

The cultural resistance to educating girls in Dagbon is evident in the enrollment statistics. There is the continuing feeling that a girl does not need education, because her husband will look after her (Wayo Seini October 14, 2005; Oppong 1973). The persistence of the custom of the aunties, not a cultural practice in southern Ghana, is symptomatic. Mary Boforo was a member of parliament, representing Savelugu.

> We still have fallout in education so far as girls are concerned in education. Because we have the custom, whereby you give the child to your brother and your brother gives the child to the sister. And that child is presumed to be the servant of the house . . . There comes a time almost all the children in the house will not be in their parental homes, they'll always be in their aunt's house, who do what they want with them. [this is only the girls?] Only the girls. Not until we are able to address this problem, I don't think we will be able to . . . (Mary Boforo June 8, 2006)

This is evidenced in the bridge generation by the relative paucity of women who made it to even middle school. If the practice of "going to the aunties" continues, the deprivation of education for girls will continue. It is far worse at the university level. Girls from the general population in Ghana are less likely than boys to attend. For the northern girls, it is that much worse. Professor Ramatu Alhassan, chair of the Department of Agricultural Economics at the University of Ghana at Legon, is herself an extraordinary example of luck, happenstance and gumption. She went to university though neither parent was educated nor was anyone else in the family. But while in secondary school sixth form in Tamale, she and her classmates all thought that if you wanted a good job, you needed to go to university. She went to UST in Kumase, she was well-mentored and graduated with a first class degree. She ended up in Pullman, WA (Washington State University) doing a master's in agricultural economics, based upon a faculty member's recommendation, and then Iowa State for a PhD. In talking to her, she was not particularly deliberate about how she made the choices—some of it was financial, some was life circumstances—she had married while at Tech and got pregnant, returning from Pullman to have her mother-in-law care for the baby. She is deliberate, however, about the gender imbalance and the need to correct it.

> Take entry enrollment into the University of Ghana—there's a disproportionate number of young men. There are a number of factors, all those traditional factors that limit girls' ability to perform having to do with kinds of work in the house and other things, and also maybe they do not have role models, and I could be blamed for that—role models to show what is possible. I am a bad role model because I'm not the outgoing type so I tend to keep to myself . . . Fathers, if they see role models, will also want the actual girl to become like that. (June 9, 2006)

In all of the testimonies I have supplied, the latter has been true for both the men and women who are members of this new elite. Patriarchy and the power of a powerful male family member makes the difference in whether or not a child is pushed forward in schooling. This is also the case for the boys. The father of Dr. Yakubu Alhassan, a tropical agronomist, was a farmer who had been raised by his mother's brother. The uncle had graduated from Achimota, in the first generation to go to school, but he did not educate Yakubu's father, "At that time not married. So it was only my father who was his companion. So he didn't go to school!!! I cannot explain the circumstances. . . ." But Yakubu's father recognized the importance of school and supported his son while his own educated uncle who raised him denied him the same.

Summary and Conclusion

A negative legacy of colonial policies in the region is the lag in establishing secular schooling. This has been partially responsible for the contemporary situation of adult illiteracy and lack of schooling in the northern three regions. The new Dagomba elite managed to clear the hurdles and as with so much else, luck and timing have been paramount. When the 1.5ers were growing up, the district assemblies helped in their schooling, for example "providing us with uniforms, fares to school—and boarding was all paid for by Government" (Fuseini Baba April 28, 2006). The lucky ones, almost all boys, went on in their schooling, to such an advanced level that they became doctors and lawyers, engineers (contractors) and architects, teachers and members of parliament. Kwame Nkrumah's importance to the educated Dagomba elite is invariably tied to his insistence on the introduction of free and compulsory education in the north.

This cohort of modern educated Dagomba, initially segregated, largely impoverished and disadvantaged, has become a powerful bridge linking Dagbon and the Dagomba diaspora. Through their perceived success, they wield considerable influence on those in the north with little or no Western education. They are opinion leaders and are socially, spatially and occupationally mobile. While societies throughout Africa and all societies in Ghana make use of the "big man" system, it is core to social organization among the Dagomba (Kirby 2003). Big men, i.e. patrons, control small men, manipulate them, own them. The highly educated Dagomba, these members of the new social order, fit the role of patrons who mostly live outside of Dagbon in the south of the country. They wield authority and enjoy favor and respect. Their education and their occupational rank give them old-fashioned status in new-fashioned clothes. Many have gotten involved in national party politics. And some have figured out how to access development aid—"the windfall pouring in from International NGOs, development organizations, and governmental ministries with IMF and World Bank financing . . ." (Kirby 2003, 182). But they are also attached to the hometown area. The rural pole provides social security for the elite urbanites, while the latter function as a bridgehead to the outside world for the former, thereby reinforcing a pattern of mutuality (Geschiere and Gugler 1998).

The issue today that some of this new elite worry about is how to obliterate the discrimination against the north, not just in its educational infrastructure but also the societal models that work against sending all children to school. The members of this new elite have all educated their children (or tried to do so), gender notwithstanding, whether they live in the north or the south of the country. But they are a tiny proportion of the Dagomba population. During both the Nkrumah (1951–66) and Rawlings (1981–91) periods, government sought to deal with educational inequalities through infrastructural expansion and increased access in participation (Quist 2003). And as every member of the newly educated elite reinforced to me, the project of universal primary education began in 1951 under Kwame Nkrumah. Most of these men and women were prime recipients of the new policy. Their access was bolstered by personal family elements. In one case, the father had travelled south for his occupation— for example as a domestic servant—and there he was exposed to a new environment where Western education really matters; in other cases, the fathers were born in southern Ghana, educated there, and then moved back to Dagbon, bringing along the educational values of the south. In other cases, the boys were sent to stay with an agnate, who was educating his own children. And as has been true for so much else about the life trajectories of this generation, serendipity played an enormous role.

Is there still a role for the state? The state is providing free compulsory education. But they have to also provide the facilities for basic education.

> Who's responsible for helping to develop these areas? It's a problem. You want universal education, you want every child to go to school. If a village has about 1000 people—with children and there's no school. And they have to go about 4–5 miles to the nearest school. The tendency to send the children to school is not there. Because maybe the child is so young and he cannot walk that distance. The parents aren't going to take and pick him up. So need to develop infrastructure in the villages. That would encourage them to send the children to school. So government needs to do a lot. (Abdulai Yakubu November 23, 2005)

Is there a role for the traditional authorities? Some believe that whatever few resources are available, the chiefs and people are benefiting. They could use the resources to set up schools for the people, to send the children to school. Each village needs one school—at least a primary school. And the land is not that expensive. People claim they want universal education, they want every child to go to school.

And is the educational model appropriate? In Tamale, one sees untold numbers of young men hanging around. Professor Ramatu Alhassan wonders, "The sad part is that most of those young men who have been to school at some point, they have dropped out, and so the question is, why did they drop out? Is it the education system—are they not getting what they expected from the system?" (June 9, 2006).

Some would say that education, even as it is crucially important, has also contributed to government interference, documentation, to distortion, to manipulation (Issa Naseri September 28, 2005). This has been especially so in Dagbon, where the proportion of educated people is so small and the position of the patron (in the modern world, the educated professional) carries such sway. And it has been particularly evident in the issue of chieftaincy. In the north, where no chiefs existed, it was the educated who created them. As I discuss at length in Chapter Six, chieftaincy in Dagbon carries great salience; over the last eighty years, it has been corrupted by the educated elite. In some cases, the educated got in as employees of the Native Authorities, because in this colonial outpost, you became teacher, joined the Native Authority or medical staff or veterinarian services. Thus those who got into traditional councils as clerks became important in documenting and managing disputes of succession.

NOTES

1. The Omanhene is a paramount chief in the Akan kingdoms in southern Ghana; Atandansu is in the south in the Central Region.
2. According to Ferguson (1972), Islam rapidly expanded in Dagbon in the early eighteenth century. Its spread was associated with a Wangara teacher from Timbuktu, Shaikh Sulayman Abdallah Bagayugu, who arrived there a century earlier, at the time of Ya-Na Luro. He brought the Wangara tradition of scholarship and pedagogy. According to the mid-eighteenth century manuscript *Ta'rikh al-Muslimin*,

   ... it seemed that the Sultan, the King of the Dagomba named Na Luro, loved this his religion of Islam ... then this great shakh came to Yendi ... And the Amir of Yendi, Na Luro said, "I have heard of you Muslim people, for example, of the way you improve yourselves ... I would like you to stay among us, and make these times better, teach us, the people of Dagomba, to read and such other things." (Ferguson 1972, 62–63)

   Thus it appears that Sulayman arrived in Yendi in the mid-seventeenth century.
3. These include religion, with many Muslims resisting mission schooling for their children, lest they be converted to Christianity. Dagomba have characterized themselves to me as conservative and as believing that they are superior to others and thus not needing to adopt the customs or institutions of others. Huudu Iddrisu recounted a wonderful story (June 28, 2007) from Tolon-Na Yakubu (the divisional chief of Tolon). He was chief when the then CCNT (Chief Commissioner of the Northern Territories) visited the various divisional chief of Dagbon when the British were leaving to say good-bye. There was a durbar in Tolon. In addressing the crowd, the CCNT told a proverb. The Tolon-Na's linguist (Na-zo) slapped the chief's leg laughing and asked the chief, "so these people too they are sensible?"
4. Dr. Abdulai is the founder of the Shekhina Clinic, located in Tamale. He sees thirty new patients a day and doesn't receive a salary, hence his nickname. His clinic is funded by donations. He houses lepers, HIV/AIDS patients, the mentally and physically disabled and the destitute – all of whom would otherwise be left to die (https, //journalism.nyu.edu/publishing/africa dispatch/2013/07/03/the-mad-doctor-of-tamale/).
5. This is interesting, because it is similar to the excuse for not sending children to secular/Western school.
6. I heard this complaint from almost all of the educated Dagomba I interviewed. The father of one man had attended Achimota School in Accra, but he was not allowed to stay in the south over vacations, lest he pick up southern attitudes.

CHAPTER 4

Paths to Careers

> When I went to the Law faculty, they would admit 80–90. At the end of the first year, they select 40 to read LLB, 20 BA. When I entered, the first lecture was Contracts. A "friend" asked about me. I told him everything, and he wrote me off. "You trained as a teacher? Oh, you can't compete!" I left that year as one of the top 10 percent.
>
> —"Lawyer" Inussa September 14, 2005

During the pre-colonial period, the north of the country engaged in agriculture and trading. The people consumed what they produced, for example millet and guinea corn, trading the surplus. The geographical position of the region enhanced trade. "Its position constituted the 'meeting place' of various itinerant traders from areas north of the region and the southern fringes of the Sahara, and also for traders due north from the southern sections of what is now Ghana" (Plange 1979, 7). Through their wares, Mande and Dyula traders linked the north with North Africa, Southern Europe and southern Dahomey and Nigeria. Asante exported kola and gold, the Ga and Ewe coastal peoples sent up salt and fish. The traders carried south shea-butter, leather goods, local cloth and livestock. Thus, in the nineteenth century, Yendi was prosperous due to its position as the entrepot for trade, "an intersections of east-west and north-south trade routes unmatched elsewhere in the region" (MacGaffey 2013, 23).

Today, poverty is endemic. The three northern regions comprise 15 percent of the national population and house 43 percent of the country's poorest. Only two percent of the country's highest quintile are located in the Northern Region (Mazzucato 2008). Related to their low economic status is their educational and literacy rate, which is only 20 percent, a legacy of British policy. The Dagomba new elite I write about have made it out and made it big. How did that happen?

As shown in Chapter One, poverty and its consequences are not simply due to lack of resources but rather the British colonial policy of neglect that has been the bane of the region ever since. The north under colonialism was treated by the colonial government as a labor reserve. This impeded the educational infrastructure, expansion of horizons and embrace of modernity. When the Dagomba new elite were growing up, Ghana was just achieving independent statehood. Work opportunities in the north were limited. Their parents were engaged in the same occupations as their parents and their parents' parents before them. They were largely occupied in hunting and farming, work foundational to traditional northern life. Education was limited. Six years after the end of World War II, Tamale Secondary School opened. Secondary education had finally come to the north, almost 100 years after the first secondary school had opened in the country, on the coast.

Core to the story of this in-between generation is that access to professional occupations, not to mention higher education, was absolutely not a given when they were coming of age. Secondary school had barely arrived. What my conversations with these men and women reinforce, and what my detailing of their professional trajectories should make clear, is that for a variety of reasons, including intelligence, luck, circumstance, and parental/family interest, a small cohort of Dagomba got educated. This opened the doors to change, to new forms of accomplishment, professional and financial success, a different life-style and considerable influence. Theirs is a striking story of success, accomplished in only one-half of a generation. When they were children, the years following World War II brought new developments to the country, but it was the south that gained exposure. The north was left behind. The place and its population continued to be defined out of the development narrative.

This chapter looks at the occupational milieu in which the Dagomba patrons came of age, and their (often accidental) avenues to professional careers. Education, as discussed in the last chapter, has made professional careers possible, even as access was not always straightforward.

The educational grounding, historically denied northerners, has clearly enabled them to prosper. As the former journalist A. B. Fuseini said to me, "In terms of academic competence I don't think we suffered—in fact to the contrary, most of us who came from the north, we came out very well. There was no disadvantage at that point—the disadvantage was to even go to school" (May 3, 2006).

This is a paradox: on the one hand, the path to school was littered with obstacles. On the other hand, after northerners had been so disenfranchised for generations the government and the educational structure put in place bent over backwards to be sure that they had access. And once they gained access, they excelled. They told me that, with a bit of surprise but with pride. This is where the opportunity met ability. What A. B. Fuseini was saying was quite simply that they *were* competent, ethnic and regional stereotypes to the contrary. It happens generally, it happened with the Dagomba women, just as it happened with the Dagomba men, though the women's access was more encumbered by tradition. And because many of this cohort came from impoverished circumstances, the obstacles were magnified. It was fine to gain access to secondary school, to be fed and clothed once there, but walking there barefoot was arduous. Having to travel for twenty-four hours to get to an interview was tough. Was it worth it? Yes, because it opened doors for them. The members of this group had the facility and the wherewithal. That is why they succeeded in school and succeeded professionally.

The British had transported to the colonies the education—occupation—financial success formula. The colonial model supported academic schooling—that would get you the trappings of a good life. This filtered down through members of the ensconced elite to their subordinates, like employees and viewers from afar. The aspiring professionals bought into it—influenced by parents, relatives, an interested mentor.

Those involved obviously subscribed fully to the vision that education opened up prosperous futures. This was a golden period of opportunity, especially for members of social groups the state wanted to better integrate. The kind of social mobility that education permitted is far less possible today. This becomes clear when we look at the occupations that the Dagomba new elite carved out for themselves and how they did it. In addition to the change in the education infrastructure in the north, there was also national service placement following university. But perhaps most important was often some kind of personal support—normally from family—and parental aspirations that transcended their children's education, hard work and good fortune.

I go on to detail the work trajectories of the members of this group, in journalism, politics and the civil service, finance, research and medicine, architecture, building, and cultural aims. These are as remarkable in their variance as they are vastly different from the hometown possibilities. I finally consider whether there has been an occupational transfer from traditional work to modern ones and whether the particular kind of job transfer meant the transmission of status from members of earlier familial generations to those in the current modernizing one.

Home Ventures

Northern Ghana is covered primarily by orchard bush (tree savannah), with grass as a ground cover (Pogucki 1955), composing the Ghana Savannah woodland, "watered by the White Volta and its tributaries to the west, the Oti and its tributaries to the east" (Oppong 1973, 16). It is not very hilly and too dry to support a forest, therefore it cannot produce profitable forest tree crops. While the economy of the southern sector, on the one hand, was transformed into an export economy by commercializing agriculture and through mining, the north, on the other hand, perpetuated the traditional subsistence economy. The trees of economic importance have been the shea butter, *dawadawa* (locust bean), baobab, kapok and mango. Trees carry especial importance, in addition to providing commodities for ritual and supernatural reasons (Oppong 1973).

Dagomba are farmers and there are two kinds of farmed lands, compound farms and bush farms—the latter the more important that are also fallowed periodically. By customary law, political control of the land is lodged with the Ya-Na, the Dagomba king, who in turn delegates rights to divisional and village chiefs. Individual householders gain rights to the land, and they can pass those rights on (Oppong 1973). On the other hand, ritual control belongs to the *tindana*, each the master of a particular locality. "He allocates use of unclaimed land within his *teng* [locality] in return for ritual, not economic gifts of first-fruits" (Manoukian 1951, 65).

While ownership of most land is vested in a lineage, the "rights to use a separate piece of land for food growing purposes are in fact individual rights" (Birmingham et al. 1967, 29). Colloquially, local people refer to rights to use the land as "the right to farm," that is, to engage in agriculture. This has not included the right to the produce of fruit-producing trees or to minerals found on the land—the latter go to the *tindana*; the same is true for stray cattle. Rights in trees are distinct from the land they grow on and vary according to whether they are sacred or fruit-bearing. The former again belong to the *tindana*, the latter (including dawadawa or locust bean, shea nut and mango) may be claimed by the *tindana*, although another may have rights to the fruit; those in the bush are claimed by the *tindana*.

When William Bossman was exploring the area in the late seventeenth—early eighteenth century, and later, agriculture was a primary occupation. In northern Ghana, the main farm crops were cereals, such as millet, guinea corn and maize, as well as rice and okra. These and salt, slaves, gold, and livestock were produced and traded within the Dagomba territory (van Hear 1982). Yams became the main root crop, both for diet and cash income They also cultivated and wove cotton, and along with tobacco, traded it with the Mossi.

Near the major markets and within Dagbon and the Gonja state, production was based on slavery—production which was disrupted by long-distance trade. The historical influence of north to south—for example, the north to northeast and northwest trade routes that brought in goods that made it south—changed with European arrival on coast.

Despite an increase in the amount of land cultivated and food produced and marketed during the first decade of the twentieth century (van Hear 1982), the potential for cultivation clearly in evidence was blocked by the European decision to use the north as a labor reserve. For example, the cocoa boom of the mid-1930s and an increase in mining activity led to more labor recruiting, some legal some not. The colonial government also recruited laborers for railway and road construction in southern Ghana. Voluntary migration started not long after the first forced migrants had returned from southern Ghana. Most of the early voluntary migrants were attracted by good labor opportunities in the booming cocoa sector (Van der Geest 2011). This drain on village agricultural labor diminished cultivation.

From the mid-nineteenth century till the eve of World War II, the agricultural landscape differed little from the earlier period. Export agriculture was generally ignored, though some peoples, such as the Dagomba and the Gonja, became interested in cotton as an export. The British had promoted cotton growing (instructing the locals and installing a cotton gin and press in Tamale), but because farmers needed to produce food for their households, they could not put enough energy into cotton production to make it worthwhile. Moreover, transport costs were high and the numbers of strong men were reduced because they were drafted to work in the gold mines. Those who emigrated south to work were impressed by the wages and decency of living conditions, an enticement to the young men.

In the late 1930s, "wage earning jobs, which might have productively retained labour in the region, were scarce in the north" (van Hear 1982, 174). Wages in the north were lower than in the south—because they were "adequate" and because most workers were also cultivating farms and thus did not rely only on their wages. This contributed to the seasonal migration of northerners south. "Having experienced underdevelopment in their home areas, these youths wanted to witness something better. Although frowned on by some northern administrators, such a world view was an inevitable result of colonial policy towards the north" (van Hear 1982, 177).

By World War II, export agriculture was still unknown. Food farming was still guinea corn and millet and yam—the same as for a long time. The low crop yield continued. There were still large unoccupied tracts of land, because land had not increased in value. Experimental stations were established in Dagbon at Tamale, Tolon, Savelugu, but farmers were not enthusiastic about crop rotation or mixed farming, which were being promoted (Dickson 1969).

In 1960, when the future Dagomba new elite were growing up, the north had only 6.3 percent of the country's population. And speaking to a very different kind of life than in the south, in northern Ghana, less than one-twelfth of the population lived in localities of 5,000 or more inhabitants (Birmingham et al. 1967).

While there have been very high densities immediately around Tamale, there has also been an abundance of land and comparatively scant population density—in 1960, the population density was eighteen persons per square mile, the lowest in the country (the average for all of Ghana was seventy-three, for Accra 494)—and thus no problems in getting and utilizing land. The savanna is a reserve of unutilized space, its marginal productivity from the point of view of the economy as a whole close to zero (Birmingham et al. 1966), thus here the land does not have economic importance.

Enid Forde (1968) explains the north-south dichotomy in terms of the dualistic nature of the economy and the respective development of economic infrastructure. "In less developed countries, especially those in Africa, the evolution of the economic infrastructure has had a great influence on the rate of economic development. An indispensable part of progress in economic development was the provision of adequate transport infrastructure in railways, ports, roads, and later, airways" (p. 80). Transport facilities were crucial to export of products. But with time, this infrastructure broadened to include the production of electricity, communication, public utilities and education. If we consider the southern and northern regions, the south had cocoa and minerals for export, urban areas with populations of 50,000 and more, and better transportation via railroads and a denser road system. It was costly to move produce from north to south, impeding economic change in northern Ghana. And in addition to urbanization and mobility, of course, the south also had education/literacy. At the time that my study population was growing up in the north, provision of education for everybody was probably more important than the need for a high level of education for everybody.

In the 1960s, five sixths of the working population in the north were employed in food production, which correlates with little migration. If one had work farming, one did not move around. The Kingdom of Dagbon lies within this region, where subsistence agriculture has predominated and the cash economy has been of minor importance. Farming methods still consisted of the wooden hoe, blades and at time the plow. Workers rotated farmed plots, trending toward a system of better tools, methods, and marketable surplus. Within Dagbon, as elsewhere in the north, the farmers engaged in shifting cultivation. Cattle and poultry were sent south. The agricultural work was based on the collective labor of members of kinship groups. Because older men with sons tended to oversee the work, the hardest agricultural workers have been the young men, primarily boys of twelve to fourteen-years old. They begin, for example, hoeing and digging the yam mounds. Given their contribution, fathers are often loathe to relinquish their labor for the sake of education.

In 1966, the National Liberation Council (NLC) overthrew Nkrumah's First Republic. They then drastically scaled back financial support for large-scale farming, pushing private entrepreneurship. The Busia regime, which succeeded the NLC in 1969, maintained the policy. There was a boom in private tractor sales to large-scale farmers given loans, which led to Tamale becoming the most mechanized district in the country in the early 1970s. There was a fertilizer project and improved seed was introduced. Many laborers lost their jobs while the large-scale farmers continued to benefit—they had first under the state-run mechanization of the Nkrumah regime and now it was buying up machinery cheaply. And then there was a coup in January 1972. The National Redemption Council (NRC), led by General I.K. Acheampong, instituted "Operation Feed Yourself." Large-scale rice farmers benefited from subsidies. "Most of the farmers who participated in the state sponsored rice boom were Dagombas, mainly from Tamale and other large towns in the Northern Region" (van Hear 1982, 299).

In the 1970s, official economic policy was focused on agricultural improvement, especially, rice growing, and indeed, the rice revolution and investments in cotton production did positively affect the region. Most Dagomba farmers who participated in rice farming did so as part of the state-sponsored rice boom. Rice had been grown on a small scale in southern Ghana prior to WWII. It was after the war that the Department of Agriculture gave rice special attention, particularly in the north (van Hear 1982).[1] As the market price of rice increased, in west Dagomba farmers intensified their production of rice, so in 1952 there were seven sites selected there. A semi-skilled agricultural labor force was trained to work in mechanized rice schemes. In the early 1960s, the state agricultural sector imported many machines and implements, largely from eastern Europe. Large numbers of northerners were mobilized for employment as tractor operators. By the mid-1960s, "the expansion of large-scale farming had created a substantial labour force composed of school leavers" (van Hear 1982, 290). The majority of these workers were members of the first generation in the expansion of the rice industry in the early 1970s.

Sadly, by the late 1970s, it was clear that the country's agricultural program, and especially rice production, "had failed in its major objective of making the country self-sufficient in food" (Antoine 1985, 337). Because of the success of rice cultivation in the 1970s, some of those I interviewed in 2006 mentioned General Ignatius Kutu Acheampong (a disgraced former head of state) as one of the two politicians (alongside

Kwame Nkrumah) who had had the greatest positive impact in Dagbon and, indeed, the whole of northern Ghana (see Antoine 1985).

Alhaji Mahdi, who is from Kunbungu, thought back fondly, "when there was farming, at Christmastime instead of celebrating (and Muslims like to celebrate), we were in the bush harvesting rice. Midnight. And so happy harvesting rice" (Mahdi September 16, 2005). Those currently living up north, observing the amount of unemployment in the region, would refer specifically to the Acheampong time, perceiving it as one when, specifically because of rice, everyone had work, men and women. Huudu Yahaya Iddrisu reminisced about that period with me:

> Up north people will always remember Acheampong because of Operation Feed Yourself. Eating what you grow and growing what you eat. Gave a boost to rice farming—became an alternative to cocoa. Even people from the south migrated to do rice farming, and it was on large scale. Hundreds of acres. And people made some money and it transformed their lives. New neighborhoods grew up. People were in saloon cars and sending children to private schools. And then, the economy of the country collapsed. (November 28, 2005)

The agricultural economist Professor Ramatu Alhassan observed to me that the program's sustainability required subsidies.

> But then you have to look at subsidies not in terms of cash and cost but in terms of the social implications. And I don't think people have. The collapse of the rice industry led to the emergence of this young *kayayi* [a girl who has gone south to work as a porter]. And it's a big social problem. So what does this mean in terms of cost for subsidies? Maybe the subsidies weren't being managed. What we should have done is how best to manage the situation and not abandon the program. But that's the problem. And we don't have the political power to change some of these things in terms of decision-making . . . Because of the poor infrastructure, you can't get investments. No one wants to go there. What we have now are incentives for producers but they have to produce first. (June 9, 2006)

And now the majority in the north have also not been to school. As this is "an important tool for human capital development" (Yeboah 2010, 49), they also do not have work.

Agricultural livelihood has traditionally been supplemented by livestock production and hunting in the Dagomba economy (Blench 2012). The Dagomba raise cattle, sheep, goats, pigs, dogs, cats, donkeys, horses, rabbits, guinea-pigs, chickens, ducks, guinea-fowl, turkeys, pigeons and bees. Cattle are prized possessions and may be family or individually owned. They are often herded by Fulani boys and men. The horse has been particularly important. In the past they were the base of the chief's military and political power (Oppong 1973). Today they are owned by chiefs and eminent men, symbolic of their status and playing largely a ceremonial role.

Hunting has been historically significant among the Dagomba (though it matters less today). The hunter was a considerable, prestigious figure and was associated with the ruling classes. Until recently, wildlife populations made the hunter a significant contributor (Blench 2004). Rights to hunting are so-called "rights of common character"—"Anybody can hunt in the bush, and anybody can kill game, which he may find on somebody else's farm without committing trespass" (Pogucki 1955, 41). Historically, bows and poisoned arrows had been used for war or hunting. In the mid-nineteenth century, they were superseded by Dane guns, the owner adorned "the stock with cowries and charms and reckon[ed] his weapon as his most valuable possession" (Northcott et al. 1899, 37). Since then, among the Dagomba guns have been an "icon of manhood" (McCaskie 2008, 439). They are a part of traditional northern life, as most men are socialized to hunt, and owning a gun is a sign of accession to manhood. In the last few decades, Dagomba iron specialists, who had produced weapons such as knives, arrowheads and spears, started producing guns and bullets for chiefs (Oppong 1973; Sowatey 2005). Today a few old men still use muskets, and the warriors of Dagbon carry muskets whenever they attend ceremonial occasions. For example, according to tradition, immediately following a Ya-Na's burial, there is much firing of guns (Cardinall 1921). This is also true on the occasion of the regent's/king's enskinment. On April 6, 2006, the day before Kampakuya-Na's installation as Regent of Dagbon, the warriors of the divisional chiefs descended upon Yendi. Hundreds of them, adorned with protective amulets, carrying guns, marched through town, tamping down gun powder, shooting, and filling the air with thick black dust.

Trade and crafts such as drumming, smithing and divining which require professional skills and involve apprenticeship and training continue to be practiced by exclusive groups (Oppong 1973). Wage labor has become more important, for both men and women. Women have traditionally cultivated gardens. Research shows that in the 1960s, there was low participation of women in the labor force in the north—less than 20 percent; women were characterized as "home-makers" (Birmingham et al. 1966). Cultivation, even when pursued, has been insufficient to support the family, let alone as a source of wealth. Thus, even women have been migrating south—to work and save money to support their families and build capital for their entrepreneurial aspirations.

Until the 1980s, the north-to-south labor migration trend in Ghana was historically male-dominated, because the job opportunities in southern Ghana were in mining, timber, and cocoa plantations; these were considered male jobs. Young men were lured to the southern towns to buy luxuries unavailable in the north, depleting agricultural work "of many of those on whom it most depends" (Oppong 1973, 20). Women were not supposed to migrate on their own (Tufeiru 2014).

Women who now are migrating south to work speak of this enabling them to acquire accessories such as cooking utensils and clothing—needed for marriage—because of their earning power in Accra. While some of these non-elite migrants work in the informal economy making and selling foodstuffs, the Dagomba women tend to engage in portering (*kayayi*). When asked to explain the swelling ranks of settlers, the Nachin-Na (an Accra Dagomba chief) told me, "Poverty is the first reason. And Dagombas have only one job and that is farming. If it fails, you have to wait a year. Some who come down go back for the harvest" (September 4, 2005).

In her study of *kayayi* in Accra, 70 percent of whom were Dagomba, Muriel Adjubi Yeboah found that 80 percent of the women had never been to school, compared with ten percent of the men. (This aligns with statistics on the northern regions' gender disparity in formal education (Asenso-Okyere et al. 2000). Yeboah also found that the majority of the women are temporary migrants, whereas the men are "rather permanent" (2010, 50). They may remit to their families, but the amounts are small. Many make return trips home to visit, to help at harvest time, or to try to start a business venture there.

Professional Educational Grounding

The cohort of Dagomba I have focused on have done remarkably well in their occupational histories. Access to professional occupations was not a given when they were coming of age. They have become professionals, in law, politics, the medical sciences, university and research positions, architecture and engineering, and management of various sorts. The positions they attained required a good educational foundation, in most cases university and post-graduate training. There is no question that education is necessary but insufficient for professional success. This is the starred generation, the in-between group (men), who because they got to school and because the country was trying to exhibit unity of opportunity and to diversify occupations, succeeded. Is it true today? Probably not, and certainly not in the south. There are may schools, many smart, well-educated men and women, who took the lesson from the British (long gone) not to learn trades but rather to become white collar and professional workers. And there are not enough positions for them, so they struggle with unemployment. This cohort of new-elite Dagomba are similar to the 1.5ers who sociologists have written about in East and Southeast Asia. They are the generation in between who hit the jackpot.

Following graduation from accredited tertiary institutions, like all Ghanaian students they are required under law to do a one-year national service stint. It provides practical exposure on the job, both in the public and private sectors. The Ghana National Service Scheme Act, 1980, was established for all citizens of Ghana, eighteen years of age or older, by constitutional instrument. It included all of the following fields, agriculture, co-operatives, education, health, local government, the military, rural development (including surveying, physical planning, civil engineering and rural industries and youth programs. In addition, the board could prescribe other fields when appropriate.[2] Many of the prospective Dagomba new elite were assigned to teaching posts, often back in Dagbon. From there, they were free to go on in post-graduate study or to begin work. Some ended up in professions that they had been introduced to for their national service.

Members of this bridge generation were not the very first northerners to be educated, as I wrote in the last chapter, a tiny number of individuals had been sent south to The Achimota School starting in the 1920s to be trained as teachers for the north. Those I am writing about, however, are among the first to have come of age after secondary education was established *in the north* and to have attended school there.

Those students aspiring to university had to also complete the A (advanced) levels, an extra two years following completion of O (ordinary) levels. "O" signify the end of a student's secondary education. A few went to school in the north but out of the region—to Navrongo, a good school and the first in the region to include A levels, to Bawku in the Upper East, and also to Lawra, in the Upper West. In the Navrongo choice, for those already there for O levels it meant not having to change schools to continue on.

Areas of Expertise

The Dagomba patrons span a surprising range of occupations. Most of their positions have required not just tertiary but graduate training. A few used that training and a profession as a jumping-off point to a new career. Some trained through life's lessons or being socialized by a savvy parental figure. Many became politically involved in college, which set their path in life—whether as a journalist or as a lawyer. To provide an overview of this cohort's accomplishments and give a sense of individual life histories, I have gone into some detail, categorizing them according to their areas of occupational expertise. While the material seems "raw," it lays out the specifics of the paths taken in these various endeavors and I have included all of those I interviewed. What is significant is 1) their provenance as northerners, 2) the fields they have gotten into, and 3) the success they have attained. All of this is what combines to make them patrons. They are at the top of their fields, they are well networked, and they are in positions to help those who seek them out.

Journalism

It is interesting that a number of the Dagomba went into journalism, given their own linguistic marginality growing up. Moreover, the major media outlets have not had news bureaus in the north. When need be, someone has been sent up to report or a local "stringer" has been used. Iliasu Adam was a stringer for the BBC and I first got to know him after seeing an article he had published on the Yendi conflict for the British press. Iliasu, who is from Tamale, attended the Ghana Institute of Journalism. He did post-graduate studies in journalism, receiving a master's degree at the University of Cardiff. He worked for Ghana News Agency and because there was no northern news bureau, he was contracted by the BBC. Unlike most of his educated age group, he did not want to live in the south. But he also became dissatisfied with journalism and after several years, he moved over to working in development. He pursued a second master's degree abroad in public administration and is now finishing a doctorate in sociology. His media interests which were political at heart mesh with the needs in the north for development in many sectors.

"Major" Gomda was also able like Iliasu to, in his father's words, "attend school to the fullest" (May 2, 2006). Like Iliasu he went to the Institute of Journalism in Accra, because he wanted to work with public relations directors of the military. To that end, he then went on to the military academy for officer training (hence the moniker "Major"), but because it was not a good fit, he left. Like many in Ghana, during the difficult times in the 1980s and early 1990s, he went to Nigeria where he worked for newspapers for ten or twelve years. Upon his return to Ghana, he got involved in the local news industry, ultimately starting the *Daily Guide*, where today he is chief news editor.

Like all of the others in this group of new elite, Major's occupational path clearly grew out of the secondary school and then college training he pursued. There are four other members of the cohort who went into the field of journalism/communication. But as with many of the other achievements of the cohort, making it in communications did not require a specialized academic degree. Indeed, Adisa Munka'ila did not go to university at all. But given her age—she would be one the oldest in the 1.5 generation—at the time she was becoming professionally groomed, a university credential was unnecessary. After finishing sixth form at Achimota, Adisa returned to Tamale and was employed at Tamale Girls School—by then it had become a secondary school—while looking for a permanent job. Siddique is younger, is also a radio broadcaster but unlike Adisa ("people thought I had a good voice" [November 10, 2005]). has not worked on air—he is a station manager at the University of Ghana. While both are in broadcasting, Adisa has really had a nose for politics, Siddique for management. Much of Adisa's professional life involved state politics, for example representing the Tamale market women for the Third Republic Constitution Commission in 1974. Siddique has stayed with the radio, taking over management of Radio Universe, the University radio station, when he returned from his MA overseas. He has had an extraordinary impact on radio broadcasting in Ghana, as currently, employees at every radio station in Ghana have passed through his training shop. While his education was important, his father's work in the military, and living at military bases, are ties into modernity.

Two other men in the Dagomba cohort work in newspapers, having arrived at the world of journalism in very different ways. Haruna Atta is the publisher of the *Accra Mail*, which he founded in 1999. Unlike the cases of Iliasu, Adisa and Siddique, his father was one of the early educated northerners, who was a trained surveyor. Haruna's father had the same attitude as "Major's" with respect to education, "go as high as you could go" (May 29, 2006). In secondary school and at the University of Science and Technology (UST) in Kumase, Haruna was politically involved—in secondary school he was in the Ghana United Nations Student Assn (GUNSA) and president of the Northern Students Union, and in university he was a member of the Student Representative Council. The latter "gave me an insight into what election democracy is all about. It was for me the beginning of my interest in the electoral process, to move an agenda forward." This apparently fed his pathway into print journalism—as a way of presenting the news and taking positions.

He studied graphic design and art at UST, then worked in film production, "the graphic art training opens your eyes to visual and word literacy. And that to me is what journalism is all about." The NDC ban on politics in Ghana was lifted in 1992 and newspapers were springing up. Haruna began writing a column for *The Statesman*. After a year, he was given the editorship. But he ran into trouble with Mrs. Rawlings, wife of the president (and former military head) and was jailed. Upon release, he went out on his own, founding the *Accra Mail*.

Media savvy has been important in the Dagomba issue of conflict, of making positions and facts known. Some of the journalists have taken the Abudu side through their output, some the Andani. The abilities of all have made it possible for the information (or propaganda) to reach a wider reading and listening audience. It has also helped the cause of one side or the other. And it has increased the profiles of the individuals involved.

Those who have worked in journalism/communication have been leaders—two founding newspapers, one a groundbreaking woman who did community work and served on the Third Republic Constitutional Assembly which led her into politics ("I never went in because I wanted—but when called to do something I did it" November 10, 2005)—one overseeing the university's radio station.

Political Office

In Ghana, there is widespread support for democracy. At the same time, there are deficits in the political culture. Popular understanding of the political process is underdeveloped and there is a weak sense of civic responsibility. Moreover, "voting patterns indicate persistent ethnic and regional chauvinism" (Gyimah-Boadi 2009, 149). After the murder of the Ya-Na in 2002, the parliamentary ratio for the Northern Region flipped, NPP, the government in power whom many in the Dagbon area held responsible, lost all but one of its seats. It was a one-issue election for them. Given the unrest in Dagbon, the political fervor of many of these men and women is understandable. A number of the Dagomba professionals who would not earlier have been so inclined ran for and won office.

The largest occupational group in this Dagomba new elite consists of politicians—elected as members of parliament (six), vice president, member of the Constitutional Convention, and as political appointees (northern regional executive, regional director of education, ministerial position, ambassador). Perhaps not surprisingly, six of the twelve politicians have law degrees. One of the journalists used his natural interest in politics as a springboard into electoral politics.

One can posit all sorts of reasons for this. This is a collection of men and women who understand how fortunate they were to get to school, not to mention a profession beyond, and who also understand the historical obstructions they were surmounting in so doing and have wanted to apply their talents to effecting political change. When queried, they shrug—there was the opportunity and they saw it as a chance to help. Adisa Munka'ila used her education and professional abilities in the 1970s to lobby for groups, which helped interest her in community work. It was through her participation on the committee writing the Third Republic Constitution that she gained national exposure, and in 1979 she was appointed Deputy Minister for Labor, Youth and Social Welfare. This, she told me, gave her the opportunity to learn and to do service for her people in the north (November 10, 2005).

But politics is an uncertain profession. When there was a coup in January 1982, she was arrested and spent three months in prison. After being a minister, it was very difficult to get a job—"who's going to take you?" She subsequently took advantage of new opportunities, like speaking on women in politics, which got her into NGO work on the street children problem. Her last formal political position was as a member of the President's Council of State in the early 2000s.

This occupational choice is perhaps an obvious change for a newspaperman. A. B. Fuseini from his former position as editor at the *Daily Graphic*. He is now the MP from Sarnarigu, just outside of Tamale. Rather than writing the news, he is now shaping it. Fuseini came from an uneducated background, though his mother, a textile trader, was very enthusiastic about sending her three boys through school, and she bore all of the incidental costs. It was his major of political science as a University of Ghana undergraduate that helped guide him into his career—although, he had been writing for some time—in secondary school, he was very active in a writing club, and then, after graduating from Legon, for his national service he was sent by the Ministry of Education to the *Ghanaian Times*, a daily newspaper, where he was on the news desk and then features. "And that is where I actually started my journalism career May 3, 2006)." The *Ghanaian Times* wanted to retain him—"they must have been impressed with what I had to offer." But he left for the *Daily Graphic*, initially as a reporter and ultimately night editor. It is from this position that he moved into politics.

Involvement in politics while in university served as a natural springboard for others who went into state politics—for example, Dr. Alhasan, Huudu Yahaya and Haruna Iddrisu . The training grounds were NUGS (National Union of Ghana Students) and Northern Students' Union. Dr. Alhassan, the eldest of the three, was until his death in late 2016, a practicing architect. But he was also very involved politically: while at UST, he was active in northern politics, becoming the General Secretary of the Northern Student's Union. In 1979 he was elected to parliament, but that role ended with the December 31, 1981 coup d'etat and the dissolution of parliament. After a one-year stint as head of architecture in the Engineering Faculty of University of Ibadan in Nigeria, he was appointed Provisional National Defence Council (PNDC) Secretary for the Ministry of Public Works and Housing in Ghana. By the time I got to know him, he was the head of Development (architecture and building) at the University of Ghana. No longer a politician but in an academic institution. As an older member of the generation, he remembers his father wanting to send him to school in Tamale in the early 1950s when he was around eight years old. The school head said "if my father can manufacture a chair and a table they would fit me, and this is what happened. My father saw a carpenter, bought wood and they made me a table and chair. I carried it to school, and they admitted me into the classroom" (May 14, 2006). He began in a classroom and ended in a classroom.

I'd known Huudu Yahaya's name for years before meeting him. He has been an important figure in party politics since Jerry Rawlings led his December 31 (1981) coup. Huudu had been politically active in secondary school and then as a student at Cape Coast University joined NUGS from 1975 to 1979. In 1979, his senior year, "we engineered the school closing down" (November 28, 2005). In study groups, he and his pals tried to understand the reason for the backwardness of the Northern Region, writing papers on how to move forward, criticizing the elite (the intelligentsia), who had come out of Acheampong's operation and had become spokespeople in the development of the region. As a political class, money had gotten into their hands.

> If you have got the means and instead of being agents of development you rather are becoming sources of negative development . . . So we did social-political-economic analysis. And as young people we had a lot of enthusiasm. We had to fight because there were so many reactionary leaders. (November 28, 2005)

After his national service, which directed him to Tamale Secondary School as a biology teacher, Huudu was admitted to Howard University in educational technology. But before he matriculated, in 1982 he heard Flight Lt Jerry Rawlings, the charismatic new military head of state, on the radio. "Political involvement as a student made it easy to slide into national politics" (November 28, 2005) he told me.

And slide into politics he did. He was appointed regional minister for the Northern Region, the longest serving regional minister since colonial times and the first northern minister who hailed from the north. "It was very challenging as someone born and raised there" (11/28/2005). The Northern Region literacy rate was under 10 percent and doctor: patient ratio the worst in Ghana. These were issues he sought to remediate. He subsequently served as Minister of Labor and Social Welfare, Minister of Trade, Minister of Tourism, and since the political party National Democratic Congress (NDC) was formed, he has served in various leadership roles. Huudu has a law degree, he is trained in public administration and international relations—politics is his love but not necessarily his meal ticket.

Huudu's junior colleague in the NDC (National Democratic Congress) from Tamale, Haruna Iddrisu, is a Member of Parliament for Tamale. He studied sociology for a deeper understanding of human behavior within the context of human society—to know why people behave as they do, why society does what it does, how society is organized, to understand social structure, and so on. Then, he thought, pursuing a professional career like law would help him "enhance the assets of my people" and work for social justice. NUGS was perhaps a political jumping off point for him—he was president at the University of Ghana in 1996–97.

"In those days to be NUGS president from the north—you know in Ghana there have been prejudices with respect to the north . . ." I first heard about him in the context of northern politics and how things had turned around politically in the north following the Ya-Na's murder in 2002. In 2000, Haruna Idrissu had run in the NDC parliamentary primary and come in last in a field of five. When he ran again in 2004, he won— as did most NDC candidates in Dagbon, because of the Andani, NDC/ Abudu, NPP alignment. Haruna's was the lone voice in parliament who (successfully) lobbied for resources for the north when the Africa Millennium Grant was awarded to Ghana.

There are others who were elected to parliament, who are also lawyers and also held political appointments. Malik Yakubu was Second Deputy Speaker of the Ghanaian parliament when I first met him. Earlier, he was part of a group of young professionals, some of whom he met in university, who formed the Progress Youth Club. After Rawlings led a coup in 1981, the group would speak out against the regime. When political pressures cemented in Ghana to go democratic, the Progress Youth Club became the Youth Wing of the political party NPP. Malik had trained as a lawyer and worked at the Ghana Cocoa Board. In 1991, he got into politics as a member of Constituent Assembly that drafted the new Constitution. Then in 1992, when he returned north, he was asked to run for parliament. But his party boycotted the election. Four years later he was elected from Yendi and went to parliament in 1997. From 2001 to 2002 he was Minister of the Interior, a position he relinquished following the murder of the Ya-Na. Recriminations had emerged, questioning whether he had done enough to prevent the carnage. He returned to the parliament.

As was true for most of these Dagomba politicians, all of Mohammed Mumuni's family were engaged in traditional occupations. He qualified for university, but he says it "wasn't easy at all. Because I came from a particularly poor family" (May 1, 2006). They were incapacitated financially when his father went blind during Mumuni's middle school days.

His mother encouraged her son. After an undergraduate degree in law, he became a magistrate. Then in 1980, he resigned from the judiciary, returned to Tamale and practiced till 1997. When I asked him why he went into the law, he said there was a popular lawyer he knew, who had a flamboyant way of speaking in court, and he was Mumuni's inspiration. But then he left law to go into politics. In 1996 while still in Tamale, he stood for elections from his hometown Kunbungu and won. He was then appointed Minister of Employment and Social Welfare. While his party NDC lost the presidential election in 2000, he won his seat, and in 2004, he was the vice-presidential candidate. He had to give up his seat to run, but he did so because, he said, he was "looking forward to growing, serving the country. I also gamble" (October 20, 2005). It was a gamble that he lost. But five years later, during which time he practiced law in Tamale and in Accra, he was appointed by President Atta-Mills to be Minister for Foreign Affairs and Regional Integration, a position he held till 2013. And now, he lives in the north where he has returned to farming—considered one of the largest private farmers in the north.

Both Inussa Fuseini and Abubakar Sumani were also elected to parliament as practicing lawyers. "Lawyer" Inussa was initially trained as a teacher and when he then chose to go to university, he needed a study leave. He could not get one for law, because it is not a teaching subject, so instead he opted for political science and sociology. He switched over to law, where his professor "told us we were getting an opportunity to gain higher status. Law and lawyers were among the first class of people. I thought that would be wonderful, to jump from being a village boy to first class. He told us, the person in front of you, the person in back, on both sides—they are in competition with you. By beating them, you prove you are capable of being a student" (September 8, 2005). His specialty is litigation, "Have to learn to think on your feet" (September 8, 2005). In 2006, one of the MPs from Tamale, Wayo Seini, "crossed the carpet," leaving his party to run as an independent. Inussa ran on the NDC line and won. After a number of years in parliament, he was appointed Minister of Lands.

As I have argued throughout this book, the professional trajectories of many of the 1.5ers are the result of unanticipated events and the vagaries of life. MP Sumani's case is a good example of how genealogy, politics and health can shape one's path. After receiving his law degree, Sumani joined the attorney general's office in Accra as an assistant, then sent to Koforidua as state's attorney. Under military rule, he found it hard to operate and got a job in the legal department of the State Insurance Corporation. With civilian rule, he moved to the Northern Regional Development office. But December 31,1981 witnessed the second coming of Rawlings and there was a violent upheaval in Tamale. Along with a few prominent men, Sumani was called a counter-revolutionary. A friend from law school warned him to get out, and he ended up spending eight years in Togo, without his wife and children. He returned to Ghana in 1991, but as an Andani, he was tainted by Dagomba chieftaincy politics. The government sent him to Saudi Arabia, the Gulf States and Pakistan as ambassador, "I was sent there so I would not be brought down here to be a minister and disrupt their plans. I took my family. I was there almost 7 1/2 years, from '94-'01" (June 2, 2006). He was brought back when the government needed him to stand for parliamentary elections rather than the party lose the seat. He was persuaded and narrowly won. He retained the seat from 2004 to 2012.

Six others have also held political office, the first three as Abudus in NPP administrations. Tijani, the current Deputy Minister of Foreign Affairs and MP for Yendi, was DCE of Yendi when I met him; as an Abudu, he has gained political appointments under NPP governments. He was also one of fifteen men remanded for trial in the case of the Ya-Na's murder. Joshua Hamidu, a lieutenant general, from the royal family in Sunson, was appointed High Commissioner to Zambia, National Security Advisor to the Kufuor Government (NPP) and High Commissioner to Nigeria. Aliu Mahama, vice president for eight years in John Kufuor's administration, was a trained engineer. He was not a politician but he was brought in to balance the presidential ticket regionally. (He was also criticized by Dagomba up north for not doing much of anything for Dagbon.)

Two other MPs in the group were both voted out of office in 2016. Dr. Alhassan Yakubu, a "village boy" from Mion has a PhD in Agronomy from Imperial College (UK). Mary Boforo. He utilized his educated expertise when he was made Deputy Minister for Agriculture. Mary Boforo is interesting on a couple of counts. First off, she is a woman; secondly, she never attended secondary school, as a result of the 1966 coup, her father was a member of parliament and also ambassador to Mali. He was arrested, "and some of us had to fall back in our education, so I went to vocational school" (Mary Boforo June 8, 2006). She went to school to learn seamstressing, a classic female job. When her father was released, Mary went into rice farming with him. "Some of us had to assist him in his farming activity. He even won many awards in farming and I've taken after him too. I'm a farmer now and I've also won many awards" (Mary Boforo June 8, 2006). In point of fact, from farming she went into baking, was voted in by bakers to be a member of the Constituent Assembly, one of those who drafted the 1992 constitution. After nine months in Accra, she returned to Savelugu and got involved in agro-forestry. The local MP decided that politics did not suit him and came to her, "when there's to be an election you should stand, *because you are for the people, you know how to play your cards*" (Mary Boforo June 8, 2006; emphasis added). Mary Boforo like many of the others expressed a real sense of duty in serving her community. She has understood how unusual her position is *as a woman*—she escaped drudgery in an auntie's household, has excelled in traditional village occupations, and spent eight years in parliament.

What is remarkable is the background, the want, of the Dagomba politicians—they made it against all odds. But it is also because of their backgrounds, knowing what marginalization and neediness look or feel like and utilizing the skills that they had—writing, speaking, lobbying, farming—that pushed them in this direction.

Civil Service and Extra-State Roles

Governmental posts that are not political are held by civil servants. These are the actors who basically run governmental offices. Throughout the public administration literature, there is debate about the issue of the representation of minorities in the public bureaucracy. At issue is the development and implementation of policies to enhance the involvement of minorities in public services, that is, representative bureaucracy. Ghana has grappled with this with respect to women and the undermining of equitable representation of women in society. "Since 1957, and especially since the early 1980s, it has instituted measures to ensure a fair balance in gender representation in the Ghanaian bureaucracy" (Adusah-Karikari and Ohemeng 2014, 568). Yet women's underrepresentation increases as one moves up the ladder of responsibility, with men dominating the upper echelons. The expression "representative bureaucracy" hails from 1940s Britain and the work of J. Donald Kingsley, whose concern was that the policies of the governing party "should be reflected in all in all aspects of democratic institutions," an eventuality made possible by administrators who are sympathetic to the needs of all social classes. While representative bureaucracy might not be responsive to all, its goal is a bureaucracy "that reflects the diversity of the general population [and] implies a symbolic commitment to equal access to power" (Adusah-Karikari and Ohemeng 2014, 571).

In my study, the population suffering "subtle discrimination" from society at large is ethnically different from the majority; the gender factor is an add-on that actually originates among the Dagomba themselves. In the current bridge group, I include Gifty Mahama and Fuseini Baba. Gifty is at the Ministry of Lands, where she has the title of head of administration, what used to be called principal secretary. As I wrote in the last chapter, Gifty comes from a family exposed early to education, in part because of their close connection with J. S. Kaleem. Following university, she joined the National Service Secretariat, where she rose to the position of acting national director. This was a political position. She said that the Abudu-Andani division "nearly affected me in my job" (March 27, 2013). This is because in 2000, when the NDC lost the election, the head of the secretariat (appointed by the outgoing NDC government) lost his job. After being made acting head, Gifty was terminated in 2001, she believes, because an NPP higher up said, "if you leave this girl there, she'll put so many Andanis there." In other words, 400 miles south of the conflict, Dagomba in Accra were implicated in the Yendi problem. And "representative bureaucracy" was not to include a *sub*-group of the ethnic minority. She was told to report to the Ministry of Education, yet there was no position for her there. As a result, she abandoned politics and applied to the civil service, joining in 2002, where she's been ever since.

Fuseini Baba is the son of the former chief butcher of the Ya-Na, signified by his second name, actually a title, "Baba." "Amongst all the butchers, he's also the Ya-Na of the butchers" (April 28, 2006). He himself, while quite attached to Yendi and its traditions, went into economics and finance. When he returned to Ghana from Lagos, where he had done an MBA, he wanted to work with the banks—"doing finance and with a math background, I thought could work in any area. But you know the system in Ghana, you don't know anybody it's difficult. [Northerners weren't just not connected]. They weren't even in the system" (April 28, 2006). A friend suggested he join the civil service. "I got the form, applied, interviewed . . ." (April 28, 2006). He was hired at the Ministry of Finance, rose through the ranks, and was in line to be promoted to chief economics officer.

There is a symbolic aspect to the Dagomba's inclusion in the ranks of the civil service—they have made it and become models for the younger generation—but there is also an instrumental aspect—representing the interests of people other than the southerners. While it might not actually happen, it might happen, or happen in part. It brings pride to the northerners and possibly advances their interests.

Money and Management

Yakubu Andani is not a civil servant; he is an accountant. From Savelugu, his father was illiterate, his mother slightly exposed to schooling. Of her siblings, she was the only one who was taken out of school. The others became highly placed in society, leading her to understand the importance of education. After sixth form, he went to the Institute of Professional Service where did accountancy, then enrolling at the Institute of Chartered Accountants. He went into accountancy because he did not like basic science but was gifted in math. And he thought, since I cannot go into medicine, better go into accountancy, because these are the professions that pay.

Yet another man in the economic sector outside of the state is Alhassan Andani. His father had been a primary school teacher, one of the men who was sent to Accra Training College in the 1910s and rose up to become the principal teacher. He retired to become a full-time village chief. He was insistent upon his children's education. "That was the only option. The old man just put everybody into school and you just have to go. And even when he died, school was the only thing that dragged you along" (June 13, 2008). Indeed, his older brother Dr. Andani was the first Ghanaian to be sent overseas to medical school. While "my dad, with a burning desire wanted all of his children to go to school, he knew that his sisters who were taking his daughters away were not looking after them in school, he couldn't do anything. He could not interfere" (June 13, 2008). And none of Alhassan's full/half-sisters were educated. Alhassan went to school and did sciences, chemistry and economics. At the University of Ghana, he did a BSc in Agriculture, but his national service was at SSB bank, and harkening back to his economics major, this was the beginning of his lifetime career as a banker. He moved over to Standard Charter, then Barclays, being posted in different regions and moving up the hierarchy. While in South Africa, Standard Bank in South Africa offered him the job of managing director for Stanbic Bank, the subsidiary in Ghana.

Like others, both Yakubu and Alhassan bring up the inequity that girls have faced. In Chapter Three, I discussed the Dagomba system of sending daughters to the aunties, illustrating this through the case of Salamatu Abdulai, the daughter of a very prominent chief who escaped detention at her father's sister home, because her father decided to send her to primary school. After finishing school and working in mass education for some time, a friend told her that GBC (Ghana Broadcasting Corporation) was hiring. So Salamatu went to see the director in Tamale,

> "Oh Madam, I know you can speak Dagbani well." I said "Yes." "Would you like to be the Dagbani speaker at GBC?" I said yes. "But I know accounting too." So I said I would prefer to be on the accounting side. So I was employed as an accountant staff, in Tamale, at GBC here. (July 17, 2017)

She has been an inspiration to her children, four men and four women. One of her daughters, Kusum Tahiro Brown, has a shop in Accra. She is married to Dr. Mutawakil Iddrisu, the neurosurgeon. After secretarial school in London, she worked at British Gas. While she was in London, Dr. Iddrisu came looking for her—his first marriage had ended. Kusum heard that his mother "kept singing in his ear, to marry someone from a respectable family and a northerner. So he thought of me" (May 11, 2013). But he did not find her, because she did not hang out with the northern Ghanaians there. She left for the United States and she did "this marriage of convenience thing;" the sham marriage ended quickly, but not before she got her papers. She moved to Connecticut and worked in an office at Yale. The doctor located her in the US, persuaded her to marry him and return to Ghana. He did not want her to have an office job, so she did cosmetology in Queens, NY. She owns and manages her cosmetology shop in Accra.

Research, University and the Sciences

Of the sample of people I was able to spend time with, six have research and academic positions. Those in research include four university professors and two men at research institutes.

Alhaji Mumuni Sulemana, Dr. Nasser, Professor Ramatu Alhassan, Alhaji Sule and Dr. Wayo Seini are all on the faculty of the University of Ghana at Legon. Sule is a professor in the Department of Religion. Sule claims he became a university professor by chance. "Teachers have always been my best friends. Since primary school. They were interested in me. I was timid. Got confidence from a university teacher. Wanted to live up to expectations. Did so well asked to be a TA. After national service, I came and did the MPhil" (October 21, 2005). Of his father's senior sons, only one is educated and he became a lawyer and core to the family. He was lucky to have been sponsored by his father to go to London and get a degree. He has pioneering status. He was the ambassador to Germany. He began his career in Accra at Lands, then practiced in Tamale and became a politician. In 1979 he became the MP for Tolon/Kunbungu.

Because he was a good student, the University of Ghana (Legon) had sent Dr. Nasser abroad for the PhD. He came directly back to Legon. Where, because the university had sent him, he was guaranteed a faculty position. Dr. Nasser never held any political position while at university but went to demonstrations, NUGS (National Union of Ghana Students) meetings. He was first motivated to go into politics in the mid-1990s, when he returned from doctoral work in Moscow. He was struck by the poverty in northern Ghana—poverty he believes is not the natural condition in Dagbon—and by the unemployment. With the virtual collapse of the rural agricultural economy, "so many idle hands and they are the potential recruiting grounds for demagogues" (April 30, 2006). Something, he felt, could and should be done. He decided to float an idea among the Dagombas in the diaspora that there was something we needed to do urgently in order to halt that decline and if not, the economic crisis would affect the social stability and cohesion. He came up with the Dagbon Development Plan, which included agricultural education, vocational training and artisan technology. "When that failed, I had to go in for political office. So that I could use that as a platform, to promote the program . . . That's how come I went into politics" (April 30, 2006). He has stood for office multiple times.

Academic training and work, like the law, can lead into a political career. Dr. K. A. Busia, an Akan who was elected prime minister in 1969, was born into a royal family in Brong Ahafo. After university he worked as an administrative officer in the colonial service—one of only two Africans to do so—then returned to Oxford University for a doctorate in sociology and became a professor at the University of Cape Coast. Dismayed over what he saw as the radicalizing of national politics, he became the accidental leader of the opposition; he went into exile to avoid imprisonment by the Nkrumah government, only returning after the coup that overturned the First Republic. Three years later, he was elected prime minister. Two years later, his government was overthrown. To many he symbolized the dilemma of the intellectual in politics—the man of thought forced by events to become the man of action.

But this has not stopped others. Wayo Seini, a Tamale man, became a member of parliament after starting out as a research faculty member at the University of Ghana. He initially studied agriculture in Kumase because of his family background. At Wye College in London, he did a PhD in economics. After working as a lecturer in the Economics Department at University of Ghana, he established an MA in Development Studies at the Institute of Statistical, Social and Economic Research (ISSER).

He told me that since childhood, he has followed elections. When he got to university, he became interested in international politics, American politics, and took sides; from the time of Kennedy, he supported the Democratic party. But in Ghana, he always supported NPP, a more conservative party. People questioned him—you belong to NPP and yet you support the Socialist party? All of these things, he said, have to do with personalities. He supported NPP because he had a personal liking for the flag bearer, Prof. Busia. As a background person, he wrote manifestos and policies for the party. He was elected national vice chairman of NPP in 1998. He quit in 2000, three months before John Kufuor was elected president. After the murder of the Ya-Na in 2002, he felt everything was political and joined the opposition party, the NDC. He was first elected in 2004, when one Tamale MP decided to step down. But then, on March 2, 2006, he resigned from the NDC and "crossing the carpet," ran for parliament as an NPP man. Losing to Lawyer Inusah Fuseini, Seini returned to academe at ISSER.

Professor Ramatu, one of the few women in my study, was in a different situation from the other academics for a variety of reasons, not the least of which that she is a woman. Women in Ghana generally confront obstacles to societal participation, all tied to the labor force, their relatively low rates of literacy, low participation in tertiary education, and low participation in professional occupations. When Ramatu tells her story, she is matter of fact, she went to university because she saw no alternative—"we thought if you needed to get a good job you had to go to university. That was the understanding in school. So from sixth form on, that was your aim" (June 9, 2006). She received a First in Agricultural Economics at UST, got a scholarship to Washington State University because of a visiting professor, had a baby (who her husband's mother cared for) and she went on to do a PhD at Iowa State. "I was there for 4 years at Iowa. I never came back, but after the first year in Iowa I had my child sent to me. My husband took my son and it took some time until we could establish a relationship. He was then four, and he was with me for the next four years" (June 9, 2006). "I had applied to this university [University of Ghana] and I had also applied to my former university [UST] and also to the Bank of Ghana, so when I came, December 1984, I took a position in this department and I've been here ever since." When I spoke with her, she was chair of the Department of Agricultural Economics.

After admission to UST by taking a science exam instead of doing the sixth form, "Prof" Walter Sandoh "liked university, liked university more than going to school [laughing], because in those days they were taking care of me, you know, three square meals and oh, a single room to yourself" (May 29, 2006). He studied agriculture and then when offered a chance to do his Master's at University of Wisconsin, he jumped at it. He returned home because they needed him to teach at UST, but after three years was awarded a Canadian Government scholarship to study at the University of Guelph. There he did a PhD in animal science. He then taught for fifteen years at UST, Ahmadu Belo in Zaria for four, then went to Bauchi, Nigeria, as dean of agriculture for five. He returned to Council for Scientific and Industrial Research (CSIR) as director of the Animal Research Institute and after a few years, as director general. In his retirement, Prof Sandoh has been at Forum for Agricultural Research in Africa (FARA), working on the Program for Biosafety Systems (PBS).

Figure 4.1. Dr. David Abdulai, the "mad doctor" (photo by Deborah Pellow).

Two other research institute scientists are Abdul Majid and Dr. Gomda. Abdul Majid was at the Centre for Economic Policy Analysis, having attained a MA at University College London. His interest lies in development projects, but along the way, like so many, he accidentally fell into politics through his friendship with the vice president, leading to a stint as Minister of Mines but without election to parliament.

Dr. Yahuza Gomda worked in animal science at the Ghana Atomic Energy Commission after completing his BA and PhD overseas. Other members of the medical sciences include four doctors, Dr. A. E. Abdulai, a maxillo-facial surgeon, who has both a private clinical practice and was on the faculty at the University of Ghana Medical School, Dr. Mutawakil Idrissu, a neurosurgeon, whose considerably older brother S. I. Iddrisu served in President Nkrumah's cabinet, Dr. Mohammed Mahama, who trained in Russia and China, and Dr. David Abdulai, a child of severe poverty known as the "mad doctor," so-called because of his *pro bono* policy at his clinic.

Two others, in allied professions, did not make it to secondary school. A Tamale resident Abubakari Alhassan was the son of an uneducated man but his father's elder brother, a veterinarian, was among the first at Tamale Secondary and then took courses. It was he who oversaw Abubakari's education, which began in Yendi with six years of primary school as a boarder, then middle school. Abubakari returned to Tamale to farm but then went to the Veterinary College in Tamale for four years and became a technical officer, i.e. the doctor in charge of direct care of cattle, sheep, goats, dogs, cats. In effect, it was his uncle who decided he should become a vet, wanting one of the children to take up his profession "when he was no more" (Abubakari Alhassan November 17, 2005).

I wondered whether Fati Isaka's brush with being sent to the "aunties" influenced her career choice. Her auntie had been harsh on her, which was particularly hard on her as she came from a home situation where she had been pampered.

> I was given to my auntie, my father's sister . . . I don't remember if it was a year, I was too little then—but my grandmother came and collected me from her, because she felt she wasn't looking after me well. So I came back with my grandmother and then lived with my auntie, my mother's sister . . . Then my cousin, who was in Takoradi, came and took me and gave me to his wife. I stayed there for some time, then my auntie came and took me back to Tamale. (November 14, 2005)

She was also encouraged by her mother's brother. Had it not been for him, she would not have been sent to school. He knew the value of education "and convinced my parents that I needed to go to school, because they didn't see the need."

In Tamale, she went through Government Girls' Boarding School for middle school education—the only middle school for girls in the north. She had written the common entrance for secondary school but got sick during exam and did not do well. Her uncle advised she go to nursing. "For girls in the north then it was either nursing or teaching. Since I was sympathetic, I was sent to nursing" (November 14, 2005).

There was no place for her to train in the north. A person from the nurses' training college in Accra, the only such training college in Ghana (the then-Gold Coast), would travel the country interviewing prospective students. She interviewed Fati, sent her to Korle Bu Hospital in Accra. She was subsequently transferred to a variety of hospitals in Ghana and also to Oxford for a year. Because her husband worked in Accra, she moved there, did a two-year course at the University of Ghana, and continued in her profession, being transferred to various parts of the country. When forced to retire in 1997, she had risen in the ranks from a staff nurse, national officer, senior national officer, deputy director of nursing services in the Upper East to head nurse Northern Region to Accra head office, and finally chief nursing officer.

Most remarkable was her post-retirement career. "During my nursing period I met a lot of abandoned children, motherless children. There was one particular one—she didn't live long and died. That was 1972. I was thinking, if I ever get the chance, I'd try to bring up one or two. So it was in my mind if possible I'd start something like that" (November 14, 2005). And she did. She returned to Tamale and opened an adoption business to contribute to society. In poor rural areas, many women were still dying in childbirth, orphaning the infant. A few were even abandoned, perhaps because of hard times. Some she thought were babies of *kayayi* who gave them away.

She used her own money, renovating her house. She started with one child. She was in one room with the child in the same bed. And then, the children started coming: "two, three, and then I saw that I couldn't keep then all in one place" (November 14, 2005). She gave one room over to them. She got to about six. "If I told people the place was full, they wouldn't understand. Thought I just didn't want to admit their children." So, she used the land behind the house to complete a building for the children. As in nursing, in this post-retirement career, she triumphed.

Design and Construction

Ghana was crucial in the creation of "tropical architecture." During World War II, the British architect Maxwell Fry and his partner/wife Jane Drew were hired to develop and plan areas in southern Ghana, and they became the founding figures of tropical architecture. Fry was appointed advisor for Town Planning in Accra from 1944 to 1946. Both he and Drew had trained in London and were motivated by architectural and social modernization. In 1957, the Faculty of Architecture was established as vocational training in Kumase, at what became UST (Pellow 2014). The German architect-planner Otto Koenigsberger was invited to re-develop UST's architecture curriculum, bringing in John Lloyd, a tutor at the Architectural Association in London, who re-structured courses in line with an Africanist approach. Architectural training at UST was ground-breaking. This was also the case for engineering. It was exclusive. For the northern boys to get in was significant, especially with the marginalization of the north.

A number of the Dagomba men in my study trained at UST in Kumase in architecture and engineering. The two architects are Dr. Abubakar Alhassan and Issifu Sumani. Dr. Alhassan, from Tamale, almost went into the Air Force, when he found out that he was accepted into architecture

Figure 4.2. Fati Isaka with some of the children in her orphanage Amfani (photo by Deborah Pellow).

at UST. He did his first degree in the natural sciences and then completed the professional diploma and was selected to teach in the University in Kumase. While in Kumase he met his first wife, Dr. Ramatu Alhassan. It was his mother who cared for the child so that Ramatu could finish her doctoral program in the United States and he could continue his studies. A Danish architect working at UST pushed for him to go to the Royal Danish Academy in Copenhagen, interceded on his behalf, and Alhassan received a Danish fellowship. After three years at the Royal Danish Academy, Dr. Alhassan did a PhD at the University of Copenhagen. Back in Ghana, he ran for and was elected to parliament, was thrown out after the 1981 coup, went to Legon to set up an architecture program at the University of Ghana, became Undersecretary for the Ministry of Works and Housing for a time, and spent the rest of his professional life shuttling between UST and Legon. He retired to Tamale.

The case of Issifu Sumani, another architect, is interesting because he comes from a long line of educated men and his professional career is a modern version of his forefathers. As I noted in Chapter Three, he is from the royal butcher family—Fuseini Baba, the economist, is his father's brother's son. His father's father, who was sent to the trade school in Yendi, graduated as a general builder, carpenter and mason. As an enlightened person, he sent Issifu's father to school—the latter rose to become the district director of education and educated Issifu and his siblings.

Given his father's father's role as a general builder, Issifu was exposed to architecture, domestic and community structures, traditional building techniques and materials. He went to UST in architecture and did his National Service in Redco, a building and developing company. He has been there ever since, playing the role of consultant and working with contractors.

Three other of the Dagomba new elite who went to UST trained in engineering. Aminu Ahmadu is in the direct line of the chief imam of Yendi—his father, his father's father, his father's father's father. Aminu was sent to Western school—"they sang hymns all the way from primary to secondary school and made us go to church. These were not mission schools—they were all local authority schools. But they were Christian and that's why Muslim communities in the north are not educated—[the school systems] couldn't penetrate them" (December 5, 2005). After secondary school in Tamale, he went to UST. He realized he had an aptitude for mathematics, and engineering was very popular for those who did math. He graduated as a civil engineer. He got a job with State Construction Corp., living wherever his projects were, largely overseeing road construction. After a dozen or so years, he moved over to work in a bank, as the chief engineer in charge of building and road projects. When I asked him if he would call himself a businessman, he said no, "I prefer to be an engineer. Anyone can just declare himself a businessman. An engineer is not just for anybody."

Abdulai Yakubu, nickname Sabon Kudi (Hausa, "new money"), comes from a prosperous Tamale family and his father was passionate about education. S. K. went to UST (Vice President Aliu was his classmate) and then did his National Service in Tamale. Then Rawlings led his revolution and S. K. went to Liberia for two years to lecture. When he returned in 1984, he started working with the State Housing Corp and after about four years, started his own company. Seventeen years after receiving his first degree, he went to Ghana Law School. "After working for so many years as an engineer, I thought I needed something else to wake up. Need for pedagogical development. After achieving certain things, my focus started to change. At the point of going to law school, I was no longer concerned with making money but could do other things. Develop myself in other ways (November 3, 2005). While he was in law school, the Dagomba issue of the two gates, Andani and Abudu, came up. He read the various court cases. A year after the Ya-Na was murdered, he decided to write a book on the conflict (Abdulai Yakubu 2005). He also opened chambers with the lawyer and former politician Mohammed Mumuni, who was subsequently appointed Minister of Foreign Affairs. S. K. does not work as an engineer but he does have a warehousing business outside of the port city of Tema.

Yet another UST alum is "Savannah," Mahama Sherif's nickname from his construction company. He got to UST without having gone through all of secondary school, but he did a course at polytechnic and then took an exam which gave him admission to university (UST). He did architecture and planning and then a three-year diploma course in physical planning. After a number of years in the field, he realized that he was wasting his time with town planning, because projects were awarded to contractors—even just demarcating blocks and layouts. So he went into construction. He settled in Tamale and created his own company, bringing in his brothers. They started tendering for new buildings and roads—only doing culverts, not grading or gravelling. Now they also do gravelling. But he complained that his work has become politicized, with the NPP government in place for eight years in the first decade of the 2000s, and with whom the Abudu identify, NDC contractors did not get bids on projects (May 14, 2006).

Related to Savannah, the last of the contractors is Alhaji Mahdi, the husband of Savannah's sister. After finishing secondary school, he did not go on to university. Looking for a job, he saw an advert for a position with State Insurance Corporation. After working there in Accra for a few years, he was posted to Kumase, where he spent thirty years. They brought him down to Accra several times to GIMPA (Ghana Institute of Management and Public Administration) to do management courses. When Flt Lt Jerry Rawlings led a coup in June 1979, Mahdi was asked to transfer to Tamale to take over there. He declined: "Too many controversies." When they asked him to go to Aflao on the eastern border, he decided it was time for a change. He used his leave to see what else he could do. All along, he was farming in the north and selling wood in Kumase. Wanting to try his luck at something else, in 1987 while he continued farming, he also moved into construction. Construction work, he said, involves a lot of courage, but he saw that he could make it. So when his leave was up, he resigned from SIC. To concentrate on construction, he dropped the wood and rice farming in the north. He is based in Accra, while doing construction in Tamale, for the Ministry of Education, and in Accra. "I fought my way through seriously" (September 16, 2005) and became successful.

Culture and Civic Pride

Issa Naseri was born in Ashanti. When he was still young, his father, who was in mining, brought the family back to Tamale. Issa is very much an intellectual who reads a lot about society and politics and thinks a lot about what he calls "flashpoints" for change (September 28, 2005). He was one of five children growing up together in the compound but the only one who made it through school—none of the others went past Middle Form. Because he had to help support the family, he did not get to university until five years after finishing his A levels. He taught and farmed. As Huudu Yahaya reported for himself, Rawlings' revolution in December 1981 made Issa an activist. "I became a leftist and read a lot on social formation, capital, working class, bourgeoisie—had reading circles" (September 27, 2005). This was when he began reading in the social sciences, to better understand the issues affecting people.

Like Yahuza Gomda, Issa went to Eastern Europe to university, to the Academy of Social Sciences and Social Management, Bulgaria. He learned a lot about class struggle, the progressive forces that include liberation movements, working class movements, the socialist international. All of this gave him a different world outlook and skills, which he wanted to apply in Ghana. He got a job at the NCCE (National Commission for Civic Education) where he has remained. He believes strongly that "if citizens are aware, know their left and right, can participate in governance, they will stand up for constitutionality, for democracy" (September 27, 2005). This he believes is the charge of NCCE—it is an educational institution—which will help broaden social consciousness, show people how to participate, how to elevate the institutional framework. "We don't need the world community to do this for us –we need organizations" that will teach people and then empower them.

"Difficult to say where I come from—where I end up is where I come from, because my umbilical cord is buried, but I'm a grandson from Yendi" (Tuya-Na November 9, 2005). Like most, he is from an illiterate farming family, the first of his mother's children. Nkrumah had just established the GET (Ghana Educational Trust) Schools—charged with opening secondary schools and teacher training colleges. Although his father was not happy about his being educated, Tuya-Na was sent to Navrongo Secondary School to do late entrance, passed and was one of pioneers there in 1960. After teacher training and classroom teaching, he went to Legon to do drama and theatre. There, he was the "darling boy" (research assistant) of Efua Sutherland—playwright, director, children's author, poet and dramatist, who founded The Ghana Drama Studio.

After the 1981 coup, the man who had invited him to be a teaching assistant at Legon was made the first Secretary for Culture and Tourism, and he invited him to come and join his team. Tuya-Na was then appointed acting director of the Arts Council of Ghana, now the Center for National Culture. Meanwhile, his former boss at the Ghana National Association of Teachers was grooming Tuya-Na as a "teacher's politician" (a lobbyist for teachers). He was appointed regional director for Culture from 1982 till 2004, when he retired. The role of his agency was to propose and disseminate the culture of the people of Ghana, culminating in a national culture. This included drama, music, dance, literary writing, poetry, and art and culture. Their charge was to unearth the hidden talents in the society—running workshops for poets, writers, dramatists, musicians, as well as festivals. In keeping with his vocation and sensibility, he became a traditional leader and was enskinned in 1986.

I include Henry Kaleem in this category, because to my mind, his real-life work was recording the culture, traditions and stories of Dagbon. Henry was a remarkable informant for me, because he had so much recorded that he could give me (lists of chiefs, Ya-Nas, wives, and successions) and because he was the spokesperson to Otumfuo, the Asantehene and head of the Eminent Chiefs Committee that was trying to negotiate a peace plan for the two clans. He was their advisor on the custom and tradition of Dagomba and spokesperson of Kuga-Na, the Dagomba kingmaker. While there are those who believe Henry (as an Andani) was biased, I did not see that.

Henry was born in Yendi, because his father J. S. Kaleem moved there in the mid-1930s to run the primary school there. J. S. Kaleem had been trained at Achimota and became a revered educator. His father's father was Dakpema in Tamale (the *tindana*), his mother's grandfather was in the first generation of northern literates and because of his way with language, he became an interpreter for the law courts. J. S. Kaleem had four wives and sent every one of his children, boys as well as girls, to school. "My first interest was agriculture, but my grade placed me teaching" (Henry Kaleem May 12, 2006). He was dismissed from agricultural training college and went back to teaching. He went to try nursing, but the British refused to let him. So he ended up at teachers training college. Subsequently he became a Catholic and the Catholic mission sent him to Rome and later to England to do social and political science. He completed his degree in London in a Catholic institution affiliated with LSE. Because of the military coups in Ghana, he remained in England and did private studies in corporate management—librarianship, budgetary control, policy. In 1990, Henry met up with his father in Denmark and was pressed to go home to Ghana. When he left England in 1992, he had been there for thirty years and was deputy to the principal of service, London Borough of Hackney. Henry expected to stay a week or two. His father forbade him from leaving. In 2002, his father died. A regent was chosen for the now vacant skin and Henry was planning on going back to England when the Ya-Na was murdered. He was chosen as the Kuga-Na's representative, so he never left. In 2006, he was made Dakpiem Zobogu Naa, one of the six landed elders of the Tamale Dakpema. He died in 2017.

Status Transfer

One of my puzzlements is whether one's traditional status or that of a significant member of one's network translates into modern status. Throughout this book I've stressed that when these men and women were growing up, societal expectations, especially in the north, did not include modern professional success. As I have written in this and the previous chapter, the vast majority of fathers (and mothers) were uneducated. The 1.5ers did benefit from exposure to education and work possibilities, not just from immediate family but from various significant others; those significant others may not have been educated themselves, but through their work and travel they were exposed to the benefits of education. Another interesting slant is the traditional social and work status of the parents and significant others of this generation. Did that status transfer in different form to the new generation? Are their professions somehow related to those traditionally practiced? A. B. Fuseini, once a newspaperman, now a member of parliament, characterizes J. S. Kaleem as a pioneer of education in the north, a man whom he and his classmates saw as a model. How does a model for something new transfer over from traditional molds?

Seventeen of the men and women had a chief as their primary support when growing up (usually father, but in some cases a brother or uncle). Four other "royal" connections were father as imam or as chief butcher. An imam might not be "literate" in the Western sense of the word, but he is certainly educated. This could have a carry-over into the next generation's inclinations toward modernity. Imams like chiefs would be men of high regard, the children growing up in the glow of their reputations. They might not opt for chieftaincy—they might not be in the direct line to become a chief—but they understood the importance of that position to the community and might look to mimic that in their own lives. The father of Abdulai Yakubu ("new money") was not educated, but he was a member of Tamale's elite when Yakubu was growing up. Theirs was the first house in town to have electricity.

Fathers were engaged in the "modern" sector, the sole one without education was a driver. Others included a transport owner, a judge, an MP, an ambassador, a surveyor, a couple of educators (mass literacy). All of them, through their work or through travel south, were exposed to the value of education and they brought it back to their own households. A number of the fathers did not hold traditional elite status and were not themself educated yet gained exposure to the advantages that education would bring their children (especially sons). Some of these men attended adult literacy or worked in an environment which encouraged Western education. Some of the 1.5ers also went into professions that were in effect a redefinition of what a father or grandfather had done. For example, Issifu Sumani is an architect. His grandfather was not educated but went to trade school and became a contractor. He was known as a general builder, including erecting swish buildings. He also used bricks, leaves and sandstone, building his own house from sandstone.

Few if any of the mothers of this bridge generation were educated or carried traditional status, and yet a number of the new elite spoke warmly of the enthusiasm and encouragement their mothers provided, which translated into small monies for food and transportation.

So parental background may or may not have provided a path to the children's upward mobility. I saw no evidence of a repudiation of ethnic identification, that is, as Dagomba. The Abudu-Andani clan situation muddied the waters for some; at least two men reported that their marriages fell apart because of the split. In one case, he was Andani and his wife Abudu, another because he is Abudu and his wife Andani. All speak Dagbani but many have not schooled their children in the language. Only nine of these eminent men and women report maintaining farms, although siblings and other family members in the north—especially those without education—do. This is not to say the attachment does not inhere—as I have observed throughout the previous chapters and will detail in the next chapter, it absolutely does.

Conclusion

As with access to education, access to *professional* occupations was not a given when these Dagomba men and women were coming of age While an educational background is necessary for the positions that members of the Dagomba elite landed in, *it is not necessarily sufficient*. As I have tried to establish, a combination of factors made all of this possible. What if, today, a Ghanaian came home with a PhD from Denmark or Romania? Can one say that he/she would surely be hired in the area for which he/she trained? Throughout the developing world, we hear about the brain drain, of individuals getting advanced training abroad and not going "home" but staying abroad and working.[3] This is defined primarily in terms of the exodus of the highly talented from the Global South to the Global North. "Why the brain drain has grown in scale may be attributed to recent developments in modern electronic and information technology, the widening gap between North and South, and the spread of corporate globalization, as well as increasing political instability, civil wars, and social and religious strife in many Southern and African countries" (Sefa Dei and Asgharzadeh 2002, 31).

This is a particular problem for them. They have maintained a tie to home, a tie that they demonstrate even today. They may not live in the north, they may be living in so-called First World surroundings, but they are in the home country, and they are involved with affairs in the home town. They own land if not homes in the north. They stay in touch. And their professions, which give them real community standing, empower them in the eyes of their northern brethren.

When they went off to school in preparation for careers, it was a golden time for the northerners I got to know. The country had the political will to enable their success. But even then, we see how few in fact "made it." The north in its entirety was devoid of models for modernity. And indeed, to become modern professionals, this aspiring group had to leave the homes and surroundings they knew and loved. Would their children, who have been raised under modern conditions, with the built-in assumption of schooling and professional advancement, be willing and able to endure the privation their fathers (and mothers) report?

Over and over, in story after story, we are awed by the impressive accomplishments of members of this group. The thread that runs through this chapter is that of "accident"—of one's place in the birth order, of a supportive person, of a chance meeting with the right person. But success is also made possible by intelligence, a changing opportunity structure, and in many cases real grit and gumption. It is the ability to see beyond the models—to imagine alternatives to what has been, to what one's family or society knows and understands. It is also the ability to buck certain elements of tradition.

What other threads emerge? Accident can be many things—place, timing, family limitations, the appearance of a mentor. At the time that these people would have been considering occupations, none came from highly Western-educated households. Agriculture, an obvious route, was considerably weakened, leaving those so engaged to do subsistence farming. It is unclear how significant—other than in an accidental sense—family background mattered. For example, four of the men became medical doctors. The father of only one had any education at all, and that was through middle school. Another had a much older brother who became a minister in Nkrumah's administration. And the father of a third was a Tamale sub-chief. The fathers of three of the elite were chiefs, and four others had a close family member who was a chief or royal. How does this translate into the professions? Seven are lawyers, four are medical doctors, three are research scientists, six are in communications, four university faculty. And there are those in the human services, who are architects, managers/administrators, and military men. Perhaps the truly interesting figures are the twelve who are politicians, six of them lawyers. Given the discrimination the north has suffered, and continues to suffer, going into fields that may level the playing field makes sense.

NOTES

1. I am providing a very brief encapsulation of the northern rice schemes. See van Hear 1982 for a rich and extensive accounting and analysis of the rise and fall of rice.
2. (www.nss.gov.gh/home/nss-act, accessed November 14, 2017).
3. I do not know how many did not succeed, given the training, and I also do not know how this group was affected by the brain drain. I detailed the example of Henry Kaleem, who after spending two decades working in London, where he was able to buy a house, returning not just to Ghana but to his father's house in Tamale.

CHAPTER 5

Living in Between
Patronage and Hybrid Modernity

The new-elite Dagomba are a bridge generation, 1.5ers. As described in the literature, the 1.5 concept has been applied to international (trans)migrants (Brettell 2016), "to describe youth who were born abroad but educated primarily in their receiving country" (Haayen 2016, 69). I am using the relocation of the Dagomba new elite from northern to southern Ghana *as the equivalent of* a transnational move. It is not translocal in Low's sense (2016) of a space which "embodies diverse cultural spaces simultaneously for many of the people who spend time there" (p. 201). I speak of it as transnational, because for these Dagomba who have relocated there, it is qualitatively different from their place of origin in the north *in the same way that* New York City is different from Accra. Their relocation to the suburbs of Accra is the equivalent of moving from the Global South to the Global North—the qualitative difference between their places of origin and their new homes in the south is one of transnationality. And they have a foot in both places—they shuttle between the two. Thus, I have characterized them as an *internal* transnational population (Pellow 2011). Based on my research among this new elite community of Dagomba, I argue that this analytical framework works to understand the experience of migrants who move within a country, not necessarily from one country to another. They are born and bred in one socio-spatial system, working and living in a very different one, but with ties to both. Their bridge spans the gulf between the hometown and the south, provinciality and cosmopolitanism, between their growing-up years and their children's, between chance and entitlement. As they adapt to a new localism, they produce hybrids, combining old and new in design and in lifestyle.

They link the two regions through their involvement in hometown politics and their patronage of northern individuals seeking help. Their lives are culturally and spatially complex. As members of the new elite, while custom has continued to matter, as has been true for the southern Ghanaian elites that preceded them, Western values have become a new reference point for their modernity. Their bridge has taken them from a very underdeveloped indigenous area to a highly developed modern one, from places that are integrally African to those that are infused by the West. They live with one foot and their heart in each place.

The new elite was disposed to understanding the new class conditions for the good life and to reproduce them through "practice-unifying" principles, i.e. class habitus (Bourdieu 1984). Their belongingness is tied to place(s) (Raffaeta and Duff 2013), the place they come from has socialized them and produced a collective organization of local identities. Its material aspects are valued. And it has created good feelings and comfort. The compound house, whether old or new, in its social and spatial dimensions, is an instrument of enculturation—it represents a microcosm of the social system of which it is a part (Pellow 1991). The new place, Accra and its suburbs, its new spaces and the practices and understandings inscribed, have similarly been agents of socialization, introducing the members of this relocated population to and enabling new identities and understandings. In effect, people produce and reproduce meaning; their change in practices often erase or obscure ethnic differences among the people, who in turn adopt styles of behavior; and their new behaviors and practices carry economic and cultural capital (Bourdieu 1984, 77).

I wrote years ago (1991) that the urban compound in Accra is a transition space for the migrant living among strangers, as it provides a familiar space in which to adapt to unfamiliar roles. Within the domestic space people learn social distinctions and the behaviors that accompany them. The new home and its spatiality help socialize the newcomer. Traditional African housing enabled community living. The individual rooms were used little during the day, opening onto the courtyard where daily activities and interaction occur. People feel attached or are attached to the compound yard because of what it offers, because of the actions that are a part of its system. Activities define this space. I would argue this is no less true in the modern home. The spaces, the layout, the organization differs from the hut left behind. But they also carry new meanings, that enable new activities and behaviors, and they help enculturate into the new social order. These structured practices are indicators of a new sociophysical space, they symbolize a version of modernity.

This chapter focuses upon the Dagomba patrons as a bridge—their new resources, lifestyles, spaces—but along the way it also outlines two other social parameters of the Dagomba who live in the south—the elite-non-elite and the Abudu-Andani divides. The patrons are people in-between—in-between the homes they hail from and the new spaces and behaviors they cultivate in a very different locale, between who they were and who they have become—who many of the non-elite look to for resources, in some cases material, in some ideological. Cross-cutting both the elite and the non-elite is gate identity. There are Abudu, there are Andani. They originate in the same towns and villages. Gate notwithstanding, they have all had more or less the same opportunities. They are equally attached to their hometowns. The attachment of the elite plays out in individually focused patronage. As patrons, these individuals play a significant role in the development of Dagbon, largely through individuals. They have harnessed their knowledge, resources and influence to help those less fortunate, but also to aggravate the Abudu-Andani split. They have become modern, but their modernity itself is a hybrid, as are the spaces they inhabit.

Hybrid Modernity

The materiality of modernity is mass-produced and standardized, which makes globally available similar kinds of building materials, construction techniques, electrical/water/sewer infrastructure, and sometimes building and fire codes. Much of this was emanating from Europe during the late nineteenth and early twentieth centuries. Modernity also created a new spatial ordering, colonial designers destroyed or overlaid traditional or indigenous architectural forms through urban planning and modernist design (see also Boyd 1962 for Imperial China, Winters 1977 for Timbuktu).

In the mid-nineteenth century, the Gold Coast (pre-Independence Ghana) experienced the arrival and impact of modernity through the British colonial occupation. In 1877, the British moved their administrative headquarters to Accra. Accra's population had been growing through migration, as did commercial and residential space. The city expanded and new neighborhoods developed, similar to the old Ga towns, with distinct locations and names. As they established themselves, the British imposed European-style town planning. They built up Victoriaborg as a European quarter, implicitly cut off from the African town by the racetrack (functioning as a *cordon sanitaire*). They created a social and spatial compartmentalization of Accra.

The plague hit downtown Accra in 1908. Consequently, the government decided that sanitary improvements were essential, they condemned much of the housing in the old quarter to relieve population density, and they laid out new town sites to relocate those affected (Pellow 2002). This included a series of *zongos* (Hausa, stranger quarters) primarily for Hausa or "strangers" (northerners) who were Muslims. As I have written elsewhere (2002), "Accra exemplifies the spatial impact of the colonial system of organization on the urban landscape, with regional inequalities complemented by sociospatial inequalities of density, modernization, and residential exclusion" (p. 113). They thus transformed this relatively homogeneous small-scale community "into a heterogeneous large-scale community" (Acquah 1972, 28). Africans thus encountered various material modernities in their cities under colonial rule. When the British built housing for British administrators and civil servants, they utilized the design of bungalows. These were different spatially from the compound houses of the indigenous people and enabled different social organization and behavior.

European colonial elites departed, and an African elite arose, emulating their standards of living. "Throughout Africa, the members of this emergent class became visibly distinguishable from the rest of society" by their locations in structures of power but also their material existence, activities, values and behaviors (Diamond 1987, 577). In Ghana, senior civil servants moved into the bungalows originally built for British civil servants in the government area; wealthy Africans moved into the European suburbs. They also copied the European house form. And they built different kinds of houses. The classic British bungalows at Victoriaborg and The Ridge gave way in the 1960s and 1970s to sleek one-story structures at Cantonments and the Airport Residential Area. These new built environments represented new habitats of meaning and of social organization.

For many of the locals, the European-influenced spaces and things symbolized what became important to the status and identity construction of those aspiring to a modern lifestyle. People adopted modernist designs because they wanted to appear different from their traditionalist contemporaries—they wanted to be set apart, not just by symbolic association, but because the physical forms allowed, or even required, them to also live differently. While the patterns I discuss are dynamic and not peculiar to the modernizing Dagomba, I have been specifically interested in the manner in which the Dagomba have incorporated cosmopolitanism into their social and spatial idioms and carried "traditional" or "local" behaviors over into the modern space.

African cosmopolitanism is, empirically, the acquisition and use of knowledge gained across sociocultural and spatial boundaries—often boundaries shared with the West, but certainly not restricted to these. The actions and interactions among individual people as well as groups of people across space and time result in the sharing of knowledge and practice across boundaries of difference. Like migrants throughout sub-Saharan Africa, they have formed and maintained among themselves social networks; like the iconic Hausa long-distance traders, they have created diasporic communities, through which they maintain feelings of connectedness to the homeland, in this case Dagbon (Cohen 1969; Works 1976; Pellow 2011).

In today's world, the distinguishing mark of the educated elite's self and social involvement is that s/he straddles modernity (Lentz 1994). Members of the Dagomba new elite, like others in much of Africa, may not be completely westernized, though their modernity is generally linked to westernization, via conceptions of modernity and global connection (Hannerz 1996). And their modernization is manifest in their social life as well as their material existence. Modernity is especially evident in the urban context, where individuals feel freer to improvise on their behaviors and interactions with others.

But they are also not completely modernized. Like the educated Dagara in Ghana's Upper West, a distinguishing mark of the Dagomba new elite's self and social involvement is that of straddling modernity (Lentz 1994). They straddle the old and the new—they have the ability to identify with both their new and their home cultures and values in varying ways, but with the ability also to switch those identifications. Lentz writes that Dagara social mobility is largely through education, kin networks, and ethnic loyalties (1994). For the Dagomba currently ascending into the elite, the same is probably true. Lentz asserts that the Dagara elite are important as culture brokers in solidifying ethnic ties. For the Dagomba I spent time with, it is certainly education that mattered, kin and ethnic loyalties less so. In fact, among the Dagomba, such reinforcement has rather been at the sub-ethnic (gate) level, because of the internal Abudu-Andani conflict.

The Dagomba elite I got to know have developed a bicultural orientation as part of their experience of migration from the north. They are open to divergent cultural experiences. As Brettell (2016, 144) writes, "they preserve customs and maintain ties with the old, but they also celebrate cultural impurity and hybridity as they take leave of the certain to intermingle with new kinds of people and engage in new practices."

The 1.5ers characterized in the literature left their hometowns before secondary school and were schooled in the new country. As I have already detailed, for the Dagomba 1.5ers that has not been the case—all but four of those I spoke with went to secondary school in the north. They moved south or overseas later than the 1.5ers both Haayen and Moran

(2016) both write about; the Dagomba moved for university and then their professions. This afforded them more time as young adults to absorb local custom and practice and may have bolstered their attachment to the hometown and their in-between-ness.

Their transformation has been unique, in part because it has occurred in one-half generation. Each member of the Dagomba new elite has gone through a "process" whereby they "became" 1.5ers, through luck, ability, indecipherable parental motivation and the accidents of life, they gained good educations, became successful professionals, created socially and materially very different lifeways in a new place, socially and spatially distant from their childhood. They have developed dual loyalties, bridging the gap between the rural, impoverished and underserved, and the urban, privileged and cosmopolitan. As newly minted professionals-in-the-making, the college-bound Dagomba moved from the "traditional" north to the "cosmopolitan" south. While there may be a gulf between the hometown residence and a "cosmopolitan home," there is also an interdependence between the two.

Once occupationally secured and socially mobile, they were exposed to and embraced different lifestyles, practices and modes of expression. The materiality of their contemporary housing in the new milieu encapsulates and enables old and new practices, old and new identities and statuses, a multiplicity of modernities, that is, a variety of modern alternatives and entanglements. Much of this occurs through repurposed spaces. I characterize the spaces and lifestyles of this new generation as hybrid or "multiple modernities," their consciousness "metropolitan."

Like other members of Ghana's urban elite, they have embraced modernity—in the aesthetics of their lifestyles and of their everyday life. Their social relations are embodied in goods (Mauss 1990[1950]), a materiality that is also achieved through houses built and occupied. Like other goods, the house is "consumed to achieve lifestyles . . ." (Dant 1999, 3). The Dagomba new elite understand the new style of house as "better," symbolically and functionally, because it enhances their prestige and their lifestyle (see Miller 2010). These Dagomba, as members of the professional elite, move into houses that are "new spaces of transaction" and configure "a new 'place' for places" (Simone 2001, 16). The spheres of activity delineated in the spatial layout embody orientations and sensibilities, which can constitute a mixture, not always easy, "of external imposition and local redeployment of selective appropriations of that imposition" (Simone 2001, 18; see also Coquery-Vidrovitch 1991) along with spatial elements of traditional sensibilities and orientations. So just as Zambian villagers are not complete prisoners of Ferguson's "localism" (1999) as they open up to a wider world, the Dagomba urbanites I am writing about have not thrown out all northern traditions and materialities even as they become "cosmopolitan."

Anthony King once asked, "What can we understand about a society by examining its physical and spatial environment?" (King 1990, 23). For example, homes everywhere have the means for preparing meals. But how and where is that preparation done? Food preparation may take place in a room that is outfitted with built-in infrastructure, which includes piped water, gas, and electricity. Or perhaps cooking may be done on a coal pot that can be carried between spaces, with water fetched in a bucket or a rain-catching container. Of course, there are gradations between the two extremes. And society grades these differences.

If one thinks back to rural African life, cooking is done in the courtyard—indeed, the primary "room" in the compound is the central yard (see Chapter Two, Figures 2.4, 2.5). The "kitchen" is a communal facility, which all of the adult women use. Cooking is labor intensive—without plumbing, water carried in, at best there is a spigot in the yard; coal or wood is the fuel; no refrigerator means the daily trek to the market and back. Given the cuisine, vegetables must be peeled, parboiled and ground with mortar and pestle. All work is done while sitting on low stools. Following the meal, eaten communally by age or seniority cohort, bowls have to be washed. Multiple wives are the norm, especially for those who can afford them.

The professional Dagomba men and women I met in Accra (and in Tamale), like those of other members of Ghana's elite, aspire to a different kind of materiality, a different kind of lifestyle than what they left up north.

> Taste classifies, and the system of classification generates practices adjusted to the regularities inherent in a condition . . . it generates the set of "choices" constituting life-styles, which derive their meaning, i.e. their value, from their position in a system of oppositions and correlations [and with a change in social position, taste] . . . commands the practices objectively adjusted to these resources. (Bourdieu 1984, 175)

In her study of households in north London among the aspirational middle class, Alison Clarke reminds us that "the construction of the household as an expressive form has been associated with the consolidation and formation of middle-class identity" (2001, 24), as people seek to fabricate an ideal social world. In such a circumstance, the "ideal" home is not a trivial fantasy but a notion of quality of life, and the chance to "actualize beyond the limitations of their particular domesticity"

Figure 5.1. Courtyard at a home in North Legon, Accra (photo by Deborah Pellow).

(p. 28). Focusing on the materiality of the Dagomba new elite's suburban homes—the design, the technology, the practices, and relationships embodied—the comparison with their childhood homes in the north is stark. Whether living in Agbelenkpe, East Legon, Airport Residential, Roman Ridge, or any other of the suburbs of Accra, there are basic infrastructural elements such as electricity, plumbing, and water. But because pipe-borne water delivery is unpredictable, many if not most home-owners in suburban Accra pay to have water delivered monthly, stored in huge poly tanks. All have satellite dishes and cable hook-up, surrounding wall, gatekeepers.

Perhaps the biggest difference from the northern compound is the square/rectangular, *never round*, spatial idiom in the south. Moreover, in terms of sociability, the compound yard is no longer where people cook or hang out but where they park cars. Socializing most likely takes place on a verandah or a downstairs room that functions like a Dagomba chief's *zana* (a mat shelter in the compound yard), where the resident rests in the afternoon and/or receives visitors.

All of the Accra houses have an indoor kitchen (see Pellow 2015). This modern space and its accessories when designed in the West carried the intention of changing domestic behavior, of streamlining the activities associated with preparing meals, of introducing convenience and efficiency. Gas stoves dispensed with the dirt and hassle of wood or charcoal. The kitchen sink eased the labor involved in the food preparation—vegetables and meat could be washed in the sink, and following the meal, washing up could be done inside without carrying water or stooping. The new Dagomba elite, like their suburban neighbors, have all accepted the idea of the modern kitchen, outfitting it with appliances such as gas stoves, microwaves, refrigerators, and freezers. They have put in tiled floors and granite counters. They have built cabinets and piped running water. Such kitchens speak to the modernity and status of the user.

And yet—daily cooking (of Ghanaian foods) occurs outside. Some households have the coal pot and other utensils, such as wooden mortar and pestle, on a verandah (Figure 5.2), or by the back door, or behind the "boys' quarters." Some have even installed a stove outside, with the traditional equipment nearby. In most cases, it is the woman of the house who oversees the cooking by extended family or hired help, if she does not do it herself. One can argue that this is practical, frying foods can be smelly and messy, pounding yam noisy. This of course is true. But then, why bother building a fancy kitchen? The modern kitchen is for show, it bespeaks a new status. Following Clarke (2001, 29) it is "an expressive practice."

Some spaces and practices have changed, others replaced. Some, like the courtyard, always a semi-public space, have been reinterpreted. Activities that went on in the courtyard, like socializing or engaging in domestic chores, have not ceased to exist; they have moved elsewhere. Family members and friends still eat together, even by age cohort or position, though inside or in the outside "room." The location or space may be different, but the concept and practice are similar. The working kitchen, on the other hand, has remained outside, while the status-bearing modern kitchen, which is incorporated into the home, is barely used for cooking.

Residents acquire new commodities and live in new circumstances, privileging them in new ways, giving them different lifestyles, practices, modes of expression, and new kinds of social power (Miller 2005). For example, as I detailed in Chapter Two, childhood for the vast majority of this new elite group involved extended family living. Fathers had multiple wives, who in turn had lots of children. Of all of the educated Dagomba men I spoke with in Accra and the north, only three have more than one wife—and two of the men are particularly well-educated, one of them a bank president, the second an architect with a PhD. Of the seven women in the study, only one is married to a man with other wives—and she is a

PhD who was chair of Agricultural Economics at the University of Ghana when I knew her.

This shift to monogamy is extraordinary but clearly fits the modern pattern. One apparently does not require multiple wives to indicate one's status. Huudu Yahaya, the NDC politician who was also the northern regional executive in the 1980s, told me his mother one day asked him why he did not have a second wife. Did this not mean he had no power? This change, according to contractor Aminu Ahmadu, is due to Westernization.

> My people cannot understand why I have only one wife. They cannot. People back home in family know if I want any woman "I will get" but I'm not interested. And difficult to explain to them. Difficult to explain that the thing is economic. If you can afford—according to Islam, if you can look after them well—but now also the women have refused to accept polygamy. Women will not cooperate. If they won't cooperate, why make problems for yourself? Our mothers cooperated, they accepted it. When my father was going to take the second wife, my mother was in charge of it. She would make sure the ceremony goes all right. There's no way now you're going to have a woman be in charge of a ceremony that is going to bring her a rival! (December 5, 2005)

Their ways of being and their subjectivity have altered, resulting from or expressing new kinds of socio-cultural mobility. More than simply embracing foreign aspects of culture and materiality, the Ghanaians in general, and the Dagomba in this case, have played with them and adapted them, innovating on the originals. I call these cultural hybrids.[1] They are creations of mixed ancestry in all realms, from the aesthetic and symbolic to the behavioral. Cultural hybridity matters, because it can produce social, political and economic conditions for cultural reflexivity and for change (Werbner 1997). My use of hybridity does not imply a kind of enlightened diversity or a way to describe developing countries with unsophisticated tastes. But in Ghana it does speak to those who have acquired and use knowledge gained across social, cultural and geographic boundaries—often boundaries shared with the West, but certainly not restricted to these. Such people are cosmopolitans—intellectually and aesthetically open to divergent cultural experiences and able to make their way into other cultures (Hannerz 2005, 201).

Having relocated, the Dagomba cosmopolitans express the change in their social position through contemporary homes. Buchli (2002) tells us that the cornerstone of the anthropological study of human society is the material culture of architecture (p. 208), with "the home as a critical site for investigation" (Buchli 2002, 210). As I have written elsewhere (Pellow

2015), changes in the materiality of domestic space can be a lens on the social change of a group. The dwelling can be thought of as a symbol of identity (Rapoport 1982, 6), which can communicate various identities, of the individual or group, of who or what the person or group is, of what makes them unique or part of a larger whole, and of how their social persona is spatialized. In other words, people's identity, and what they aspire to, is "embedded in design." The building, as a material form, is shaped by cultural man and, in turn, shapes social action. Like material objects, buildings can condition human actors and socialize them as social beings (Dant 2005). "Individual biographies are embedded in objects and furniture through collecting and keeping" (Dant 1995, 83).

The elite Accra-dwelling Dagomba I have portrayed clearly have a different design sensibility than their brethren up north—rich or poor—and the underprivileged Dagomba also living in Accra. Those with their own homes in the north live differently than they do in the south, where they have adapted modernity to accommodate features and behaviors of the traditional socio-spatial idiom. Their Accra homes display new materialities and a multiplicity of modernities in their interpretation of design.

Modern designs incorporate a particular intentionality of the designer, whose aim may be to change people's perceptions and behaviors through material forms. But African cosmopolites do far more than embrace foreign aspects of culture and politics; they express innovative identities and belongingness, blending and juxtaposing elements of modernity with elements of tradition. In her work among the Marakwet in Kenya, Moore (1986, 152) shows how domestic layouts, like all societal spaces, can be read as "ideological representation[s] of the real" (1986, 152). Men symbolically display modernity, those who want "to declare their allegiance to a changing way of life" choose to live close to the modern settlement of Tot (Moore 1986, 133) and build square rather than round houses, the most prominent indication of modernity. They also reorder interior space. I would argue similarly that the Dagomba new elite may be buying contemporary homes in suburban Accra to proclaim through the built form their new identities and status aspirations, inscribed by designer, resident, social inference. But, also like the Marakwet, while they are affected by particular traditions from abroad, they are simultaneously bound to the traditions into which they were socialized, themselves products of deep historical interconnection. Thus, the new homes also enable old practices that are tied to an ancient materiality, the spatial organization of the house, traditional roles, food preparation and consumption. In traditional culture, the commonality of built forms carries generally agreed upon meanings, meanings inscribed by community implication in the material/built environment.

These contemporary forms express cultural hybridity through alternative or vernacular modernities in modes of doing business, raising a family, designing new spaces for living (Knauft 2002). Connections are made, continuity experienced, modernity negotiated (De Brujin et al. 2001) across a multitude of internal and external boundaries of difference and rootedness.

People buy and create clothing and environments according to their aspirations of who they want to be—they construct their identities around these material expressions as they experience a shift in consciousness in who they are and how to express it. This follows exposure to new ways. So for Dr. Iddrisu, a neurosurgeon, it may have been through living with his much older brother who was a politician in Accra and then spending thirteen years in Europe as a student. Dr. A. E. Abdulai also spent time in Europe and the US as a student, and southern Nigeria on a medical fellowship. Professor Wayo Seini went to graduate school in the UK, Dr. Nasser in Moscow, Dr. Alhassan in Denmark, Dr. Gomda in Romania and Germany, Issa Naseri in Bulgaria. Alhaji Mahdi is in construction in the south of Ghana, the outward-looking part of the country, and as he builds for others must be conscious of housing possibilities.

Foreign concepts and products can be procured through global and local markets and media, inspiring local residents and newly arrived migrants to produce new homes and new localities—what Appadurai calls "ethnoscapes" (1996). According to architects in Accra,[2] more people are building with professional designers and when they see something interesting, they come and say "*sibi mami*" (Twi: "I want the same thing"). They may see a picture in a magazine or an actual dwelling in a local development or even when visiting overseas. And they may want this same house or feature because they believe it will give them status. Extreme extroverts use their house to make a statement to society. If someone they know (and who they think is below them socially) has a particular architectural ornament such as pillars, they may want that as well but taller or bigger. They can afford to buy whatever they want to buy and through the accretion of features, create their own value.

When critics charge Africans with not following the correct protocol in their approach to modernity, for example building houses that are of different proportion or using materials that are regarded as garish in the West (Menon 2001; Ferguson 1999), they unwittingly apply ethnocentric meanings and interpretations to what may be novel appropriations. African cosmopolitanism has always been vernacularized, expressing cultural hybridity and opening new avenues for meaning and interpretation, as well as action.

Dagomba (Sub) Communities in Accra: The New Elite

Diamond (1987) has written about the pivotal role of patron-client relations in Africa in structuring access to power and resources. For those living in southern Ghana, the physical distance to Dagbon is great, and the Dagomba patrons (urban elite) play a significant role in defining a regional identity for their home area; this depends upon the resources they bring with them and their ability to mobilize followers (clients). One wonders why the Dagomba professionals in Accra care so much. Some depict the educated elite *and* the chiefs as both wanting power—the chiefs locally through financial gain, the elite through giving direction (Henry Kaleem March 19, 2013). The chief links up with the power broker, the power broker manipulates the chiefs. It becomes a way for the elite to demonstrate that they themselves have power (through influence). The Bishop of Yendi, an important neutral player in the resolution of the chieftaincy crisis, confirmed Kaleem's opinion. Many chiefs are illiterate and need direction, and even though the Accra patrons are well-to-do professionals, the Bishop believes that as Dagomba, their main aspiration is to become a chief (Bishop Boi-Nai March 17, 2013).

Growing up in Dagbon, the Accra-dwelling patrons, whose ideas carry weight among their Dagomba clients, all lived in extended families, with various mothers who were equally responsible for their food and welfare and with half-siblings who were treated like full siblings. People were indeed family oriented. Yet compounds were open to the outside, to community residents, all of whom knew each other. The compound was not exactly "private" though it was walled and it was guarded by the "eyes of the house" (see Jacobs 1961). Can the time spent as adults in modern housing, living much more as nuclear families, make a difference in concern for others? Can it make a difference in concern for others than one's kin or individuals carrying connectedness to the patron? To what extent does one's tie to the private home, with its spatiality and new materiality, its upscale trappings, incite a change in loyalty to the larger group?

On the one hand, the men I spoke with primarily see community development in governmental terms. For example, people say they want universal education, that every child should go to school. But what if the closest primary school, for example, is four to five miles away, the child is too young to walk and the parents won't organize the child's trip to school and home? Alhassan Yakubu, a middle-aged businessman/lawyer from a well-to-do Tamale family observed, "You need to develop infrastructure in the villages. That would encourage them to send the children to school. *So government needs to do a lot*" (November 23, 2005; emphasis added).

When he and the others were going to schools, it *was* the government in the form of the district assemblies that made going to school financially possible. An academic observed that the only places undergoing development are on the main road and close to Tamale, for example on the road to Bolgatanga (to the north). The only visible government development besides the Tamale-Yendi road is the Tamale Hospital. And then there is concentrated development in Tamale, like the construction of new houses, which may have led to stagnation in the other towns. This is different from the south of Ghana, where the people "go to their hometown and build. We rather build in Tamale. So if Tamale is destroyed, the whole of Dagbon is destroyed" (Yakubu November 12, 2005).

The northern politicians have not helped development in the region (Mopson Abdulai March 13, 2013). When the Tamale-Yendi Road was paved in 2000, it was done as a sop to the voters in the run-up to the election by the party (NPP) that lost big in the north because of the murder of the Ya-Na by Abudu men and the alignment of gate and political membership (Andani: NDC, Adubu: NPP).

For the eight years that John Kufuor was president of Ghana (2000–2008), his vice president was Aliu Mahama, a Dagomba from Tamale. Mahama surrounded himself in his office with family and other Dagomba. And while he was in government, Dagomba people enjoyed the fact that he continued to hold a party in Tamale at *Id al Adha* (VP Aliu Mahama June 19, 2006). But many Dagomba, Abudu and Andani, complained bitterly that here he was, in this highly important and visible position for eight years, and he brought no resources to his hometown area. While Kufuor's party (and Vice President Aliu's, the NPP) was in power, Andani businessmen in Dagbon complained that they were not considered for state contracts.

The general lag in development help from the state (going back to the British administration into the contemporary period) has set the region back. Huudu Yahaya, well-known in political circles, was the longest serving northern regional executive. In 2005, he noted that Yendi looked no different than it had for years. He gave an analogy, "If a Dagomba has this smock [the traditional man's clothing] his grandfather gave to him, he will keep it. Which is why the new palace looks exactly like the old. Tradition is very important"(November 28, 2005). But it is also about stability. Once the murdered king was buried in April 2006 and the regent was installed, things calmed down and building in Yendi picked up. A modern guesthouse was built on the main road east of town center, and cement block houses were going up in 2013. As the regent said to me, when there is peace, people invest. Alhassan Andani, the bank president from the royal family in Sarnarigu, has plans to rebuild their palace. While that

Figure 5.2. Ad for The Vteng Mall, Tamale, in process (photo by Deborah Pellow).

might not benefit the town directly, there is always a trickle-down effect. There is also a symbolic impact.

There is no question that today there is a place for the state in development. For example, in looking at Tamale, said to be the fastest-growing city in West Africa, Huudu Yahaya asks, how can one set up central planning, bring education or health up to standard, without the help of the state? Decades ago, people had been on the farms and you could hardly find an individual out there without work and pay. Then, in the 1970s with the virtual collapse of the rural agricultural economy, many men and women were idled. That and a variety of northern conflicts set off the migration of the uneducated, looking for jobs. And that is how the local Dagomba elite became more important. Many agree that their position is a draw to those in need. Their nostalgia matches contributions that make a difference in peoples' lives.

The fact is individuals do aid community development up north. Dr. Muta Iddrisu lives in Accra. Born and bred in Yendi, he continues to support his family's (father's) house there and some years ago, he built a mosque nearby in honor of his father. "Mopson" Abdulai, A. E. Abdulai's half-brother, has a PhD in land economics and anthropology from Cambridge University. He has built a home in Tamale, and he splits his time between northern Ghana and the UK. He has brought aid to the local communities. Both men have underwritten local development, which most of the local people cannot for lack of resources.

Chiefs also matter. Many complained to me that the chiefs have taken the main resource, land, and have been selling it off—the very land that people should be farming (Mopson Abdulai March 13, 2013). One wonders whether the way that the Dagomba chiefs progress from one skin to another, from one level to another climbing toward the top, obstructs a real commitment to a given community.

And yet, there are powerful counter-examples, when the chiefs are educated. After returning from Dubai where he was Ghana's ambassador, in 2015 Yakubu was installed as Chief of Vteng, an area of Tamale. As a contractor (and a patron), he decided to put his professional abilities to use and is building Tamale's first mall. He began construction December 2017 (see Figure 5.2). He hopes to be done sometime in the near future. This is "the kind of service we can provide. When we make a bit of money we spend it in Accra. But we are in extended families—should not keep all of your wealth for yourself" (Yakubu July 14, 2019). As an educated person, he observed that the illiterate chiefs participating in meetings are afraid to speak up. "We [educated] say things others cannot."

It was through his educational and thus professional success and connections that Yakubu was made ambassador to Dubai. His commitment to his hometown and his resources led to his chieftaincy when he returned to Ghana. And his professional expertise fed into his project to build a mall (Tamale's first!) for his hometown.

There is also the remarkably progressive chief of Sunson. He was lucky as a child. Perhaps this impacted his future vision.

> J. H. Alhassan, Minister in Nkrumah regime, he was the best friend of my father . . . [My father] supported him to win the election in our constituency. There was nothing he could pay him back—take me [to give me] a future. He told my father, "I want to take this your son to prepare him sufficiently. Tomorrow chieftaincy will be competition. It will be on education basis, not I am son of chief. You must be a scholar before you can occupy the skin. So, I need this boy to prepare him." So he was able to convince my father to take me to Accra and he was able to get me to school. (Sunson-Na June 25, 2008)

Like so many other members of the new elite, his father's network was key.

Figure 5.3. An informal photograph of the Sunson-Na, Na Mahama Shani Hamidu (photo by Deborah Pellow).

When he was in the second form of secondary school in 1965, Maj. General Bawa, a Dagomba, was going from school to school looking for northern boys who were educated to join the army. And he persuaded him to enlist.[3] Na Mahama Shani Hamidu was in the military for twenty-five years. His father died in 1985 and Na Mahama's brother, Joshua Hamidu, should have succeeded the father as regent, but he was in exile for political reasons. So Mahama Shani returned to Sunson and took up the chieftaincy (See Figure 5. 3). Remarkably, or perhaps because of his training in the army in combination with some secondary schooling, he figured out how to negotiate NGO-land.

> My people were suffering guinea worm. I said no. The water we drink gives us guinea worm. So I quickly asked NORIP [Nordic Reference Interval Project, a Finnish NGO] to come and give me bore holes—4, for the community. The schools you are seeing—I put them, not the government. My clinic is over there—I put up a clinic. For my people. Nobody will live in peace with hunger. I went to British High Commissioner. I told him my plan, about my honey shop. I need support. There is an NGO known as Action Aid. He said, Wise man, he was

surprised. When he came to the country, no chief ever called on me. But this Sunson-Na is a wise man. He came to my office, he want help. So go to Sunson and give him all the support. We signed an agreement for ten years. Project after project, project after project. And I took them to Yendi, to our Traditional Council. I was told that that Council was built in 1936 or so. I said this is where we sit down and deliberate. So—can you help us to put a new building for the Traditional Council? They said, why not. So they give me the schools—primary, secondary school—clinic, and a nursing quarters. Now I have 3 nurses here. Taking care of my people. So if someone is sick, a nurse, otherwise they can refer the one to Yendi. And now, the irrigation dam . . . (Sunson-Na June 25, 2008)

The dam is a terrific boon to the local farmers, made possible without state finances in a region which has historically not received state help—both during the colonial and the post-colonial eras. When Kwame Nkrumah was president, he had a small dam built in Sunson. But there was no state oversight. Over the years it fell apart, until it appeared like a natural water hole. The Sunson-Na had an idea. The World Bank was funding projects in Ghana. Sunson-Na caught the president's attention. World Bank money came to his community to construct a new dam. Summer 2008, when I first visited Sunson, the work was beginning, one single Chinese engineer was overseeing the project. He stayed throughout the construction. The plan was to be able to irrigate 100 hectares of land—to alleviate the farmers' dependence on the rains, they installed valves. "When I die and go, that dam will survive me" (Sunson-Na June 25, 2008). The dam was completed in 2013. The Sunson-Na handed it over to the Ministry of Agriculture. July 2019, when I visited Sunson, members of a Ghanaian NGO were there teaching local women to plant/transplant crops. They had planted four test acres—three of pepper, one of maize. They were expecting their first harvest a few days later.

This is an unusual story. While education may have something to do with it, the Sunson-Na is clearly a born leader who is committed to his people. As I will detail in the next chapter, his behavior fits the ideal of Dagomba chieftaincy to keep the community together (Sunson-Na June 25, 2008). Additionally and significantly, he has provided progress.

In speaking of the elite group in general, "Lawyer" Inussah spoke of Dagomba community closeness—"we're [the elite] still small, so we know each other" (March 7, 2013). I would argue that this ethnic/sub-ethnic closeness begins at the level of the compound house. As I observed in Chapter Two, in the north in all of the households, when it was a given wife's time to cook for the husband, she cooked for everyone—the husband, all of the wives, all of the children. And all of the children ate together by cohort.[4]

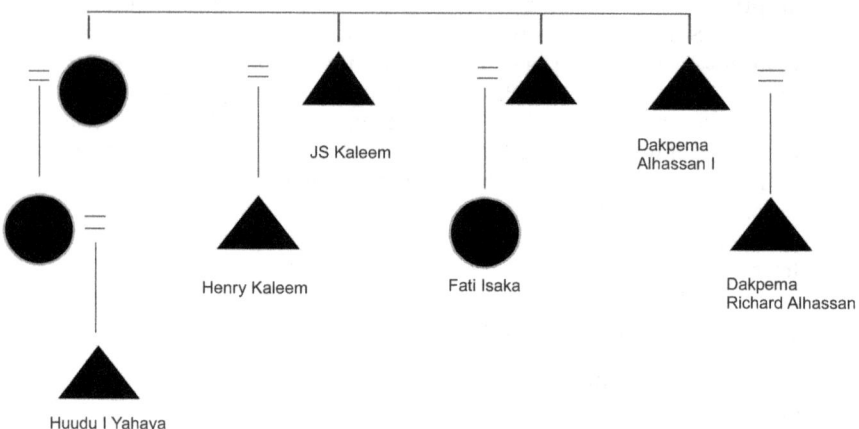

Figure 5.4. The interconnection of Henry Kaleem, Tamale *dakpema*, Huudu Yahaya, and Fati Isaka (created by Deborah Pellow, computerized by Matt Coulter).

Thus, they grew up in well-knit homes and many married one another. At that time, gate membership was not relevant, in the household or out. Examples of their genealogical connectedness abound, an index to the interconnectedness and insularity of the bridge generation. They mostly came from similar circumstances, they became successful. They are related or married to one another.

The following sample charts testify to the intra-group connectedness. I begin with the patriarch J. S. Kaleem, known apocryphally as the first educator in the north; the Dakpema Alhassan I, an educated man trained as a pharmacist, was regarded as the "chief" of Tamale. The two were brothers. Thus, their sons Henry Kaleem and Dakpema Richard Alhassan were first cousins (Figure 5.4). J. S. Kaleem, the educator, and the mother's mother of Huudu Yahaya, the modern politician, have the same maternal grandfather; J.S. Kaleem's father and the father of Fati Isaka, the nurse-turned-adoption-agency creator, were brothers, as was the Tamale Dakpema.

This is a fascinating family. Traditional politics run through, as members of the various generations have occupied roles of chieftaincy and custodianship (*tindana*), at the same time that they have gone through secondary if not tertiary education and succeeded at modern professions. After his years as an educator, J. S. had become the Chief of Nyankpala. His son Henry, who had worked in Britain for three decades, was persuaded by his father to return to Ghana, where he became something of an archivist for the Dagomba and in 2006 was made Dakpiem Zabogu-Na,

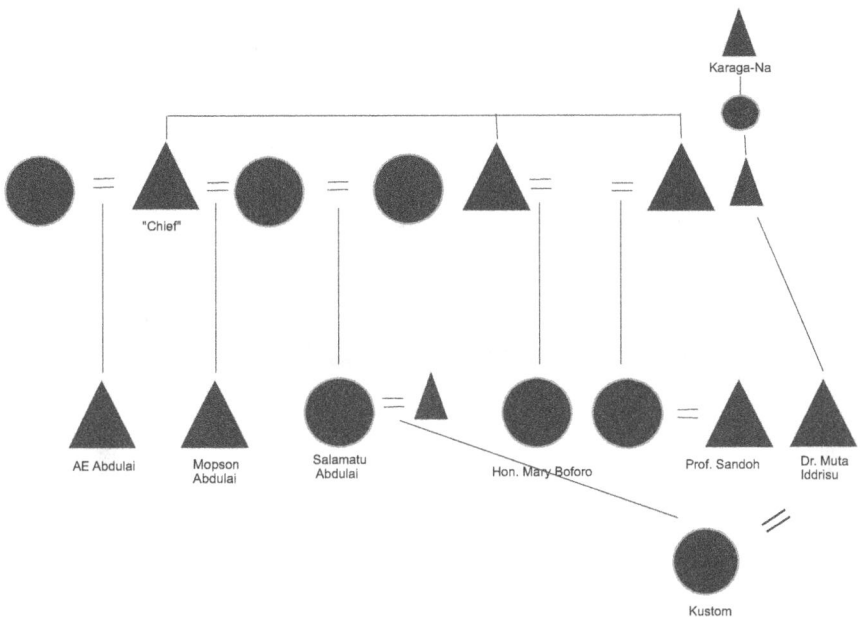

Figure 5.5. Chief Abdulai, three of his wives, two of his brothers, and the interconnection of their offspring (created by Deborah Pellow, computerized by Matt Coulter).

as one of the six landed elders of Tamale's custodial body. J. S. Kaleem was junior brother to the Dakpema Alhassan, who was not educated. But Dakpema Alhassan sent his eldest son, Dakpema Richard Alhassan to school. "I was trained as a nurse. I was trained as a dispenser. I was trained as a laboratory technician—three in one" (May 12, 2006); he became a traditional leader and gave up the medical field. Huudu Yahaya is one generation below the other three members of the bridge generation on this chart; he referred to Henry as his "uncle" which bespeaks the closeness he felt. Whenever he was in Tamale, he would drop by the house to greet him.

A. E. Abdulai, the maxillo-facial surgeon, is from Savelugu, where his father Chief Abdulai was the Yo-Na, the Savelugu chief. As Figure 5.5 shows, the family interconnections are complex. Seven of the members on the chart participated in my study—although I arrived at them from different directions. I met Dr. A. E. and Dr. Iddrisu early on through an Accra friend who knew them both professionally. A. E. led me to Mopson, his half-brother. Dr. Iddrisu led me to his wife Kustom and through her I

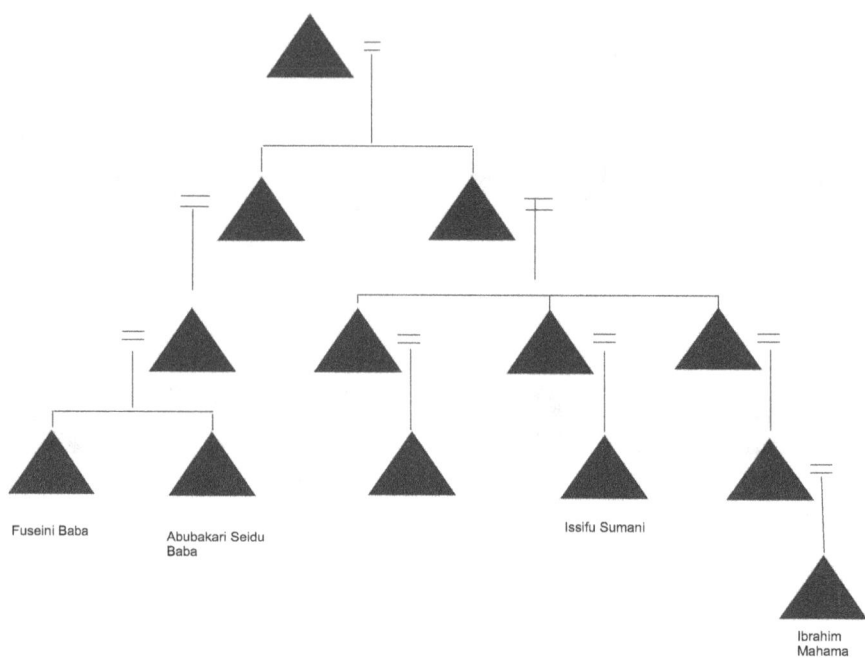

Figure 5.6. Three generations of Issifu Sumani's patrilineal descent group (created by Deborah Pellow, computerized by Matt Coulter).

met Salamatu her mother, the half-sister of A. E. and Mopson. Keeping in mind that according to the chief's daughter Salamatu at some point her father had as many as thirty-three wives, I have included in the chart three of the wives and one child of each—Salamatu, AE and Mopson—and some of their connections with others. Salamatu is the eldest of the three. Her daughter's husband Dr. Iddrisu's father was not Dagomba but a Hausa man from northern Nigeria; his mother, however, was the daughter of a former Karaga-Na, like the Savelugu chief, chief of one of the three gate skins. Dr. Iddrisu's family house is in Yendi. The Honorable Mary Boforo, MP from Savelugu, is related to the three "Chief" children through her father, their father's brother. And Professor Sandoh, an animal scientist who was in part trained in the United States, married a daughter of another of Chief's brothers.

I was continually amazed by the kin connections that popped up. Another professional offshoot of the Abdulai family is Yakubu "Accountant," whose father was "Chief's" brother. In the context of Accra, these are seemingly dissimilar men, who are patrilineal first cousins.

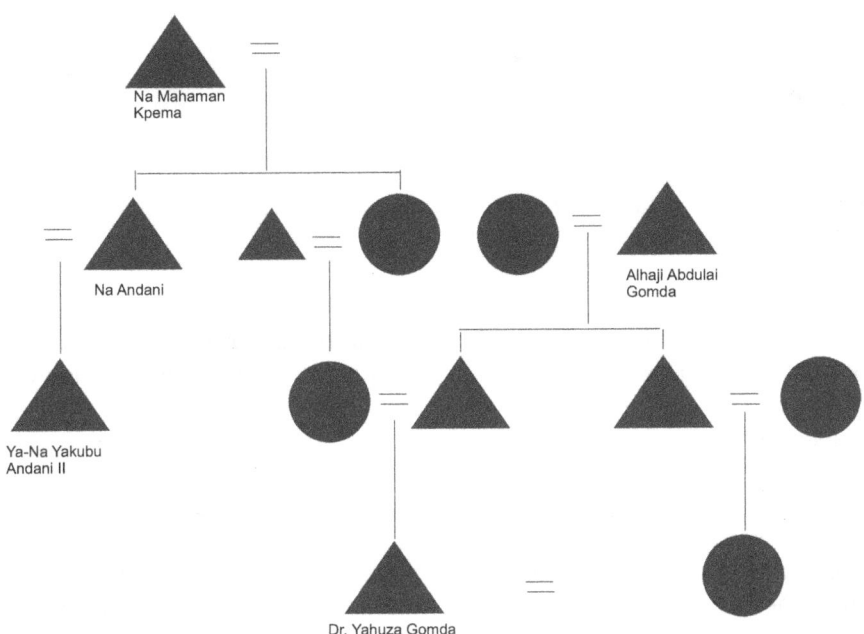

Figure 5.7. Dr. Yahuza Gomda's royal connections (created by Deborah Pellow, computerized by Matt Coulter).

As drawn in Figure 5.6, Abubakari Sumani and Issifu Sumani were cousins. Abubakari was a lawyer and one of the three MP's for Tamale. Issifu Sumani, his father's brother's son, is an architect. Issifu's paternal grandfather was from the chiefly butcher's family but didn't practice as a butcher—rather he was in building and farming. The surname Baba indicates the butcher profession. Among those two generations up from Issifu, it was only Issifu's grandfather who got to school. This was when the first school opened in Yendi, not a grammar school but a trade school, where he learned the building trade. When Issifu's father was in middle school, Issifu's paternal second cousin (his father's father's brother's son's son) Abubakari Seidu Baba was an assistant teacher. Seidu Baba is brother of Fuseini Baba, the Ministry of Finance economist. That Issifu's father got to school and in fact rose to district director of education was highly unusual and apparently due to his relationship with J. S. Kaleem. But his father's father had, in a sense, done the equivalent by going to trade school—there was no primary, middle or secondary in Yendi in those days. Ibrahim Mahama, while of the next generation below the MP,

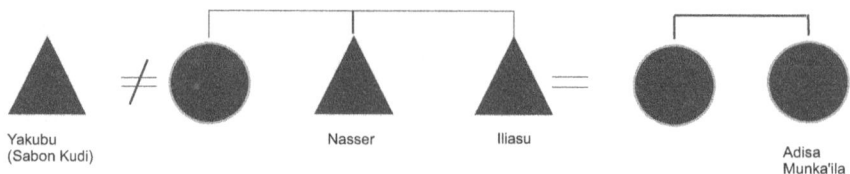

Figure 5.8. Iliasu Adam and his familial connections (created by Deborah Pellow, computerized by Matt Coulter).

Fuseini Baba and Issifu is actually considerably older. A lawyer who has written a good deal about Dagomba law and custom, he was the lawyer of Ya-Na Andani, his nephew, and known colloquially as the kingmaker because of his political clout.

Dr. Yahuza Gomda, the nuclear animal scientist, is another connector to Dagomba royalty. As one sees in Figure 5.7, his mother's mother's brother was the father of the Ya-Na Yakubu Andani II. He feels this connection keenly, evident in his fierce reaction to the murder of the Ya-Na. His father's father was the chief imam, Alhaji Abdulai Gomda, also a significant traditional role—religious but also one wielding political power. Thus Dr. Gomda has royalty on one side, the imamship on the other. Intriguingly, he and his wife share the same lineal relative two generations up—his wife's father's father is also Dr. Gomda's paternal grandfather.

Figure 5.8 delineates members of Iliasu Adam's family. Iliasu is one of the younger members of the cohort I worked with. He is a younger brother of Nasser. His wife is a younger sister of Adisa Munka'ila, who was one of the older members of the cohort and died in 2019. At the time a freelance journalist, Iliasu was an extraordinary help to me from before I formally began this project—talking me through the intricacies of Dagbon politics. Adisa, in all of her graciousness, was a real pistol. She had been a real force as a professional, and after she moved back to Tamale, she bought a water truck and started a water business; when water became an issue in town, she sold to locals. Iliasu's sister was the first wife of contractor, lawyer and chief Abdulai Yakubu (nickname Sabon Kudi: "new money"), thus Sabon Kudi is also related to Adisa Munka'ila. Trained in engineering and construction, Sabon Kudi went back to school, got a law degree, published a book on the history of the Andani-Abudu, was appointed Ambassador to Dubai and is now a chief in one of Tamale's divisional chieftaincies. Thus, like many of the patrons, he has gone back and forth between the trappings of modernity and tradition, using the former to help the latter.

There are many more such interconnections through descent and marriage, such as that of Alhaji Mahdi, the contractor in Accra, and the contractor in Tamale Mahama Sherif, aka "Savannah." Savannah's sister Amina is married to Alhaji Mahdi. Amina's mother and Savannah's mother are sisters. Amina's father's brother is the father of Abdulai Yakubu, the above mentioned chief of Vteng and Nasser and Iliasu Adam's former brother-in-law. (Yakubu's father may not be the full brother of Amina's father.)

The affinal and kin ties of the Dagomba new elite thread through all of the families and help cement the diasporic group. During the Abudu-Andani chasm following the Ya-Na's death, the cement was largely according to gate. In fact, a number of Andani-Abudu marriages fell apart. Aligned with the kin or kin-like ties is the condition of help provided to Dagomba in the north and the extent to which it is based upon the individualistic patron-client tie. Some Dagomba arrive from the north and approach patrons in Accra whom they do not know but have been referred to by someone in the network. Haruna Atta, the newspaper editor, gets regular visits from non-family—"some purely on political grounds, some who think my name can be used for whatever they want to do, some want advice, some want money, some want me to introduce them to some political person" (May 29, 2006). Dr. Yahuza Gomda, the research scientist, agreed. He spoke particularly of the illiterates who have come to Accra. "They go, stay there for some time, then later come back here [Dagbon]. Do some other things, send the money back home, that's what is happening" (September 15, 2005). They visit him at his house in Accra, and he visits them where they stay.

> Sometimes when they have problems, some will approach you, thinking that maybe you are in a better position. For instance, securing of job, that we may know somebody you can talk to and then you will be employed. A lot of people are approaching me.

These men and women patrons, who were born, bred and schooled through secondary school in the north advanced their education in southern Ghana or overseas. They made their way south in search of opportunity. If these patrons lived up north, many of those opportunities would not be available. Alhassan Andani, the bank president, receives visits from many he does not know.

> The amount of school fees I pay for Dagombas, I don't know them from Adam and Eve. Not even just in Ghana. Abroad! He comes and tells me he's got a scholarship to go abroad and he expected the papers—I always say, the last adverse comment I want to be made

against me is when someone is my age, "I went to Andani to help me to go to school and he did not do that." I don't ever want that comment to be made of me. (June 13, 2008)

At home in the hometown, there is a sense of collective ownership, each one is his brother's keeper. The communality of life is valued, which is why one at least helps one's kin. This has carried over to the diasporic community. "Lawyer" Inussa agrees that "it feels like a duty if you can help alleviate some of their problems" (September 14, 2005). For example, one's brother's daughter is getting married. You transfer money, call together the family and inform them.

But even in the city in the south, Fuseini Baba, the bureaucrat at the Ministry of Finance, told me,

> I took care of a friend's of mine son—he was virtually staying with me. He has completed Legon [University of Ghana] and he's done his national service at Ecobank, and we are hoping that they will take him. And he brought a friend of his when he was in pre-sec who is an orphan and he was staying with one of the teachers. But the teacher was to join the husband and he had no place to go, so he came and told me, oh daddy, I have a friend and this is his situation. He stayed with us from pre-sec through Legon and now he's also in the United States. So such things, yes. And my elder brother's son, I'm taking care of right now—he's with me and he's going to school. And the cousin I just mentioned. She has just completed University of Cape Coast. So when I see such a needy bright person, I try to help. I help in taking care of my sister's children. (April 28, 2006)

The neurosurgeon Dr. Mutawakil Iddrisu does it both ways—he helps people in Accra and also in the north. In the north, he started his cashew farm and built a retirement house. "I still want to have contact, I want to keep a home, and I want them to benefit from me. So I have a big cashew farm there and a cousin looking after the farm" (September 12, 2005). He also has a family member looking after his new house outside of Tamale. In Accra, he spends every Monday morning in his consultation office and sees people with "problems," medical and otherwise. He hired Malam Sani, a local Dagomba tailor, in 1991 as his go-between. Malam Sani brings northerners to see the doctor who need help. When we agreed to get together for an interview, Dr. Iddrisu asked me, "And do you know where I live?" "No." "Sani will bring you. Come at 3" (September 12, 2006). The reciprocity is clear, in exchange for his clientage, Dr. Iddrisu paid Sani's children's school fees.

But family often does come first. "Coming from such an environment and growing to be in this position, you become a role model. So many family responsibilities fall on you" (Dr. A. E. Abdulai March 15, 2013). As Dr. A. E. has learned over the years, his success has also meant that siblings and their children expect that much more help from him on their various projects. As vexing as these requests may be, Fuseini Baba, reminded me, "You don't have any family apart from those at home, and your roots is [sic] your roots" (April 28, 2006).

One of the few highly educated Dagomba women I spoke with, Professor Ramatu Alhassan, is the agricultural economist who teaches at the University of Ghana. Trained in the United States, it is not surprising that she married into the same educational class—to Dr. Alhassan, the architect trained in Denmark. Musing about responsibility to others, she said, "it's family oriented and you see, I've always looked at myself and thought, well even if I'm able to do that, I'm doing enough because you are the privileged in the family and you must have responsibility over the others. And that alone takes quite a bit of toll on you. So you think charity begins at home and you are able to support your own family too, helping the system but maybe not on the wider scale. It's how far you can go" (June 9, 2006).

This is not peculiar to any one person, especially where education is involved, because this stratum of society, from a marginalized and deprived region, understands the significance of education. Iliasu Adam, a trained journalist, and his brother Dr. Nasser, a university professor, are two of their father's twenty-six children. A butcher, the father regretted being uneducated, because during the independence struggle, it prevented him from taking up certain responsibilities. Thus he decided to prevent that happening to any of his children. All twenty-six were educated.

Dagomba (Sub) Communities in Accra: The Non-Elite

Spatial distances notwithstanding, socio-economic disparities and a history of ethnic violence and chieftaincy conflict (Akwetey 1996, 102) and consequent societal disruption (Drucker-Brown 1988–89; Ferguson and Wilks 1970) have contributed to the migration long a feature of life in West Africa. Thus, people migrate to new places for a variety of reasons, both push and pull. Today, while many individuals travel out of Ghana and even out of Africa in search of opportunity, the internal movement of people continues to be important. In Ghana, for example, men and women migrate from towns and rural areas in the north to cities like Kumase and Accra in the south. The burning issue that contributes to their migration is economic. Once relocated, some succeed and prosper; many barely scrape by. The former are epitomized by the Dagomba new elite, the highly educated professionals who are the focus of this study. The latter, on the other hand, are represented by most migrant Dagomba, whose home region houses some of the poorest of the poor. Many of them are "clients" of the educated "patrons." According to Fuseini Baba, when there were rice farms in the past, there was work (discussed in Chapter One). Now, because there is no work, many are coming south, "they don't have anything to do there [in the north] . . . they just sit under trees . . . The alternative is to come where they can get work to do" (May 8, 2006). They relocate—some seasonally, some more permanently. Many of the migrants who move down south from northern Ghana report as single and mostly within the ages of ten to twenty-four years of age.

The major concentration of the Dagomba poor in Accra is in Old Fadama, colloquially known as Sodom and Gomorrah. This locale may appear chaotic to municipality officials, but in fact, the area is organized. There is a Dagomba chief (technically of the youth), the Nachin-Na. In addition to the Nachin-Na, there is a Malgu-Na, an arbitrator or resolver of disputes; a Konbon-Na, who, like the Hausa Sarki Yaki, is the war chief; and a chief imam. Moreover, the residential areas are organized on the basis of peoples' town of origin—according to the Nachin-Na, there is no ethnic admixture—largely because, in a mixed setting, we "don't know who's a thief" (September 4, 2005).

Nachin-Na oversees the Dagomba squatters, a community that the Accra Municipality has periodically tried to disperse, but whose numbers have grown considerably over the last fifteen years, possibly to 40,000 (Grant 2006). When asked to explain the swelling ranks of settlers, the Nachin-Na told me, "Poverty is the first reason. And Dagombas have only one job and that is farming. If it fails, you have to wait a year. Some who come down go back for the harvest" (September 4, 2005). They travel to the cities in the south, mostly Accra, to seek opportunities to acquire accessories necessary for marriage and to support families back at home. The majority of this group of migrants is engaged in the informal sector, working at low-income jobs, primarily because they have little or no education. Many of these Dagomba men work at Avenor, a scrap dealers business area in Accra. When I asked one man why he did not live in his hometown of Tamale, he said, "there's no work there" (October 29, 2005). These men trade in used, heavy duty machinery, mostly tractors, trucks, front loaders, etc.

Cultural resistance to educating girls in Dagbon, as in the rest of the north, persists. This has resulted in a significant concentration of female migrants from the Northern Region working as *kayayei*, porters, in the market in Accra; this menial employment offers low earnings (Awumbila & Schandorf 2008; Kwankye 2012), but more than they could earn in the north. A young woman interviewed for a study of kayayei said that she came to live and work specifically at Agbogbloshie. "Since I wanted to live with Dagomba people I came here" (van den Berg 2007, 48). They also live informally. Whereas men may obtain decent individual sleeping quarters, women are more likely to live communally, "sleeping in open spaces and in wooden kiosks" (Yeboah 2010, 54). "A four-by-four size kiosk accommodates ten to twenty girls and each girl tenant, in addition to providing her own sleeping materials, must as a rule make a weekly down payment" (Aluizah 2006, 2). Residents of Old Fadama suffer poor sanitation, and women are vulnerable to sexual predators and disease. While the majority of the women are temporary migrants, the Dagomba male poor migrants are "rather permanent" (Yeboah 2010, 50).

Dagomba migrants, rich and poor, have created strong ties with the new environment, largely through social interrelations, which intersect there while the new place also produces new social processes (Massey 1994). At the same time, Ghana is a country where the hometown figures large in the collective imagination. Some years ago, John Middleton (1979) wrote of the continuing salience of the southern Ghanaian town Akropong-Akuapim to those born there, "who regard it as their 'home-town' (as they say), whether they actually live in it or not" (p. 246). Northern Dagomba towns, such as Karaga and Savelugu, are very different than Akropong; yet they too have a "ritual or moral topography" that unifies their people. Like the people of Akuapim, the Dagomba hold their state, Dagbon, as a single moral entity. They perceive of their hometowns within Dagbon as places of custom. They maintain strong ties to the people and the place from which they hail. The hometown area is the source of a primal identity, kinship, community. I would argue that like the Akuapim towns, the Dagbon towns are socially and politically stratified; for example, one can argue that the gate skin towns (Karaga, Savelugu, Mion), gateways to the Yendi kingship, are "superior" to the others; that Sarnarigu and its chieftaincy is superior to Nyankpala; that Gushiegu is superior to Sunson. And so on. In addition, there is the competition between the two Dagomba gates. All of this is "controlled, inhibited or resolved by the operation of periodic and other rituals in which 'custom' is performed" (Middleton 1979, 256).

The Split: Abudu and Andani Sub-Communities

Abudu and Andani are significant clan/gate identities that normally one would think of as ascriptive but which in point of fact are also conscriptive.

> You know sometimes some people become Abudus because of their friends; some people become Abudus because they are related to

Abudus; some people become Abudus because they are the Abudus. People have left their husbands, people have left their wives, just because they come from different parts, from different wings . . . It's unfortunate. So this is what has come into the family that are now divided. For example, I'm lucky. In my family, we are all Andanis. My senior father, my junior father, myself, my brothers, our wives and everything—we are all Andanis. But if you go to some families, the head of the family is Abudu, next to him is Andani, the wife is this, the wife is that. It has brought untold hardship.

Some time ago, some people come to us when they have problems for help—sometimes when someone comes to you, you don't even have to ask them where they come from, because if they're speaking Dagbani you know they're Dagomba. Sometimes so and so comes, you want to know where he comes from. If he is the same person who will go and sit and talk about you . . . So it's very unfortunate. This has really destroyed Dagbon. (Savannah May 14, 2006)

The ugly conflict between the Abudu and Andani gates, in both Dagbon and the Dagomba diaspora, has not been spatially based. They never lived in distinctly separate areas or streets. But the fact of the split has disrupted any sense of unity, both among the elite and the non-elite. For example, a Dagomba man in Accra was looking for a room to rent and the (Dagomba) landlord asked him where he was coming from. When told, he said he could not rent to him, because he did not know whether he (the renter) was Abudu or Andani, and if another Dagomba rented and was from the other side . . . "Now this is in Accra, so imagine up north" (Ibrahim Adam November 6, 2005). The Dakpema of Tamale speaks for many when he states that it is the people in Accra (the patrons) "who have spoiled Dagbon and spoiled our custom—because they don't know . . . they are simply Dagomba by name only" (May 12, 2006). And why do the local people listen to them? "They want to eat; they are sitting on gold mines, so they follow them."

The split due to Ya-Na Yakubu Andani II's murder, sidesteps the fact that the two originated as the offshoots of the two sons of Ya-Na Yakubu, who died in the late nineteenth century (Staniland 1975; Tsikata and Seini 2004). Moreover, as observed above, birth into gate need not be forever. Some individuals have in fact chosen their gate identity, such as the paternal grandfather of Issifu Sumani's father, who was born Abudu and identified as Andani. Many have also married into the other gate

Even in Accra, members of the two gates split. When I was first looking to make contacts, individuals called others on the spot on my behalf. It was two-plus years after the Ya-Na's murder. Andani called Andani, Abudu called Abudu. During the four-year period between the Ya-Na's murder and his burial, there were no festivities or meetings that brought together all Dagomba. When Dr. Gomda held an outdooring for the birth of his child in the middle of the crisis in December 2005, it was the Andani who attended.

Members of the two gates held separate meetings, occasioned by the murder, to talk through issues. The Andani elite were hosted weekly by Alhaji Mahdi the contractor at his house in East Legon. The scrap dealers at Avenor (mainly Andani) also attended a meeting every Sunday as a community in Newtown to discuss the issues brought up by the Ya-Na's murder. Sometimes they held a general meeting, organized by the "eminent" Dagomba in Accra. Smaller community meetings were also held in Sabon Zongo and outside Tema in Ashaimah. I attended one of these meetings, the Andani Family Association, in Accra Newtown on a Sunday, November 6, 2005. The secretary Ibrahim Adam explained,

> We used to have an association comprised of all the Dagombas, known as Dagomba Youth Association, to unite everyone from Dagbon, (DAYA). That thing [the Ya Na's murder] has brought about some hardship. Has caused divorces. Some of them have even migrated to Accra—these *kayayi*. [The festivals had not been celebrated in the four years since.] This means a lot with respect to Dagomba tradition.

In June 2010, eight years after the Ya-Na Yakubu Andani II's murder, fourteen defendants from the Abudu gate were remanded to the Adjabeng District Magistrate Court in Accra, to determine whether they should stand trial in High Court for the crime. They were each represented by an attorney and each had been served with a bill of indictment. The group included the seventy-six-year-old *mbadugu* (linguist) for the Abudu Regent, the Gbonlana, Abdulai Mahamadu and the NPP politician Mohammed Tijani, former DCE of Yendi (and current Deputy Minister of Foreign Affairs). One of the supporters in the courtroom was Dr. M. Mahama, an Abudu patron.[5] We sat together and had a brief exchange before court began (June 28, 2010),

> Dr. M. M.: if only justice is served.
> D. P.: a king was brutally murdered.
> Dr. M. M.: it was a war and he started it.

Dr. M. M. is venerated as an opinion leader in both north and south Dagomba communities among the Abudu. Like other patrons, his relationship with non-elite clients is a vertical alliance between two persons of unequal status, power or resources. Their relationship offers them mutual benefit, despite the gulf in social status (Landé 1977). Like other patrons, he also does not subsidize general community development up north, because in the Big Man scenario, the exchange is more particularistic than universal, more political than economic, essentially symbolic. Thus, even though he has not contributed much to the transformation of his hometown, Tamale, he is decidedly connected to it and to the people. His connection is social, sentimental and political. Despite his medical practice, he sat through the Magistrate Court proceedings, offering support to his (Abudu) side.

A major issue is that this kind of progress is dependent upon having access to the right person(s). The client's supplication can matter,

> Two people come to me with the same qualifications—his lineage is in the back of my head—I don't do it consciously . . . Someone comes when his daughter is old and hasn't got the grade, and someone wants to enter the training college, someone wants to . . . And those of us who are here, this is the only help we can give them. Because of our contact with other people. (Dr. Iddrisu September 12, 2006)

The patrons are important as culture brokers in solidifying ethnic ties; "leaders are never wholly dissociated from their supporters" (Daloz 2003, 278), and in the Dagomba case, they solidify sub-ethnic ties. One might argue that "gate-ism" is potent for the patron-client relationship.

In the aftermath of the Ya-Na's murder, Vincent Boi-Nai, the Bishop of Yendi, helped to organize a dialogue in Yendi, inviting elders and youth from both Andani and Abudu gates to meetings. The chairman was Abudu, the vice-chairman Andani. He reported to me that in the course of the meetings, participants would go outside to call people in Accra (patrons) on cell phones to tell them what was being discussed and to ask their opinions (June 24, 2008). The Accra people like everyone following them—it gives them power. The Dakpema of Tamale referred to the elite Dagomba in Accra as "the people who have spoiled Dagbon and spoiled our custom—because they don't know . . . They are simply Dagomba by name only" and their subordinates listen to them because "they want to eat" (May 12, 2006).

"There are faceless but powerful people in Accra and Kumasi" (Bishop Boi-Nai March 17, 2013). Because there were two elite Dagomba diaspora communities in Accra during the chieftaincy crisis (Abudu and Andani), the phone calls were made to members of the respective gate. And from Tuya-Na, the deceased former regional director of culture:

> The accusations and counter accusations came from Accra, in the initial stages. They have polluted Tamale. But ask them how many of their children we know. Some of them are even not married to northerners, let alone Dagombas. So they have nothing to lose if Dagbon is destroyed. My wife is Dagomba, my children are Dagomba, I'm a Dagomba. So where do I go? Those people from Accra—most of them are hypocrites. It's very painful. (November 9, 2005)

Where does education come in? Issa Naseri, the director of the National Commission for Civic Education (NCCE) in Tamale, talked to me a lot about transformations and flashpoints of conflicts in Dagbon, with a mixture of legal and political contributions in their resolution (September 27, 2005). In his view, education (of the elite, the patrons) contributes to government interference, to documentation, to distortion, to manipulation of the chieftaincy. "Certain people" used their education and knowledge to outmaneuver their adversaries in regard to the chieftaincy. Chiefly succession came to coincide with politics, leading to societal transformation.

Conclusion

This chapter examined more closely through the patrons themselves what being a bridge generation means in this new elite Dagomba situation. I have discussed how these individuals who have been so successful in not even a generation link the two regions of Accra and Dagbon, of professionals and clients, through their attachment to people and place—in effect the activation of their childhood activities, relations and attachments as involvement in hometown life and politics and their patronage of northern individuals seeking help. It was their growing up years in the north that instilled their cultural beingness as Dagomba. And now, they live in very different circumstances from those in the north. It is (perhaps) their very different submersion in a new materiality, a new socio-spatial environment, in combination with their deeply instilled background that has led to their invention of a hybrid modernity. That in-itself has affected their understanding and activation of patronage, the part they play in the development of Dagbon and those less fortunate than them.

The patrons accrue status while dispensing favors within personal networks. Lentz (1994, 165) writes about patrons from northwest Ghana, where "the leadership discourse allows the elite to identify with its rural 'roots' and . . . culture." The Accra-Yendi/north connection is also mutually reinforcing. The professionals become culture brokers for progress but also for indigenous culture. Their legitimacy "derives from their ability to nourish the clientele on which their power rests" (Daloz 2003, 278). Their social mobility is through education, kin networks and (sub-) ethnic loyalties, all of which emphasize not class theory but personal agency and networks. They marry one another, the kin of on another, similarly newly well-positioned, which further cements both their connectedness and their status. Their clientelistic ties are based on mutually beneficial reciprocity. Many of the educated elite have over time played a modernizing role—in part mediating between so-called tradition and modern ways.

There is not yet a substantial entrepreneurial class of which they would form a part, a class which might constitute a donor group. But there are big-men in a region where patron-client relations are core to social organization. All of those I spoke with were very aware of how fortunate they were to have gotten schooling and to have achieved a high position on the modern occupational ladder. Many use the word "lucky" to characterize their own success. With clients dependent upon them, they have become Big Men.

Like everywhere else in sub-Saharan Africa, these Big Men operate in "economies of 'affection'" (Daloz 2003, 281), where they both display power and reassure their followers of their ability to satisfy this network of clients. As patrons, they use symbols, rituals and rhetoric (sometimes customary, sometimes newly invented), in combination with money, to coordinate action beyond the local level, while also connecting with the central government (Kertzer 1988). As has been true in Sierra Leone, this elite group engages in "patterns of interaction, cooperation and coordination of corporate activities through communal relationship" (Cohen 1981, 232).

The connectedness of the Dagbon patrons to their roots is evident in their maintenance of cultural traditions and the extent to which they, as an exclusive subset, are either related to one another or married to one another. They have also acted as interventionists, even disrupters, back home, as exemplified by the Yendi tragedy of 2002. Patronage was stained with sub-ethnic acrimony, and in both the south and the north with the rupturing of the whole. Ironically it has been their connectedness to their roots and especially to 1qthe institution of chieftaincy that has wounded their unity as "one Dagomba."

NOTES

1. Arce and Long (2000, 17) prefer the words mutation (for the process) and mutant (for the product), because the changes are dynamically generated which "often rapidly and unpredictably [involve] the re-assembling of the recursive properties of entities and the redrawing of boundaries in such a way that new social forms emerge out of existing ones."
2. During summer 2010, I spoke with a group of Ghanaian architects at the Ghana Institute of Architects about the design process they engage in.
3. Sunson-Na's senior brother is Joshua Hamidu, a military man who went to Tamale Secondary School and while there was a cadet. He was taken to Accra for officer training and ultimately made it to Sandhurst. He became a general and in 1979 was Chief of Defense Staff when Rawlings led his first coup. After a major falling out with Rawlings, he went into exile until 1999.

When John Kufuor was elected president, Hamidu became his national security advisor. But he left the position after the Ya-Na's murder—he and the minister for the interior, Malik Yakubu, and Major Suleimana, member of the National Security Advisory Corps, were accused of masterminding the murder. Technically, Joshua Hamidu should have been enskinned as Sunson-Na, but he was in exile at the time.

4. I have gotten to know a Dagomba man in Tamale who has two wives and eight children. To aid family cohesion, he has mixed the children of the two wives in the two houses.
5. Members of the Abudu elite also supported one another—for example organizing attendance at the arraignment of the fifteen men held for the Ya-Na's murder—but I have no specifics on their group gatherings.

CHAPTER 6

Conflict at Home, Enflamed from Afar

Chiefly lore and traditions are core to the northern (Dagomba) imaginary. As elsewhere throughout northern Ghana, chieftaincy is symbolized by the skin—when chiefs are installed, they are "enskinned." When I began my research among the Dagomba in September of 2005, the community had been riven for three-plus years as a consequence of the murder of Ya-Na Yakubu Andani II. No one, neither na nor regent, occupied the skin in Yendi for four years. During those years and continuing periodically, disturbances broke out between members of the two gates throughout Dagbon and even in the south of the country. In Dagbon, the military presence continued. In Yendi, both the charred remains of the palace and its mosque, and the newly built temporary palace nearby, were off-limits to the public. There was still no peace plan, so that Na Yakubu could not be buried and a regent enskinned. Unemployment was rife. A general malaise had settled over Dagbon.

In April 2006, the Regent of Dagbon, Kampakuya-Na, son of the murdered Ya-Na and thus an Andani, was installed, but a shadow regent, the *gbonlana*, son of deskinned Mahamadu, was recognized by the Abudu, a reminder of the unsettled situation. The diasporic patrons, Abudu and Andani alike, continued to feel a general unease about going to Dagbon for festivals, if they were held, or family events. Crucial to Dagomba connectedness to their culture and worldview was and is the place, Dagbon. The place, while real, did not feel welcoming.

There is something essential about chieftaincy for the Dagomba, that helps fuel their attachment to home and place. The death of their king defined these ties. Many of the patrons had their own ideas about who should rule (Arhin 1985). As evidenced in the murder of the King and reactions to it, they engaged in what I would call leadership by remote control, using tools gained through education and social connections, they pulled strings from afar and manipulated politics at home. Like members of other chiefly groups in Ghana, they care about chieftaincy. They believe that community prosperity correlates with the gate in power, the chieftaincy's social, economic and political importance enables groups aligned with the ruling gate to derive huge benefits from its political alliance with the Ghanaian State. Thus they continue to pay considerable attention to the succession and who is eligible.

Since the conquest of the region in the fifteenth century, the "right to dispose of land" has belonged to the Ya-Na and delegated to divisional and village chiefs (Staniland 1975). The *tindamba*, the fetish priests or caretakers of the land, continue to perform sacrifices to maintain ritual control over the land. But as throughout Ghana, "the history of land tenure and its modern problems is intimately bound up with that of chieftaincy" (MacGaffey 2013, 144). In this chapter, I focus directly on what chieftaincy means to the Dagomba patrons, the circumstances surrounding the Ya-Na's death and in the words of one of the Tamale men, chieftaincy as a flashpoint for discord in Dagbon.

Chieftaincy Matters

Chiefs and kings in chiefly societies are structurally patrons *par excellence*. Speaking of the divine kingship of the Shilluk, Graeber characterizes them as sovereigns (2011, 2), who can victimize their subjects. But the king too can be a victim, as "at the moments when the people gather together to destroy the king" and at the moment he is transformed into a transcendental being. Evans-Pritchard (quoted in Graeber 2011) argues that divine kings are non-existent but rather that it is the kingship that is divine, that there is a tension between the kingship and the individual holding it. In examining divinity, sacrality and forces inherent in kingship, Graeber notes that it is not that the king embodies a god but that he *acts* like a god and is allowed to do so. In some cases, he may reign, in some cases govern. In all he is a symbolic figurehead (2011).

Chieftaincy matters, even to most members of this highly educated, professionally employed, cosmopolitan group of 1.5ers. An index to the significance of chieftaincy in Ghana may be that "operators at the highest echelons of Ghanaian society crave chieftaincy titles" (Abotchie et al. 2006, 103). Furthermore, the significance of traditional authority is apparent in the plethora of chieftaincy conflicts throughout Ghana *and* the interest of Ghanaians of all classes and status-groups in successions (Arhin 2006). Becoming chief is a cherished achievement, it confers legitimacy, and competition for chieftaincy positions is passionate. Many understand the chief as the social leader, the one who directs community development, provides a link to government, performs religious ceremonies, preserves ideas and lifeways unique to the group, and maintains law and order. Dr. David Abdulai reminds us that

> the original Dagomba didn't have chiefs. Kind of acephalous paying allegiance to clan heads and fetish priests. And fetish priests had no direct relationship with each other. The non-Dagomba chiefs conquered us without any resistance and put us together. They stand things on us, we don't get anything from them. For practical purposes, the chieftaincy is useless. But it has unifying aspect which is attractive. Also has a way of showing we have a culture. (September 24, 2005)

Their culture is performative, but it is also anchored to identity in a tangible sense—that is, the chieftaincy is an anchor in social, physical and temporal space, especially for those like the Accra patrons, who are removed from the metaphorical/physical place of origin.

A friend told me about a northern man, Alhaji Y, who had always derided chieftaincy—he felt it was outmoded, no longer mattered, a product of bygone days. Then one day, when Alhaji X, a friend of Alhaji Y, saw a Mamprussi chief all adorned, he dropped to his knees in deference. The chief called out his name. The chief was Alhaji Y, the very man who had ridiculed the significance of chieftaincy. "You don't know till it happens to you!" (A. E., April 27, 2006). I was at the Ministry of Finance, waiting in the Reception Area to meet up with Abdulai Yakubu, a Dagomba diplomat, in hopes of scheduling some time to talk before he left the country to take up an ambassadorial post. I was joined by three highly placed Dagomba patrons, two of whom worked at the ministry. When Abdulai Yakubu walked in, the three men all fell to their knees and clapped in the traditional Dagomba manner. The diplomat was the junior regent of Savelugu, and his countrymen were according him respect for his chiefly office.

A different Abdulai Yakubu, the contractor and lawyer originally from Tamale and who is now a chief, believes there is a place for chieftaincy (November 23, 2005). "But," he continues, "I think that chieftaincy should be seen as a repository of our culture—it should be seen as a way of preserving our culture. And beyond that, it has no other role. And I think Dagbon will have a very beautiful culture—I think that we should preserve it. So we need the chieftaincy for that role." Not, one may note, to rule. Dr. Yahuza Gomda, a nuclear animal scientist, reinforces this position.

> Without chieftaincy I think most tribes or most communities would just fall apart. People still identify themselves to these things, you know, and it's through these things you see our cultural dances, our

practices, the traditional way of doing things. Of course, tradition is dynamic. From time to time there could be some changes here and there, but it shouldn't be so radical that it would destroy the fabric of tradition. (September 15, 2005)

Professor Walter Alhassan Sandoh, who is an agricultural scientist, also affirms the centrality of chieftaincy in Dagbon.

> And if there's no chieftaincy, I don't see it. It holds society. It's a cohesion. Most of us who have left home and have raised our children down south, when I talk to my children about chieftaincy, they are not really sure what I am talking about. So maybe with the education to come, the influence of the chiefs will decline somehow. But as of now, the institution helps us pull together. (May 29, 2006)

Thus, to these men and the others, the chief matters, but in a passive manner. While he may no longer be the active decision-maker—his power is seemingly largely symbolic—in Dagbon, it is the chiefs, and the Ya-Na most particularly, who claim the right to dispose of land. There is a rapacious element, the chiefs may try to access land for personal gain and are often successful. When I was driving on the Tamale-Yendi Road in 2013, my assistant pointed to the cashew farm that was said to have been sold to the former Vice President Aliu. This ploy was complicated by the presence of the *tindamba*.[1] The land grab has made chieftaincy disputes a major source of conflict, and succession to the nam (kingship) especially trenchant, because the rules of tradition regarding chieftaincy are often differently interpreted, depending upon who is doing the interpreting. And land is an element in the tangible exercise of power in being chief. The chiefs hold much of the land in trust on behalf of the people (even as some regents and chiefs sell it off). In Dagbon, during the years that there was no Ya-Na and no regent in Yendi, 20 chiefs died and could not be replaced because there was no one in place to enskin new ones. I was told by locals in Tamale and Yendi that where there were regents occupying those vacant skins, they did not want to relinquish their respective slots, because even as temporary chiefs, they could sell off land.

Away from the big towns and cities, customary royals have considerable economic and political clout, because the state is less present. There are villages with no state presence, for example, no police station. Crimes and conflicts must be resolved, and that falls to the chief. Even where there is a police station, the chief is often the stop of first resort. The Banvim Lana is the Regent of an area that falls within Tamale South. As the acting chief, he hears three types of cases, those dealing with women, with animals, and with land (May 12, 2006). With regard to women, "it's about usurping somebody's wife. The aggrieved man comes to me, the chief. The woman can be pregnant with a different man or has sex with a man from a different community. I pose the question, 'Is it true?' I indicate the steps to take. Usually the judgment is against the man." With regard to animals, it is normally about theft. "The aggrieved person brings the problem to me. The animal is collected for the person and a charge [$] is brought to me. If the person doesn't agree to pay, he's sent to the police station." And with respect to land, the issue can be that following fallowing of the cultivated land, "a different person comes in and claims that land. If the land is vast, I may give some to the person. The Banvim land all belongs to the chief" (Banvim Lana May 12, 2006).

The latest and largest source of money and power is access to development aid. Thus, access to and control of resources can make chieftaincy lucrative and powerful, especially as it intersects with the apparatus of the state, and by extension, transnational resources. Throughout Ghana today,

> chieftaincy titles, particularly those involving high offices, are mainly given to wealthy, educated and politically influential persons who can use their contacts with government officials, local and international NGOs, donors, foreign embassies and Ghanaians abroad to bring in development projects and raise funds to administer the palace and their territories. (Tonah 2012, 5)

Furthermore, the average Dagomba man in Dagbon defines his own position in relation to the chief. Without chieftaincy, what identity does he have? Who will protect him? Is it the culture? It is patriarchy at the communal and regional levels. Haruna Iddrisu, a sociologist, lawyer and MP for Tamale South and who is leader of the Minority in Parliament, asserts that "the chief performs traditional social, religious, political, judicial and other duties. And then society accepts that he exercises some powers in the collective interests of the community" (October 26, 2005).

There are those who support the continuation of the institution, although with qualification. The political activist and university professor Dr. Nasser observes ". . . it's very entrenched in the people's psyche and the infrastructure and why not use the positive aspects. But [the educated elite, initially those who completed Middle School and/or teacher training] manipulated the chieftaincy process . . . creating confusion [during the 1940s] that has lasted up to today. . . And they were supposed to be the most enlightened" (April 30, 2006).

Some others oppose the continuation of the institution, also with qualification. Within the Dagomba new elite I interviewed, a handful (and only a handful) wants chieftaincy abolished because of the problems resulting from chieftaincy conflicts and the absence of development in the region. It is true that they remember from their childhood how important, how revered, chiefs were. In those days, before Independence and the importance of state politicians, the Ya-Na was so important that "in the Dagbon state, if you did not agree with him, you had to leave the place, you could not stay in Dagbon and fight the Ya-Na. But as soon as we had a central government, then the politician became the center of power and no longer the Ya-Na. So you could sit in Dagon, disagree with the Ya-Na, fight him . . . even slaughter him, and there would be no problem . . . That tells you how important the place of the Ya-Na is now for them . . . Even the symbolic is now lost" (Abdulai Yakubu November 23, 2005).

Support and opposition to the chieftaincy can get quite muddy, depending upon the context. As with the criteria for chieftaincy, the interpretation of its usefulness is a function of whose interests are at heart. To some extent, it could be that "with qualification" is a function of ambivalence on both sides. Some believe that chieftaincy matters to the illiterate and as more people are educated, the role of chief will become irrelevant. Others see that it has declined in importance, and they blame the decline on their educated peers. Clearly, it has mattered to the educated, else the 2002 mayhem would not have occurred. For most of the Western-educated Dagomba I spoke with who live in Accra, far from the homeland area, the Dagomba chieftaincy holds appeal. They believe the institution holds the people together—even as it has torn them apart.

Emanuel Bombande is a founder of the West African Network for Peace (WANEP). In meeting with higher ups in Dagbon during the days of "confusion" (the four-plus years following the Ya-Na's death), he said to them at a meeting, "Your kingdom needs to stay whole" (June 19, 2004). Dagbon had turned on itself, he opined, the two gates using tradition selectively when it supported their respective side, often for reason of political expediency. In 2005, three years after the murder, six months before the burial, Basharu Alhassan Dabali, President of Concerned Citizens of Tamale, asked me,

> If we have our own problem, why can't we sit down as Dagombas? . . . we lean on parties to solve our problems, thereby worsening the situation. Because political parties will come and go, governments will come and go, and we will still be Dagbon. So it is against this background that I think that any politician who is Dagomba who wants to interfere with Dagbon chieftaincy crisis should place Dagbon first before any gate he or she is coming from. Look at Ashantis—they have never allowed political interference in their chieftaincy issues. They have placed Asanteman first before any other thing . . . (October 3, 2005)

As I have argued elsewhere (2012), for the Dagomba it *is* a matter of loyalty to the group, but it is loyalty to the *sub*-group, the gate, not to the whole. What matters is whose gate is represented by the kingship. This in turn ties into patronage—whose patronage is most powerful, which in part could be due to gate politics, to the gate of the patron, and his relationship to the king. The issue of gate affiliation exploded in the 1950s when Dagomba politics became tied to national and regional politics,[2] and each of the two gates aligned with political parties, Andani with Nkrumah's CPP and Abudu with the United Party; this has continued with their respective successors, the NDC and the NPP of today.

Goody has written that "the history of monarchy is stained with the blood of close kin" (1966, 142). This has been true in Dagbon. Do we blame the Dagbon situation on the Ghanaian State? On traditional elders? On the new educated elite? The impact of the state on Dagbon has been either deleterious or remote, so that residents view traditional authority as more effective than the state. And yet, every move is interpreted according to the state rather than indigenous politics and some think the traditional side has been grossly disadvantaged by state politicians. The former Regional Executive Huudu Yahaya reminds us that "Dagombas are very very conservative. We are not easy to deal with. They want the world yesterday to still be the same today. And they will fight to maintain it. That is why this chieftaincy thing has dragged on." But at the same time, "it's too early for us to wish [chieftaincy] away. The Dagombas who are literate are a minority compared to the others. And the institution is what holds everything together" (November 28, 2005).

According to Haruna Atta, a journalist, the Asantehene (King of the Asante) is an enlightened traditional authority, who "just marries in with the modern and then it moves on . . . [the chiefs] have a role to play. But now it depends on us the people to insist that our traditional leaders must have a certain world outlook" (May 29, 2006). And be educated. The current Asantehene, Otumfuo Osei Tutu II, received an honorary doctorate from London Metropolitan University where he had years earlier earned the Diploma in Management and Administration. His predecessor Opoku Ware II did a law degree in Britain. After being admitted to the Middle Church, he returned to Kumase and opened a law practice.

The importance of an enlightened traditional leader matters, as evidenced by activist chiefs who lobby the government for development in their own communities. Sunson-Na would fall into that category—knowing to pursue NGO and World Bank money for his bore hole and dam projects. Education for the chiefs helps enormously, because that better situates them to become agents of change. Alhaji Siddique (October 19, 2005), the head of Radio Universe at the University of Ghana, Legon, says, "Chieftaincy—huh?. . . If you talk to the chiefs who have western education, they know the values, they know that if I swear by gods. . . the

Figure 6.1. Ya-Na Yakubu Andani II (Mahama Alhassan, aka Americana).

traditional system of arbitration is such that it is based on faith, it is based on trust . . ."

While many of the Dagomba educated elite would say, chieftaincy is not the priority, education should be. And yet, it is not clear that chieftaincy has outlived its usefulness. Many educated Dagomba would also say, you cannot talk about Dagbon without talking about chieftaincy. And indeed, some cared enough about chieftaincy and the occupant of the skin that they enabled the murder of the Ya-Na.

The Death of a King: Cause and Explanation

There are remote and proximate causes for the three days of death and destruction that led to the Ya-Na's death on March 28, 2002. In the Prologue, I recounted the proximate causes through the eyes of three of the Ya-Na's widows. The remote causes include the interpretation of Abudu-Andani rotation for succession to the Yendi skin.

There is no evidence of government foul play, but there were rumors of official complicity and a series of coincidences. At the time, the vice president of Ghana was Aliu Mahama, an Abudu; the minister for the interior, Malik Alhassan Yakubu, was also an Abudu; the security advisor for the state, General Joshua Hamidu, was an Abudu; and the security coordinator for the state, Major (rtd.) Suleman, was an Abudu. To investigate, the Wuaku Commission of Enquiry was appointed on May 29, 2002, two months after the carnage. It was chaired by retired Supreme Court Judge Wuaku and had two other members. They submitted their report to the president on November 6, 2002. According to the report (Yendi Events, Republic of Ghana 2002), Mohammed Habib Tijani, District Chief Executive of Yendi, stated that,

- On March 25, when shooting was going on, he tried "to solicit [the regional minister's] assistance for reinforcement, but the phone lines went down" (p.9). In fact, telephone lines to and from Yendi went down on March 25 at 5:30 pm and did not come back on until March 27 at 10:00 pm, after hostilities ended.
- The following day, according to his testimony, "the police said they could not find the key to their armoury, while the military also said their number was not enough for such an assignment" (p.9);
- and then on the morning of March 27, when he asked the military to intervene and rescue the Ya-Na, the equipment of the military detachment in Yendi "suffered dramatic failures and manpower deficiency" (p. 74)—insufficient combat soldiers, reinforcements without proper gear, the armored car out of commission because the battery was dead.

There were other less proximate sources for the trouble. Islam is considered the state religion of Dagbon.[3] It is the Ya-Na who chooses the chief imam and this follows rules of seniority. Several decades ago, the sitting Ya-Na made one Husein the Imam of Yendi. Husein died and after him the Ya-Na died. An Andani was selected Ya-Na. Husein, the former Imam, had five sons and the eldest was chosen as Imam. According to a source, a younger brother was peeved, because he had served loyally—his family were Abudu, but until this time they had maintained close relations with the Andani king. He was also better educated in Quranic studies than his brother. The Ya-Na, however, made his choice according to order of seniority.

The Imam of Yendi died. Husein's younger son, now Imam of Zohe, the village neighboring Yendi, contested for the Imamship of Yendi. But there was still another older brother and following rules of seniority, the Yendi imamship went to him. The Imam of Zohe died and his son succeeded him. It is said that the son regarded the Andanis as ingrates and not worthy of support, and he became a big Abudu booster. He died. In 2002, before a new imam was installed, the aggrieved man "robed himself" as Zohe Imam to avenge his father's humiliation.

At the time for *Id al Adha* and then *Bugum* in 2002, the Abudus sought for the first time to celebrate separately from the (Andani) king. The king and his followers felt this as an insult (Tonah 2012). The Abudus held their own *Bugum* first, which I am told was organized not by the Abudu Regent but by the Zohe[4] Imam. Their action fueled the unrest and violence that ended in death and destruction.

Even more remotely, this tale speaks to the interpretation of the criteria for chiefly succession, Andani-Abudu rivalry, the complication by state/party politics, and the larger tensions underpinning the place of chieftaincy in society. It also speaks to the place of an emerging educated elite. The Accra-based Dagomba opinion leaders, i.e. the patrons, are instrumental in (sub-) group decision-making. They have their respective agents at the local northern community level, where, as I have detailed earlier, they inserted their opinions into local (especially chiefly) politics. They fanned the fires of anger, jealousy, contention, and the cries for restitution. While the Abudu shouted that with the death of the Ya-Na, it was their turn in the chiefly rotation, the Andani roared that the Abudu could not profit from the crime they had committed. It was the correlation of gate with political party—Abudu with NPP, Andani with NDC—that the murder and blame resulted in an NDC rout in the parliamentary elections of 2004 in Dagbon.

There were immediate costs, a special team of police investigators, establishment of the Wuaku Commission, and the Otumfuo Committee of Eminent Chiefs. The government spent about seven billion cedis (nine million dollars) on the crisis—¢4.5b was spent on 395 soldiers and twenty-nine officers from the Ghana Armed Forces and 250 police personnel while ¢770m was spent on the sittings of the Wuaku Commission (Paintsill and Coomson 2002). There were other expenses that cannot be quantified, the adverse effect on production, marketing and investment on agriculture, crucial to Tamale's economy; financial institutions refusing to grant loans due to violence and insecurity; the abuse of basic human rights; and of course, community cohesion (Issifu 2015). Properties worth millions of dollars were destroyed.

In Ghana, since chieftaincy is in principle an independent body of government and also above national government, "chieftaincy disputes are to be settled at the Regional House of Chiefs, National House of Chiefs and eventually at the Court of Appeal levels, in that pecking order" (Ahorsu

Figure 6.2. The military presence near the old palace, Yendi (photo by Deborah Pellow).

and Bone 2011, 24). But there was so much disputation following the 2002 upheaval, that in 2003, President John Kufuor set up the Otumfuo Committee of Eminent Chiefs, chaired by the Asantehene, Otumfuo Osei Tutu II, with Nayiri-Na Bohugu Shirigu (paramount chief of Mamprugu) and Yagbonwura Bawa Dosie (paramount chief of Gonja), to resolve the traditional chieftaincy differences in Dagbon. "Their selection was influenced by shared characteristics of traditional administrative structures and the culture of chieftaincy" (Ahorsu 2014, 113). In addition to the governmental initiatives, there was also active peace mediation by civil society organizations, such as WANEP.

On April 10, 2006, the Ya-Na was buried. The day before the burial, his 26 widows returned to Yendi from Tamale where they had been living at the home of Lawyer Ibrahim Mahama's sister for four years. They travelled in in a mini-bus, said to be preceded by 1,000 men and boys on motorcycles and motorbikes (Iliasu April 23, 2006). As the caravan approached Yendi, youths came out on the road and began throwing stones at them. After a lapse in time, security intervened. The following morning, there was more stoning in Yendi. Concerned, National Security is said to have called one of the Abudu patrons in Accra and told him that if a problem erupted, he would be held responsible. The stoning ceased. Eleven days later and four years after Na Yakubu's death, on Friday April 21, 2006, his son was installed as regent, Kamkapuya-Na Andani Yakubu Abdullai.

The perpetrators of the Yendi massacre were never brought to justice, a trial in 2011 of fifteen Abudus (including former DCE Tijani) resulted in acquittal. The old palace and mosque remain standing, surrounded by barbed wire. There is a military presence—soldiers and sandbags—near the new palace (see Figure 6.2). All are material reminders of the three days in March nineteen years ago. They are also reminders that the old days when traditional issues were resolved traditionally, from within the group, are over.

Gate Place

Since Andani and Abudu are offshoots of the same man and one can actually *choose* the gate with which he or she is affiliated as desired, remarks by the Lamashoggu Gbonlana, the Regent of Lamashoggu, make perfect sense,

> You can't have complete Abudu, you can't have complete Andani. The only thing is, myself like this . . . we originated as Abudus. But later we felt that the Abudus are cheating the Andanis . . . so we left our families and then we are supporting the Andanis. (May 15, 2006)

The spatial element in Accra has separated out the well-to-do persons more generally; the patrons who live there have many suburbs to choose from and aside from the opposite gate, any and all are mixed in with other well-to-do ethnics, Akan, Ga, and so on. In Dagbon, especially in villages and towns where many still live in family residences, the geographic distinction is absent. This became very apparent in Yendi following the three days of fighting.

Yendi has a larger Abudu than Andani population in the vicinity of the Ya-Na's palace. There is nothing obvious to differentiate one residence from another—all are round, thatched, and so on. But, especially in times of heightened intra-ethnic tension, everyone knows which is Andani, which is Abudu. This was especially clear during the three days of rage in late March 2002, when many homes were torched.

Six years after his father's murder and no indictments forthcoming, the enskinned regent complained to me, "there [are] a lot of people arguing [the] issue. Was it an attack on the king? Was it a war?" (June 28, 2008). He came up with an idea to "prove" that the three days of fighting were one-sided. He had an artist draw up the housing layout in the palace neighborhood. It requires no interpretation (Figure 6.3),

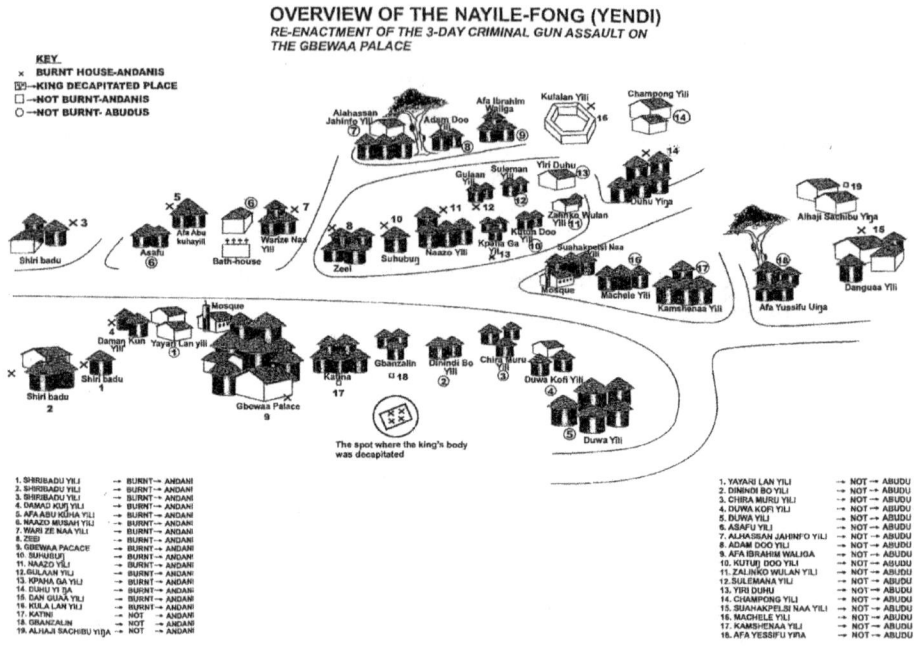

Figure 6.3. Diagram of houses burnt adjacent to the Ya-Na's palace, March 27, 2002 (Kampakuya-Na, Regent of Yendi).

> You see Andanis' houses, you see Abudus' houses. You see Andanis' houses are burnt, Abudus' houses are not burnt. Why is it that Abudu houses are not burnt? You see, this is an Andani's house and this is an Abudu's house—this house is burnt and this one is not burnt. [this was outside or within the palace?] Within the premises. You see the surrounding houses, they are mixed up, Abudu and Andani . . . You see Abudus' houses—there are about 18 and none of them got burnt; the Andani houses are 19. *Katini* where the royal mauseleum is and where the first lady is in another house—it was not burnt. The rest of the Andani, about 16 houses, were burnt. (Regent of Dagbon, June 28, 2008)

And then he said to me, "You come closer, you bring your chair here and I'll show you something [pointing at the drawing, Figure 6.3] . . ."

> This is where the Ya-Na was, this is the *Katini* and this is where the first lady of the Ya-Na is—*Gbanzalin*. When you look at the key, burned houses (Andani), that is the X. So you see this is Andani, where the Ya-Na was burnt. You see here, burnt. Etc. But when you look at this key here, not burnt (Abudus)—so look at the difference. This is the

house of Andani, this of Abudu. Why is it this one is not burned and this one is burned? They are sharing [a] boundary. You get my point? So when you come here, you see the only 2 Andani houses that are not burnt—18 and 19. Number 19, Alhaji Sachibu Yinga [an old man who is a mallam]. The only Andani house not burnt. So you begin to ask yourself, I'm sharing a boundary with somebody and we are fighting and nothing happens to his house and my house is burnt. Look at this house and look at this house, etc.

I want to show people because there is some argument that it was a war. Some people say it was an attack. So I have to come out with this thing so people can use this to *judge* . . . they say it's war in Iraq, so we know that Iraqis are dying, American soldiers are dying. But what happened in Dagbon . . . You can even see where they murdered the king, it is there. It's not in somebody's house—this is the palace, this is *Katini*, and look at where he was.

[There's] an Andani house in the middle of two Abudu houses. And nothing has happened to them. So if this is war, most of the Abudus houses should have also been burned. It's not one day, it's three days.

The spatial admixture of Andani and Abudu is clear when one looks at the plan, as is the one-sidedness of the fighting.

Flashpoints for Discord

The Dagomba appreciate hierarchy. In the words of Dr. David Abdulai,

> our uniqueness is we are very hierarchical and the one at the top likes to be there as long as it possible. But the one at the bottom also wants to get there. When you are at the top you get the allegiance of everybody else. But everybody else is also trying to get there. So it's a subtle competition for the top position. (September 24, 2005)

The conflict that lead to the death of the Ya-Na and twenty-eight of his followers in 2002 was hardly subtle.

It is within the family that competition is first learned. In the customary community, family teaches a given way of life, encompassing values and attitudes, and it provides protection to its members. Hierarchy is at the core of the Dagomba household. At the same time, with societal development and broadening of horizons, the family has diminished and thus one's responsibility within the family has weakened. Education factors in as well. The dilemma, according to Issa Naseri, the northern director for NCCE (National Commission for Civic Education), and a flashpoint, is wanting to hold onto family traditions even as the family has weakened and the place is becoming more diverse and street culture becoming more influential.

Dagomba leadership is at its heart hierarchical, by seniority, family, and merit. We see this in the operation and importance of chieftaincy. It is also visible in the ranking of the chieftaincies, with succession determined at the top, by the Ya-Na. Even the three royal provinces, the venue to the kingship—Savelugu, Karaga and Mion—are ranked in seniority with Savelugu at the top. Chiefly offices can be royal or commoner. Royal juniors suffered from their lower position, losing all chiefly rights. There are two divisions of royal chieftaincies, those for the sons of Ya-Nas and those for grandsons of Ya-Nas. There are posts for royal women. And then there are divisional and village posts, which are also ranked, Tolon and Gushiegu at the top (Staniland 1975).

Dagomba conservatism is also an ingredient. Chieftaincy is an institution that many Dagomba believe should be conserved, because one cannot talk about Dagbon without talking about chiefs. And chieftaincy can be a uniter, as I documented earlier in this chapter, those who favor chieftaincy perceive it as solidifying the group. It can be an avenue for mobilization. Yet this institution that is so central can also be divisive, exploitative, inimical to Dagomba interest. In line with conservatism, many chiefs are not educated, which can impede development and change, as well as the ability to negotiate with those who are educated and more worldly. It can also enable manipulation by the latter.

The selection of a chief creates an immediate flashpoint as the issue of succession arises. In 1948, the traditional way of selecting the king by a small group of elders following divination (see Chapter One; Staniland 1975) was amended and the earliest of the Western-educated Dagomba got involved, successfully arguing for a committee of selection. People refer back to that as the modern beginning of the problem of succession, and it became a point of tension to which many refer today.

More recently, in 2002, as soon as the king was assassinated, tensions erupted, among and between gates, among and between families. People could not pray together. The Bishop of Yendi chaired an intra-religious dialogue, but he could not get the two sides to come together to talk. Everybody became an enemy. Marriages broke down. People threw out provocative statements, "hey, where are you going? To market to buy fish? There's a big fish [the murdered king] in the mortuary" (Bishop Boi-Nai June 24, 2008).

Dagbon is a multi-ethnic state, it is a highly centralized state, and the contest is how to manage it.[5] As much as the Dagomba themselves constitute a whole, they are not mobilized as a whole; rather, the gate subdivision is what matters. But they do on occasion come together, and this is to fight. There are "mind gods," those who factionalize Dagbon (Naseri September 28, 2005); those would be the patrons in Accra. On its own, the relationship between the elites in Accra and the locals in Dagbon is nothing special. It is a society of movement; one has ties with the place one comes from, so there's nothing unique about the Dagbon situation in general. But this situation is different. Dr. David Abdulai became involved in the peace process not because he had an interest in politics but because "they were my people, and they were divided" (September 24, 2005). *"The relation between the people in Accra and the people up here is they feed them—they give them guns.* So they need them. The Accra people, the elite Dagomba, may be followed by those up north, but they are also mistrusted; everything they do is read with misunderstanding" (Bishop Boi-Nai May 17, 2013, emphasis added).

Even though, or because, they are educated, professionals and well-to-do, the Accra Dagomba elite like having followers—it solidifies their power. Many, like the Bishop, believe that the main aspiration for Dagomba is to become a chief. (Dr. David Abdulai would say, "Most Dagombas want to be recognized as being somebody" (September 24, 2005)). But a critical issue that needs to be dealt with is that not everyone can become chief. So for a variety of Abudu whom I talked to, Ya-Na Andani Yakubu II was on the skin for too long (twenty-eight years). It was their side's turn. And moreover, they complained, why can't we have the kingly funeral for Mahamadu? And if we have it, it must be in the palace, therefore you, the Andani king, must leave. It may have been a disregard of Dagomba rules of succession, of hierarchy and seniority, exacerbated by party politics that precipitated the tragedy. A theory floating around is that the Abudu intention was not to kill the Ya-Na but to scare him out of the palace so that they could occupy the place and negotiate from a position of strength for the funeral. Events got out of hand. The situation degenerated into a mob attack. This was their flashpoint.

In March of 2004, two years after the tragedy, the old palace was still off-limits to the public. There was a continuing state of emergency, with guards surrounding the locale. Despite this, a band of Abudu were able to rush in, occupy the palace for five days (until they were removed), and re-roof the palace. The offended Andani felt the Abudu were erasing evidence from the March 2002 onslaught. The conspiracy theorists wondered, could there be powerful hands behind the scene? (Iliasu June 8, 2004).

Women blame the youth for the looting, burning and stone throwing. The youth blame the imams for not doing enough for the youth. In the bishop's view (March 17, 2013), there are four elements to the problem, the political (the military takes orders from above therefore it is political), the traditional (what does custom dictate?), the criminal (society must find someone guilty) and the creation of peace (stop stone throwing, insults, etc.). Issa Naseri spoke to the major consideration of how to resolve "I have lost." What is life after a failed campaign for a skin? Why need such a loss be regarded a social disgrace that causes personal pain? They understand retributive justice—you do something to me, I have to retaliate, and a spiral erupts. They need to understand what forgiveness is, they need to learn to give and take (Bishop Boi-Nai March 17, 2013).

The polarization in Dagbon increased the politicization of the Naship and vice versa. National politics came to manipulate and exploit factions for political gain. I was told that during the 2000 presidential campaign, the NPP promised that Ya-Na Mahamadu (the de-skinned Ya-Na who preceded Ya-Na Andani Yakubu) would finally have a royal burial. Then after the murder of the Ya-Na, the NPP was said to ensure the royal funeral of Ya-Na Mahamadu. Indeed, as I wrote earlier, with each change in the state regime, it is expected that the royal Dagomba faction affiliated with it will somehow be put on the paramount skin. The carnage in March 2002, the Wuaku Commission, the trials—none brought justice for the aggrieved.

Conclusion

It is now almost twenty years after the murder of Ya-Na Yakubu Andani. Both Mahamadu and Yakubu Andani finally had their respective royal funerals. In 2019 a Ya-Na was enskinned. It is clear that what has mattered is that proper procedure be followed. Rituals count. Who is installed as Ya-Na matters socially, economically, politically. If we ask who has rights to the Naship, not only must we consider the constitutional rules specifying who is eligible, the dynastic rule of rotation, the rule of who has the authority to select the Ya-Na and coming to terms with the March 2002 massacre. Many in the north, including the chiefs, feel left out. "All of our speakers are in Accra. They will not listen to us here . . . There's no respect" (Karaga-Na November 13, 2005). We must also consider the intersection of traditional authority and state authority, of outside interference with traditional authority, indeed, of state authority trumping traditional authority. State politics come in, intertwined with gate politics, causing more conflict and a breakdown in social and political order.

NOTES

1. As I wrote in Chapter Two, while the *tindanas* have not had a "secular political" role, they did sanction the use of land. And as members of the autochthonous people, they preceded the chiefs who were created by the conquerors.
2. As detailed in Chapter One.
3. The Regent of Yendi, now Yo-Na, was raised a Catholic, converted to Islam.
4. Zohe is a village adjacent to Yendi.
5. This for example is the problem of the Konkomba, who are separate from but managed by the Dagomba.

CONCLUSION

This book chronicles the journey of a generation of Dagomba from northern to southern Ghana, from somewhat powerless positions vis-à-vis the state to elite status, examining their life experiences and how they got there. They are 1.5ers, a generation in between, who were born and bred in Dagbon, went to secondary school, and from there to professional training. They are highly accomplished, and with such resources, they have become patrons in the Dagomba community. Their social evolution is framed by place—the place they hail from, the place where they have relocated.

Place, a space with meaning, is both container of and participant in activities. This story brings the significance of place to the fore. It reveals the bonding of a cohort of people, the Dagomba bridge generation, to that place, to its people and its social practices, indeed bonding to that place *through* social practices. The hallmark of attachment to places is the affect, the emotion and feeling, that individuals and groups associate with them, such as childhood haunts. Globally, places are bridges to the past that provide continuity. This is true for the Dagomba 1.5ers, even as they have moved far away and live very different lives, as evidenced by their continuing involvement in home events and institutions, and the help they provide.

I have explored spatial location, its attachments and disjunctures, as newly elite Dagomba relocate from "home of origin" in the north across space and levels of development to their "home of adoption" in the south. I've explored the materiality and the sociability of what's been left behind, what is missed, what has been borrowed, what has been modified, what has been newly devised, as this elite group have longed for anchors of old in re-fashioning their lives in a very different place. Indeed, they have moved to a place that is a world apart from their hometown area. While socially and spatially distant from one another, Accra and the northern hometown are the two poles of this translocal Dagomba community, its social and spatial anchors. Their social and economic links with the home area contribute to the development of community both among themselves and with those "at home." They also enable the Dagomba 1.5ers to switch identities in different situations.

The place Dagbon, the hometown region, is the diasporic elite Dagombas' anchor and core to their place attachment. It is there that their kin groups, and their gates, are based. It is there that traditions are anchored in place. Some were inscribed in the compound, such as the togetherness of offspring, no matter who the mother is. This new elite grew up in the bosom of Dagomba custom, where fathers had multiple wives and little distinction was made between full- and half-siblings. Childhood memories are salient. What is remembered is inscribed in symbols and rituals, cultural rhetoric and social relationships. It takes root in narratives, engagements, objects and places. Some of the new elite carry these along with them to their new homes.

There are the northern shrines that continue to attract adherents, whose locales are sacred. There is the king, the Ya-Na, seemingly crucial to the coherence of the Dagomba people, to whom many express attachment, whose skin is established in Yendi, and who in his very being represents the place as well as the culture. Chieftaincy is an anchor in social and physical space and time, a social element that both reproduces and transforms the socio-economic environment of the respective communities. The Dagomba king's palace is the locale for the celebration of many customs.

In a very real sense, these Dagomba are a bridge: culturally, between the norms and values of the north and those of the south; socially, for a new generation of northerners to whom they act as an actual avenue for migration from one place to another; and spatially, as their lives span these physically separate locales. They have achieved their success in less than one generation. They have become "patrons" to their northern "clients," their less-accomplished brothers and sisters resident in the northern home area. The region's rate of illiteracy is 80 percent. The patrons are literate and articulate. They have education, professional standing and money, all of which has afforded them, living in Accra, greater power and influence in the affairs of the traditional state of Dagbon.

One area that they have had perhaps undue influence is in the campaigns for king and chiefs. Dagomba attachment to their northern origin is evidenced in their attachment to its king, who in his very being represents the place. Throughout the preceding chapters, I have referred to the murder of the Ya-Na in Yendi in 2002; this tragedy did not emerge out of nowhere. There were months if not years of build-up, based upon the Andani-Abudu rivalry and varying interpretation of rules of chiefly rituals and succession. In bygone times, decisions affecting Dagbon were made by the Ya-Na and his local council. Over the years, there were changes.

The 1930 Constitution, drawn up at the behest of the British administration, introduced the role of principal subordinate chiefs and the Yendi elders. And as Staniland (1975) has shown, the "traditional" criteria qualifying men for office (age and seniority), as opposed to education and adaptability, lead to tensions regarding the rules of office holding: "who was qualified to become king; who was responsible for selecting the king; and how power was distributed within the kingdom" (Staniland 1975, 106). In 1948, shortly before the death of the (Andani) king, an anonymous petition was presented to the British Chief Commissioner asking that the Constitution be amended so that the educated have a greater role to play in the selection of the king. In so doing, they took away the rule "that kings were chosen, after divination, by a small committee of elders" (Staniland 1975: 122).

By March 2002, passions ran high and some were willing to kill the king. By all accounts, the Dagomba patrons, the in-between generation who live afar, lit the match that sparked the murder of the Ya-Na and bankrolled the on-going anxiety and disquiet. This highlighted the "gated-ness" of Dagbon and the Dagomba elite, further crippling Dagomba coherence.

As I have shown in this book, those unhappy with succession would try to go through successive new governments, petitioning in Accra, so that the Dagomba elite there became important. By all accounts, the 2002 tragedy was fueled by Dagomba patrons living hundreds of miles south in the capital city, Accra. They were so drawn in by local concerns, that some were even willing to support the murder of their king. All of these elite men were born, bred and schooled in the north, but their lives as working adults evolved in the south. Highly educated, professionally trained, cosmopolitan in every sense, they continue to care greatly about life and institutions in the out-of-the-way "insignificant" place from which they hail. Distance intensifies ties and tensions, and fuels misinformation. In southern Ghana, they self-identify as a diaspora, form and maintain among themselves networks of sociality and community, feel connected to the homeland in the north, and enjoy preeminence. Their diaspora is both a coherent social unit by itself and one node in a network of mutual obligation and responsibility that ties it to the north. Like southern Ghanaians who revere their hometowns, the Dagomba patrons plan to return to theirs, to family houses or houses that they themselves have built.

It was in the late 1800s that a rotation was put into place between the two gates for succession to the kingship. But how to interpret the rotation, that has been a problem. Dagomba at home and away pay considerable attention to the succession, because they believe that community prosperity correlates with the gate in power: the chieftaincy's social, economic and political importance enables groups aligned with the ruling gate to benefit from its political alliance with the Ghanaian State. The state, in turn, has over the years been pulled into the struggle, as judge of legitimacy (as in the de-skinning in 1974 of Ya-Na Mahamadu), investigator (the Wuaku Commission, 2002), mediator (the High Court case against fifteen Abudus, 2012), or guarantor of security (the continuing military presence by the palace in Yendi). The three days of chaos in 2002 culminating in the murder was the latest salvo in a dynastic rivalry that has been going on for decades, as both sides have sought legitimacy for its position.

At heart, proper procedure must be followed. Rituals matter. Who is installed as Ya-Na matters socially, economically and politically. But who decides what is "proper"? The Europeans invented traditions for the local people. They brought new ideas and practices—reinvention of Dagomba tradition—such as the creation of the (British-initiated) Constitution and the 1948 Committee for selecting a new Ya-Na. Depending upon their position, for example vis-à-vis a new king, people interpret the rule of gate rotation in different ways, question whether there must be a ban on drumming till the Ya-Na is buried, wonder whether a deposed Ya-Na receives a royal funeral. The people take tradition seriously, but as the roiling conflicts over chieftaincy have made clear, they do not all interpret tradition in the same way. Much of the time, their interpretation of custom is political—both local and national, societal and state.

We must also consider the intersection of traditional authority and state authority, of outside *and internal* interference with traditional authority, indeed, of state authority often trumping traditional authority. Many in the north, including the chiefs, feel left out. "All of our speakers are in Accra. They will not listen to us here . . . There's no respect" (Karaga-Na November 13, 2005). In the Dagomba Kingdom, chieftaincy is both conservative and progressive—conservative in that it holds onto traditions, progressive in the manner of succession to ever-higher skins. Moreover, chieftaincy is the heart of governance in this part of the country where throughout history the state has been largely absent. It is also a chiefly system that is complicated and prone to problems, because of confusion internal to the system and also interference from outside.

Two months after the burial of Ya-Na Yakubu Andani in 2006, I asked the newly enskinned regent if things were settling down. "It's taking too long—because of the politicians . . . All this conflict in the North—it's because of manipulation by politicians" (June 24, 2008). Walter Kudzodzi of IRIN news reported on the 2002 conflict and assassination. "People are making money out of conflict situations," he observed, "therefore they don't want them to end" (June 7, 2006). The conflict lead to a break down in order, some were shot into power, and they then took control of the resources. And of course gate politics came into play, especially given the media-savvy Accra-based Dagomba elite.

This elite are the 1.5ers, the patrons. They may live at a distance, but their attachment to the homeland, and to gate, is palpable and intense, made even more so by the death of the King. As power brokers, they have exerted influence in Dagbon. Their ultimate influence has been on the succession to chieftaincy.

The opportunities for this generation when they were growing up and coming of age were complicated if not adversely affected by their background and place of origin. Place matters in term of opportunity—for school, work and professional networking. These people I got to know so well were members of the first generation to attend secondary school once it had opened in the north—opening the door to greater life opportunities for northerners. Their access was bolstered by personal family elements, by intelligence, by grit and talent, and by the determination at various times and various levels of the state to better incorporate northerners. Some say, how can education matter so much? Surely there must be other elements at play. At the time, it was a ticket to advance, in part because so few could take advantage of it, in part because society at large wanted to incorporate northerners. Thus I have dwelt on serendipity, on the accident that opened the door to education and professional accomplishment. There have been supportive family members, friends, even strangers, who made it possible. Some would say that education, even as it is crucially important, has also contributed to government interference—chieftaincy corrupted by the educated elite, as they have used their money and social status to sway the local populace.

The south as "place" has provided exposure to different values and behaviors, tastes and statuses, houses and neighborhoods, social and material realities. These patrons left the round, mud-and-wattle hut behind, settling in Accra in suburban homes. They acquired the trappings of Western materiality. The new spaces have enabled new activities and behaviors, and they have helped enculturate the residents into the new social order. But the spaces they built and live in, while different from those of their childhoods, encapsulate traditions that they brought along—traditions of sociality, of observance, of items of material culture. Their structured practices are indicators of a new socio-physical space; they symbolize a hybrid version of modernity, in the design of their homes, the spaces they inhabit, their daily activities, how they eat, dress, socialize.

It was the interactive grounding that helped fashion them into a powerful bloc. The remarkable socio-cultural *and* physical journey of this group of men (and a few women) was part of the process that made them into high achievers and a new elite. They became bicultural and multilingual, as they have easily shuttled back and forth between two very different material and social existences, identifying with Western and home cultures according to the situation. While they live graciously in the south, they hold onto the north: "You don't want to forget your roots," one of them told me.

Coming from an environment that *still* suffers discrimination by southerners, whose residents were not encouraged to pursue Western education let alone training in the educated professions, where poverty and illiteracy have been the norm, and, as they often pointed out to me, their access to opportunities was often accidental, their accomplishments are remarkable. As I wrote at the end of Chapter Four, neither access to education nor to *professional* occupations was a given. But once they accessed both, they ran with them.

Both Andani and Abudu left the north, education in hand, progressed to higher training, and they became a new elite. They became patrons to those less fortunate—who are not educated, whose opportunities are limited. They have become leaders by remote control—using tools gained through education and social connections, pulling strings from afar, to manipulate politics at home. They dictate and advise on issues of state politics (who to vote for) and tradition (concerns of chieftaincy); they are listened to and followed by those left behind. They are sought out in Accra by migrants from the north, for help in accessing school and work.

When I began this research, I did not intend to probe the death of Ya-Na Yakubu Andani II. I tried to avoid discussion of the event, because there was so much emotional baggage and associated drama. When I first sat down with one of the men in late 2005, our conversation became tense. I found myself backed into a corner, even as I had no dog in this fight. Another man I approached I assured I did not come to see to talk about the Yendi tragedy. He said, why not? It matters. We should talk about it. He then provided his own whitewash: Yendi is his hometown, and he said, "it has been very peaceful for the last 3 years!"

Over the months and years, what became clear to me was just how raw the Abudu-Andani breach continued to be, how involved the patrons were, and how salient chieftaincy still is. One might say that the death (murder) of the king further underscored gate loyalty but also peoples' ties to the place. This became particularly crucial for the educated elite who no longer lived in that place but remained tied to it socially, politically, and emotionally.

For many, there is clearly a role for the traditional authorities, just as development of the north is considered by most to be the role of the state. Traditional governance operates alongside the state; while parallel they interconnect. There is an intersection of the two that has yet to be figured out. Many believe, for example, that had the state stayed out of the Yendi confusion, the indigenous leaders would have come to a resolution. Politicians and other modern professionals believe that the chiefs, throughout the country, need to be educated and trained in how to be a leader.

One aspect of significance to this story of the making of a new elite caught in between is not unique, insofar as globalization continues to spin people across space, tying together seemingly disconnected places through the people who inhabit them and incorporate multiple attachments. In fact, the Dagbon case is a metaphor for other situations of migrants with conflicting loyalties, caught between two places and two social systems or more.

I used the meme of transnationalism in characterizing the vast difference between the area where the Dagomba bridge generation was reared and where they ultimately settled. This raises a broader question: is there such a group of transmigrants, domestic or international, who can socialize their children into such ties? Is transmigrant/transnational identity generation-limited? The men and women I asked about their children's ties to or interest in Dagbon generally shrugged. If significant extended family members no longer live in Dagbon, many stopped taking their children along to visit. When the 1.5er spouse does not speak Dagbani, it is not a given that the offspring will. Unless there is a continuing cycle of migration of the sort I have described in this book, development of the hometown is not a given either. Who will play the role of patrons to the less fortunate? This is no less true in developing areas elsewhere in the world.

The patrons today to some extent play the role of the voluntary associations so popular during the first generation following Independence. Whether traditional or modern (the monikers of the time), they helped incorporate newcomers into urban ways, helping with places to live and job prospects. This is relevant to what Simone refers to as "worlding" (2001): distinct African societies have used the transformation of cities or creation of new ones according to their "'own'" objectives (2001, 19). I would argue that different populations would similarly use the city in different ways, adapting what works. Just as urbanization may have been grafted onto inhospitable territories, the same could be said for people—whether spatial or social. It has always been about opportunities and networks. As with the importance of the urban-rural anchor so evident in the lives of the Dagomba patrons, so we see that "developments in cities enabled the rural areas to produce and organize themselves in different ways" (Ibid., 20).

The ways in which this "urbanization for engagement" was accomplished and manifested varied in different settings and time periods according to the degree and kind of urbanization that proceeded colonialism. It varied as well with the different ways in which distinct African societies used the creation of new cities and/or the transformation of precolonial ones for their "own" objectives, however diffuse, coherent, varied, or contradictory they might have been. There is a process of urban identity making and exchange—it is true for the place, it is true for the people. The city is engaged to reach and operate at the level of the "world." Some become cosmopolitans in so doing. The urban and rural are parallel to the international circuit, with exchanges and learning and adapting. One question is, who belongs? In the case of the Dagomba patrons, as they have become successful, they help in the adaptation of others. They have, in Simone's words, been able to "switch gears" (2001).

EPILOGUE

In 2003, President John Kufour constituted a Committee of Eminent Chiefs, comprising four prominent Ghanaian kings: led by Otumfuo Osei Tutu II, Ashanti King, the other members were the Paramount Chief of the Gonja Traditional Area, Yagbonwura Tuntumba Boresa Sulemana Jakpa I, and the Paramount Chief of the Mamprugu Traditional Area, the Nayiri Na Bohugu Abdulai Mahami Sheriga. The president charged them with the responsibility of finding a durable solution to the chieftaincy dispute in Dagbon. After three years of negotiation and deliberation by representatives of the two feuding gates, they signed a Roadmap to Peace on March 30, 2006.

> The "Roadmap to Peace" enumerated five major benchmarks in the peace building process. These include the burial of the late Ya Na Andani II; the installation of the regent of the late king; the performance of the funeral of the deposed Ya-Na, Mahamadu Abdulai IV; the performance of the funeral of Ya-Na Yakubu Andani II; and finally, the selection and enskinment of a new Ya-Na for Dagbon. Eight years after the signing of the roadmap only the first two proposals have been implemented with the remaining being shelved due to continuing disagreement between the two factions. (Tonah 2012, 10)

April 2006, Yendi. The deceased Ya-Na Yakubu Andani II is buried. There is no royal funeral. Ten days later, his eldest son Kampakuya-Na is formally installed as Regent of Dagbon. The Gbonlana remains as the titular head of the Abudu contingent, a shadow regent, living in the home of his *mbadugu* (linguist) Alhaji Idi.

February 2019. The person enskinned (enthroned) is Ya-Na Mahama Abukari II, an Andani, formerly Yo-Na of Savelugu. The new chief of Savelugu is the former Regent of Dagbon, the Kampakuya-Na, whose new title is Yo-Na Andani Yakubu Abdulai IV. He was enskinned February 28, 2019. The new chief of Mion is the former Gbonlana, the Abudu Regent. The first son of the late Ya-Na Mahamadu Abdulai IV, he is now Mion-Lana Abdulai Mahamadu, effective Sunday March 3, 2019.

How did this come about after an almost seventeen-year collapse in inter-gate dealings? In 2003, then-president John Kufuor set up a Committee of Eminent Chiefs (CEC) to help create a path to peace. The CEC's immediate charge was to resolve the disputes relating to the performance of the traditional rituals necessary for the settlement of the Yendi conflict, primarily the burial of Ya-Na Yakubu Andani II and the funerals of the two deceased kings. In consultation with the two gates, on March 30, 2006 the CEC drew-up and signed a "Roadmap to Peace" (Aganah 2019).

There were five benchmarks to its success:

1. burial of the late Ya-Na Yakubu Andani II;
2. installation of the Regent of Dagbon, Kampakuya-Na;
3. performance of the royal funeral of the deposed Ya-Na Mahamadu Abdulai IV;
4. performance of the royal funeral of Na Yakubu Andani II; and
5. final selection and installation of the new Ya-Na.

The burial of the late Ya-Na Yakubu Andani II and installation of his son, Kampakuya-Na Abudulai Andani as regent, supervised by the CEC, occurred on April 21, 2006, respectively, thereby realizing the first two benchmarks in the roadmap. The CEC and the two gates reached a "Final Peace Agreement" on November 18, 2007 to resolve the challenges that arose in relation to the implementation of the Roadmap to Peace. "The implementation of the remaining benchmarks, however, met several challenges as the rival gates failed to agree on exact modalities" (Aganah 2019, 157). There was a continuing disagreement between the gates on the performance of the final funeral rites of the late Ya-Na Mahamadu Abudulai. Moreover, after the change in government in 2008, the investigation of Yendi massacre was re-started and fifteen people were indicted for the murder. The government was not able to make the case against those accused and all were acquitted and discharged on March 29, 2011 by an Accra Fast Track High Court.

On November 30, 2018, representatives of the royal Abudu and Andani gates met at the Manhyia Palace in Kumase and agreed on a final peace agreement. The signatories pledged to "encourage their supporters to continue to keep the peace" (Final Peace Agreement Statement, issued by the Committee of Eminent Kings of his Majesty Otumfuo Osei Tutu II, Yagbonwura Sulemana Jakpa and Nayiri Mahami Abdulai Na Bohagu November 2018). The agreement specified the guidelines for the performance of the funerals of the two deceased paramount chiefs, and the

Figure 8.1. Ya-Na Abubakari Mahama II (Mohammed Adam Gariba).

election of a new Ya-Na. Although Na Yakubu was Andani, mediators made either gate eligible because Yakubu Andani did not die a natural death. To pave the way for a future royal position, the Abudu Regent was installed as the new Regent of Dagbon, Friday December 14, 2018.

The funeral of Ya-Na Mahamadu Abdulai IV took place December 14–28, 2018; the Abudu Royal Gate was granted permission to perform the final funeral rites at the Gbewaa Palace. The Andani Royal Gate then performed the funeral of the late Ya-Na Yakubu Andani II from January 4–18, 2019 also at Gbewaa Palace. On Friday January 18, 2019, the Dagomba kingmakers consulted the Dagbon oracles. Apparently with the support of the non-partisan kingmaker the Kuga-Na, they settled on the elderly Yo-Na Abubakari Mahama, chief of Savelugu, son of Mahama II and uncle to Yakubu Andani II. His formal name is now Ya-Na Abukari Mahama II.

The new Ya-Na officially enskinned the former Kampakuya-Na on February 28, 2019 as Yo-Na Andani Yakubu Abdulai V, chief of Savelugu. The first son of the late Ya-Na Mahamadu Abdulai IV, who had been an unofficial shadow regent to the Abudu and who was officially enskinned as Regent of Dagbon in December 2018, was then enskinned as Mion-Lana[1] Abdulai Mahamadu, effective Sunday March 3, 2019.

Thus, the two former competitors were both given gate skins—Savelugu and Mion—both of which provide eligibility for the Yendi kingship. As Mohammed Mumuni, former Minister of Foreign Affairs, observed to me, nobody got everything, but everybody got something.

NOTE

1. Mion and Savelugu are two of the three towns, the third Karaga, that are gates to the Yendi kingship.

GLOSSARY

Bugum, the Fire Festival

Damba, the celebration of the birth of the Prophet Mohammed

Hajj, pilgrimage

Id al Adha, the second of Islam's two official holidays, following the conclusion of Ramadan

Id il Fitr, the first of Islam's two official holidays, which marks the ending of Ramadan

Kampakuya-Na, the Regent of the Dagomba from 2006 until 2019

Kayayi, a porter, most often a girl who has gone south to work

Kuga-na, the kingmaker

Lana, owner, as in Mion Lana, Mion owner of the skin, Gbonlana, the owner of Regent skin Gbonlana

Luna, luntse, drummer historians

makaranta, Quranic school

Na, chief

Nachin na, chief of the youth

Nam, skin, chieftaincy

Salla, the celebration the day after Ramadan concludes

Tindana (*tindamba*, pl.), custodian of the land, of the earth shrine

Ya-Na, king of the Dagomba

Yo-Na, chief of Savelugu

Zakyi, the youth

Zong, a large round ante-chamber in the compound

REFERENCES

Abdul-Hamid, Mustapha. 2011. *Abibisem: Journal of African Culture & Civilisation*, 4: 47–62.
Abdulai, Abdul-Gafaru. 2012. "State Elites and the Politics of Regional Inequality in Ghana" Ph.D. dissertation. Manchester, UK: University of Manchester.
Abdulai, Abdul-Gafaru, and David Hulme. 2015. "The Politics of Regional Inequality in Ghana: State Elites, Donors and PRSPs." *Development Policy Review* 33 (5): 529–53.
Abotchie, C., A. Awedoba, and I. K. Odotei. 2006. "Perceptions on Chieftaincy" In *Chieftaincy in Ghana: Culture, Governance and Development*, edited by I. K. Odotei and A. Awedoba, 103–144. Accra: Sub-Saharan.
Acquah, Ione. 1972. *Accra Survey: A Social Survey of the Capital of Ghana, Formerly Called the Gold Coast*. Accra: Ghana UP.
Adusah-Karikari, Augustina, and Frank Louis Kwaku Ohemeng. 2014. "Representative Bureaucracy in the Public Service? A Critical Analysis of the Challenges Confronting Women in the Civil Service of Ghana." *International Journal of Public Administration* 37 (9): 568–80.
Aganah, Gamel Mathew Abotiyane. 2019. *State-Society Collaboration in Peacebuilding in Northern Ghana*. Ph.D. dissertation. Tokyo: National Graduate Institute for Policy Studies (GRIPS).
Agbodeka, Francis. 1972. "Sir Gordon Guggisberg's Contribution to the Development of the Gold Coast, 1919–27." *Transactions of the Historical Society of Ghana* 13 (1): 51–64.
———. 1971. *African Politics and British Policy in the Gold Coast, 1868–1900*. London: Longman.
Agyekum, George, ed. 2002. *Yendi Chieftaincy Trials of 1987: A Clash between State and Traditional Norms*. Accra: Justice Trust Publications.
Ahorsu, Ken. 2014. "A Poststructuralist Approach to the Dagbon Chieftaincy Crisis in Northern Ghana." *African Conflict and Peacebuilding Review* 4 (1): 95–119.
Ahorsu, Ken, and Boni Yao Gebe. 2011. *Governance and Security in Ghana: The Dagbon Chieftaincy Crisis*. Accra: WACSI.
Akwetey, E. O. 1996. "Ghana: Violent Ethno-Political Conflicts and the Democratic Challenge." In *Challenges to the Nation-State in Africa*, edited by A. O. Olukoshi and L. Laakso, 102–35. Uppsala: Nordiska Afrikainstitutet.

Akyeampong, A. K. 2006. "Extending Basic Education to Out-of-School Children in Northern Ghana." In *Education for All and Multigrade Teaching*, edited by A. W. Little, 215–38. New York: Springer.

Altman, Irwin, and Setha M Low, eds. 1992. *Place Attachment*. New York: Plenum Press.

Al-Hassan, Abubakr. 1980. *The Impact of Modernization on the Traditional Structure of Settlements in Northern Ghana 1400–1980*. Ph.D. dissertation. Copenhagen: University of Copenhagen.

Aluizah, Amasaba Abdul-Yakeem. 2006. "Kayaye: The Menace of Our Time." *The Pen* 1 (10).

Antoine, Adrien. 1985. *The Politics of Rice Farming in Dagbon, 1972–1979*. Ph.D. dissertation. London: University of London, SOAS.

Appadurai, Arjun. 1996. *Modernity at Large: Cultural Dimensions of Globalization*. Minneapolis: University of Minnesota Press.

Appiah, Kwame Anthony. 2006. *Cosmopolitanism: Ethics in a World of Strangers*. New York: WW Norton.

———. 1992. *In My Father's House: Africa in the Philosophy of Culture*. Oxford: Oxford University Press.

Arce, Alberto, and Norman Long, eds. 2000. *Anthropology, Development and Modernities: Exploring Discourses, Counter-Tendencies and Violence*. New York: Routledge.

Arhin, Kwame. 1985. *Traditional Rule in Ghana: Past and Present*. Accra: Sedco Publishing.

Asenso-Okyere, W. K., K. A. Twum-Baah, Adams Kasanga, Jacqueline Anum, and Claus Portner. 2000. *Ghana Living Standards Survey*. Report of the Fourth Round (GLSS4). Accra: Government of Ghana.

Awedoba, A. K. 2009. *An Ethnographic Study of Northern Ghanaian Conflicts: Towards a Sustainable Peace: Key Aspects of Past, Present and Impending Conflicts in Northern Ghana*. Accra: Sub-Saharan Publishers.

Awumbila, Mariama, and Elizabeth Ardayfio-Schandorf. 2008. "Gendered Poverty, Migration and Livelihood Strategies of Female Porters in Accra, Ghana." *Norsk Geografisk Tidsskrift* 62 (3): 171–79.

Bachelard, Gaston. 1964. *The Poetics of Space: The Classic Look at How We Experience Intimate Places*. Boston: Beacon Press.

Bahloul, Joele. 1996. *The Architecture of Memory: A Jewish-Muslim Household in Colonial Algeria, 1937–1962*. Cambridge: Cambridge University Press.

Basch, Linda, Nina Glick Schiller, and Cristina Szanton Blanc. 1994. *Nations Unbound: Transnational Projects, Postcolonial Predicaments, and Deterritorialized Nation-States*. Langhorne, PA: Gordon and Breach.

Bening, R. B. 1990. *A History of Education in Northern Ghana*. Accra: Ghana Universities.

———. 1983. "The Administrative Areas of Northern Ghana, 1898–1951." *Bulletin de PLFAN* 45 (3–4): 325–56.

———. 1977. "Administration and Development in Northern Ghana 1898–1931." *Ghana Social Science Journal* 4 (2): 58–76.

———. 1975. "Colonial Development Policy in Northern Ghana, 1898–1950." *Bulletin of the Ghana Geographical Association* 17:65–79.

Bernardo Hernández, M. Carmen Hidalgo, M. Esther Salazar-Laplace, and Stephany Hess. 2007. "Place Attachment and Place Identity in Natives and Non-natives." *Journal of Environmental Psychology* 27 (4): 310–19.

Birmingham, Walter, I. Neustadt, and E. N. Omaboe. 1967. *A Study of Contemporary Ghana: Some Aspects of Social Structure*. Evanston, IL: Northwestern University Press.

———. 1966. *A Study of Contemporary Ghana: The Economy of Ghana*. Vol 1. London: Geo Allen & Unwin.

Blench, Roger. 2012. "Aardvarks Go Shopping: Dagomba Concepts Of Living Things." Retrieved October 5, 2017 from www.rogerblench.info/Ethnoscience/Animals/General/Dagbani percent20living percent20things.pdf.

Blench, Roger, and Mallam Dendo. 2004. "Cultural and Biological Interactions in the Savanna Woodlands of Northern Ghana: Sacred Forests and Management of Trees." Trees, Rain and Politics in Africa. Oxford University. To be included in proceedings edited by Michael Sheridan and Celia Nyamweru. Retrieved April 26, 2015 from http://rb.rowbory.co.uk/Ethnoscience/Plants/Trees/Oxford percent20paper percent202004.pdf.

Blier, Suzanne Preston. 2004. "African Creation Myths as Political Strategy." *African Arts* 37 (1): 38–45, 94.

Bolaji, M. H. A. 2016. "Beneath Politicization: the Unacknowledged Constitutional Crisis in the Dagbon Succession Conflict in Ghana." *The Journal of Legal Pluralism and Unofficial Law* 48 (2): 273–301.

Bourdieu, Pierre. 1984. *Distinction: A Social Critique of the Judgement of Taste*, trans R. Nice. Cambridge, MA: Harvard University Press.

Boyd, A. 1962. *Chinese Architecture and Town Planning: 1500 BC – AD 1911*. Chicago: University of Chicago Press.

Brettell, Caroline. 2016. "Perspectives on Migration Theory—Anthropology." In *International Handbook of Migration and Population Distribution*, V. 6, edited by Michael J. White, 41–67. Dordrecht: Springer Science+Business Media.

Brown, Barbara, Douglas D. Perkins, and Graham Brown. 2003. "Place Attachment in a Revitalizing Neighborhood: Individual and Block Levels of Analysis." *Journal of Environmental Psychology* 23: 259–71.

Brukum, N. J. K. 2003. "The Voices of the Elite in Northern Ghana, 1918–1938." *Transactions of the Historical Society of Ghana*, New Series 7: 271–81.

———. 1998. "Underdevelopment and the Dilemma of Independence: Northern Ghana in Nationalist Politics, 1946–1956." *Research Review*, New Series 14 (1): 16–32.

Buchli, Victor. 2002. "Architecture and the Domestic Sphere." In *The Material Culture Reader*. edited by V. Buchli, 207–36. Oxford: Berg.

Cammaert, Jessica. 2016. *Undesirable Practices: Women, Children, and the Politics of the Body in Northern Ghana, 1930–1972*. Lincoln: University of Nebraska Press.

Cardinall, A. W. 1921. "Customs at Death of King of Dagomba." *Man* 21: 89–91.

———. 1920. *The Natives of the Northern Territories of the Gold Coast: Their Customs, Religion and Folklore*. New York: Negro Universities Press.

Carter, Donald. 2003. "Preface. New African Diasporas." In *New African Diasporas*, edited by Khalid Koser, ix–xix. London: Routledge.

Chan, Sucheng. 2006. *The Vietnamese American 1.5 Generation: Stories of War, Revolution, Flight, and New Beginnings*. Philadelphia: Temple University Press.

Chawla, Louise. 1992. "Childhood Place Attachments" In *Place Attachment*, edited by I. Altman and S. Low, 63–86. New York: Plenum Press.

Chernoff, John Miller. 1979. *African Rhythm and African Sensibility: Aesthetics and Social Action in African Musical Idioms*. Chicago: University of Chicago Press.

Claridge W. W. 1915. *A History of the Gold Coast and Ashanti*. 2 Vols. London: J. Murray.

Clarke, Alison J. 2001. "The Aesthetics of Social Aspiration." In *Material Culture behind Closed Doors*, edited by D. Miller, 23–45. Oxford: Berg.

Cogneau, Denis, and Sandrine Mesple-Somps. 2008. "Inequality of Opportunity for Income in Five Countries of Africa." *DIAL*. Document de travail DT/2008-04.

Cohen, Abner. 1981. *The Politics of Elite Culture: Explorations in the Dramaturgy of Power in a Modern African Society*. Berkeley: University of California Press.

———. 1969. *Custom and Politics in Urban Africa: A Study of Hausa Migrants in Yoruba Towns*. Berkeley: University of California Press.

Cohen, Robin. 1995. "Rethinking Babylon: Iconoclastic Conceptions of the Diasporic Experience." *New Community* 21 (1):5–18.

Comaroff, Jean and John, eds. 1993. *Modernity and its Malcontents: Ritual and Power in Postcolonial Africa*. Chicago: University of Chicago Press.

Comaroff, Jean and John. 1993. "Introduction." In *Modernity and its Malcontents: Ritual and Power in Postcolonial Africa*, edited by J. Comaroff and J. Comaroff, xi–xxxvii. Chicago: University of Chicago Press.

Coquery-Vidrovitch, Catherine. 1991. "The Process of Urbanisation in Africa: From the Origins to the Beginning of Independence." *African Studies Review* 34 (1): 1–98.

Crook, Richard C. 1986. "Decolonization, the Colonial State, and Chieftaincy in the Gold Coast." *African Affairs* 85 (338): 75–105.

Cuba, Lee, and David M. Hummon. 1993. "A Place to Call Home: Identification with Dwelling, Community, and Region." *Sociological Quarterly* 34 (1): 111–31.

Curtin, Philip, Steven Feierman, Leonard Thompson, and Jan Vansina. 1978. *African History*. Boston: Little, Brown and Company.

Dakubu, M. E. Kropp. 1997. *Korle Meets the Sea: A Sociolinguistic History of Accra*. New York: Oxford University Press.

Daloz, Jean-Pascal. 2003. "'Big Men' in Sub-Saharan Africa: How Elites Accumulate Positions and Resources." *Comparative Sociology* 2 (1): 271–85.

Danico, Mary Yu. 2004. *The 1.5 Generation: Becoming Korean American in Hawaii*. Honolulu: University of Hawaii Press.

Dant, Tim. 2005. *Materiality and Society*. Maidenhead, UK: Open University Press.

———. 1999. *Material Culture in the Social World*. Buckingham, UK: Open University Press.

Darvas, Peter, and David Balwanz. 2014. *Basic Education beyond the Millennium Development Goals in Ghana: How Equity in Service Delivery Affects Educational and Learning Outcomes*. Washington, DC: The World Bank.

De Bruijn, Marjam, Rijk van Dijk and Dick Focken, eds. 2001. *Mobile Africa: Changing Patterns of Movement in Africa and Beyond*. Leiden: Brill.

Der, Benedict G. 2001. "Christian Missions and the Expansion of Western Education in Northern Ghana, 1906–1975." In *Regionalism and Public Policy in Northern Ghana*, edited by Y. Saaka, 107–38. New York: Peter Lang.

Diamond, Larry. 1987. "Class Formation in the Swollen African State." *The Journal of Modern African Studies* 25 (4):567–96.

Dickson, K. B. 1969. *A Historical Geography of Ghana*. Cambridge: Cambridge University Press.

———. 1968. "Background to the Problem of Economic Development in Northern Ghana." *Annals of the Association of American Geographers* 58 (4):686–96.

Donham, Donald. 2002. "On Being Modern in a Capitalist World: Some Conceptual and Comparative Issues." In *Critically Modern: Alternatives, Alterities, Anthropologies*, edited by B. Knauft, 241–57. Bloomington: Indiana University Press.

Drucker-Brown, Susan. 1988–89. "Local Wars in Northern Ghana." *Cambridge Anthropology* 13: 86–106.

Duncan-Johnstone, A., and H. A. Blair. 1930. *Inquiry into the Constitution and Organisation of the Dagbon Kingdom*. Accra: Northern Territory.

Eades, J. S. 1993. *Strangers and Traders: Yoruba Migrants, Markets, and the State in Northern Ghana*. Trenton, NJ: Africa World Press.

Easterly, William. 2009. "How the Millennium Development Goals are Unfair to Africa." *World Development* 37 (1): 26–35.

Eisenstadt, S. N. 2002. "Multiple Modernities." In *Multiple Modernities*, 1–29. New Brunswick: Transaction Publishers.

Ferguson, James. 1999. *Expectations of Modernity: Myths and Meanings of Urban Life on the Zambian Copperbelt*. Berkeley, CA: University of California Press.

Ferguson, Phyllis. 1972. *Islamization in Dagbon: A Study of the Alfanema of Yendi*. Ph.D. dissertation. Cambridge: Newnham College, University of Cambridge.

Ferguson, Phyllis and Ivor Wilks. 1970. "Chiefs, Constitutions and the British in Northern Ghana." In *West African Chiefs: their Changing Status under Colonial*

Rule and Independence, edited by M. Crowder and O. Ikime, 326–69. New York: Africana Publishing Corp.
Forde, Enid. 1968. *The Population of Ghana: A Study of the Spatial Relationships of its Sociocultural and Economic Characteristics*. Studies in Geography, Number 15. Evanston, IL: Northwestern University.
Fried, Marc. 1963. "Grieving for a Lost Home." In *The Urban Condition*, edited by L. J. Duhl, 151–71. New York: Basic Books.
Fuseini, Issahaka, Joseph A. Yaro, and Gerald A. B. Yiran. 2017. "City Profile: Tamale, Ghana" *Cities* 60, Part A: 64–74.
Gergen, Kenneth J. 1994. "The Communal Creation of Meaning." In *The Nature and Ontogenesis of Meaning*, edited by Willis F. Overton and David Stuart Palermo, 19–40. Hillsdale, NJ: Lawrence Erlebaum.
Geschiere, Peter, and Francis Nyamnjoh. 1998. "Witchcraft as an Issue in the 'Politics of Belonging': Democratization and Urban Migrants' Involvement with the Home Village." *African Studies Review* 41 (3):69–91.
Geschiere, Peter, and Josef Gugler. 1998. "The Urban-Rural Connection: Changing Issues of Belonging and Identification." *Africa* 68 (3):309–19.
Giddens, Anthony. 1990. *The Consequences of Modernity*. Stanford: Stanford University Press.
Goody, Jack. 1966. "Circulating Succession Among the Gonja." In *Succession to High Office*, edited by J. Goody, 142–76. Cambridge: Cambridge University Press.
Goody, Jack, and Esther Goody. 1967. "The Circulation of Women and Children in Northern Ghana." *Man*, New Series 2 (2): 226–48.
Graeber, David. 2011. "The Divine Kingship of the Shilluk: On Violence, Utopia, and the Human Condition, or, Elements for an Archaeology of Sovereignty." *HAU* 1 (1):1–62.
———. 2008. "On Cosmopolitan and (Vernacular) Democratic Creativity, or There Never Was a West." In *Anthropology and the New Cosmopolitanism: Rooted, Feminist and Vernacular Perspectives*, edited by P. Werbner, 281–308. Oxford: Berg.
Grant, Richard, and Jan Nijman. 2003. "The Re-Scaling of Uneven Development in Ghana and India." *Tijdschrift voor Economische en Sociale Geografie* 95 (5):467–81.
Grischow, Jeff. 2006. *Shaping Tradition: Civil Society, Community and Development in Colonial Northern Ghana, 1899–1957*. Leiden: Brill.
———. 1998. "Corruptions of Development in the Countryside of the Northern Territories of the Gold Coast, 1927–57." *Journal of Peasant Studies* 26 (1):139–58.
Gugler, Josef. 2002. "The Son of the Hawk Does Not Remain Abroad: The Urban-Rural Connection in Africa." *African Studies Review* 45 (1): 21–41.
Gyimah-Boadi, E. 2009. "Another Step Forward for Ghana." *Journal of Democracy* 20 (2): 138–52.
Haayen, Lisa. 2016. "'My Friends Make Me Who I am': The Social Spaces of Friendship among Second Generation Youth." In *Identity and the Second Gen-*

eration: How Children of Immigrants Find Their Space, edited by F. G. Nibbs and C. B. Brettell, 65–86. Nashville, TN: Vanderbilt University Press.

Hahn, H. P. 2012. "Circulating Objects and the Power of Hybridization as a Localizing Strategy." *Conceptualizing Cultural Hybridization: A Transdisciplinary Approach*, edited by Philipp Wolfgang Stockhammer, 27–42. Berlin: Springer.

Halbwachs, Maurice. 1992. *On Collective Memory*, edited and translated by Lewis A. Coser. Chicago: University of Chicago Press.

Hall, Stuart, in Conversation with Pnina Werbner. 2008. "Cosmopolitanism, Globalization and Diaspora, March 2006." In *Anthropology and the New Cosmopolitanism*, edited by P. Werbner, 345–60. Oxford: Berg.

Hannerz, Ulf. 2005. "Two Faces of Cosmopolitanism: Culture and Politics." *Statsvetenskaplig Tidskrift* 107, 3:199–213.

———. 1996. *Transnational Connections*. New York: Routledge.

Hanson, Kobena T. 2005. "Landscapes of Survival and Escape: Social Networking and Urban Livelihoods in Ghana." *Environment and Planning* A 37:1291–310.

Hidalgo, M. Carmen, and Bernardo Hernandez. 2001. "Place Attachment: Conceptual and Empirical Questions." *Journal of Environmental Psychology* 21:273–81.

Hobsbawm, Eric. 1983. "Introduction: Inventing Traditions." In *The Invention of Tradition*, edited by E. Hobsbawm and T. Ranger, 1–14. Cambridge: Cambridge University Press.

Hodgson, Dorothy L. 2001. "Of Modernity/Modernities, Gender, and Ethnography." In *Gendered Modernities: Ethnographic Perspectives*, edited by D. L. Hodgson, 1–23. New York: Palgrave.

Holloway-Friesen, Holly. 2008. "The Invisible Immigrants: Revealing 1.5 generation Latino Immigrants and their Bicultural Identities." *Higher Education in Review* 5: 37–66.

Iddrisu, Abdulai. 2005. "The Growth of Islamic Learning in Northern Ghana and Its Interaction with Western Secular Education." *Africa Development* XXX (1 & 2): 53–67.

———. 2002. "Between Islamic and Western Secular Education in Ghana: A Progressive Integration Approach." *Journal of Muslim Minority Affairs* 22 (2): 335–50.

IRIN. 2013. "Ghana: Counting the cost of the Dagbon crisis." Retrieved February 8, 2013 from www.irinnews.org/report/42019/ghana-counting-the-cost-of-the-dagbon-crisis.

Issifu, Abdul Karim. 2015. "An Analysis of Conflicts in Ghana: the Case of Dagbon Chieftaincy" *Journal of Pan African Studies* 8, 6: 28+. Retrieved June 27, 2018 from https://go.galegroup.com/ps/i.do?id=GALEpercent7CA44191202 1&sid=googleScholar&v=2.1&it=r&linkaccess=fulltext&issn=0888660 1&p=AONE&sw=w&userGroupName=nysl_ce_syr.

Jacobs, Jane. 1961. *Death and Life of Great American Cities*. New York: Random House.

Jok, Jok Madut, and Sharon Hutchinson. 1999. "Sudan's Prolonged Second Civil War and the Militarization of Nuer and Dinka Ethnic Identities." *African Studies Review* 42 (2): 125–45.

Kanet, Roger E. 1968. "African Youth: The Target of Soviet African Policy." *The Russian Review* 27 (2): 161–75.

Karlstrom, Mikael. 2003. "On the Aesthetics and Dialogics of Power in the Postcolony." *Africa* 73 (1): 57–76.

Kaspin, Deborah. 1993. "Chewa Visions and Revisions of Power: Transformations of the Nyau Dance in Central Malawi." In *Modernity and its Malcontents: Ritual and Power in Postcolonial Africa*, edited by J Comaroff and J Comaroff, 34–57. Chicago: University of Chicago Press.

Kearney, M. 1995. "The Local and the Global: The Anthropology of Globalization and Transnationalism." *Annual Review of Anthropology* 24: 547–565.

Kertzer, David. 1988. *Ritual, Politics and Power*. New Haven: Yale University Press.

Kimble, David. 1963. *A Political History of Ghana: The Rise of Gold Coast Nationalism, 1850–1928*. Oxford: Clarendon Press.

King, Anthony. 1990. *Urbanism, Colonialism and the World Economy: Cultural and Spatial Foundations of the World Urban System*. London: Routledge.

Kirby, Jon P. 2006–07. "Ethnic Conflicts and Democratization New Paths Toward Equilibrium in Northern Ghana." *Transactions of the Historical Society of Ghana* 10: 65–107.

———. 2004. "Mending Structures for Mending Hearts in Dagbon." *TICCS Occasional Papers in Cross-Cultural Studies* 1: 35–45.

———. 2003. "Peacebuilding in Northern Ghana: Cultural Themes and Ethnic Conflict." In *Ghana's North: Research on Culture, Religion, and Politics of Societies in Transition*, edited by F. Kroger and B. Meier, 161–205. Frankfurt: Peter Lang.

Knauft, Bruce. 2002. "Introduction: Critically Modern." In *Critically Modern: Alternatives, Alterities, Anthropologies*, edited by B. Knauft, 1–54. Bloomington: Indiana University Press.

Kuper, Hilda. 1972. "The Language of Sites in the Politics of Space." *American Anthropologist* 74 (3):411–25.

Kwankye, Stephen O. 2012. "Independent North–South Child Migration as a Parental Investment in Northern Ghana." *Population, Space and Place* 18: 535–50.

Ladouceur, Paul. 1979. *Chiefs and Politicians: The Politics of Regionalism in Northern Ghana*. London: Longman Inc.

———. 1972. "The Yendi Chieftaincy Dispute and Ghanaian Politics." *Canadian Journal of African Studies* VI (i): 97–115.

Landé, Carl H. 1977. "The Dyadic Basis of Clientelism." In *Friends, Followers and Factions: A Reader in Political Clientelism*, edited by S. W. Schmidt, 13–37. Berkeley: University of California Press.

Lawrence, Denise. 1992. "Transcendence of Place: The Role of *La Placeta* in Valencia's *Las Fallas*." In *Place Attachment*, edited by I. Altman and S. Low, 211–230. New York: Plenum Press.

Lawrence-Zuniga, Denise, and Deborah Pellow. 2008. "The Self-Consciousness of Placemaking." *Anthropology News* 49 (9): 4–5.

Leichtman, Mara, and Dorothea Schulz. 2012. "Introduction to Special Issue Muslim Cosmopolitanism: Movement, Identity, and Contemporary Reconfigurations." *City and Society* 24 (1): 1–6.

Lentz, Carola. 2020. "Tradition versus Politics: Succession Conflicts in a Chiefdom of North-Western Ghana" In *Elites: Choice, Leadership and Succession*, edited by João de Pina-Cabral and Antónia Pedroso de Lima, 91–112. London: Routledge.

Lentz, Carola. 2006. *Ethnicity and the Making of History in Northern Ghana*. IAI. Edinburgh: Edinburgh University Press.

———. 2000. "'Tradition' versus 'Politics': Succession Conflicts in a Chiefdom in Northwestern Ghana." In *Choice and Leadership in Elite Succession*, edited by Jo˜ao de Pina-Cabral and Ant'onia Pedroso de Lima, 91–112. London: Berg.

———. 1998. "The Chief, the Mine Captain and the Politician: Legitimating Power in Northern Ghana." *Africa* 68 (1):46–67.

———. 1994. "Home, Death and Leadership: Discourses of an Educated Elite from Northwestern Ghana." *Social Anthropology* 2 (2):149–69.

Levtzion, Nehemia. 1968. *Muslims and Chiefs in West Africa. A Study of Islam in the Middle Volta Basin in the Pre-colonial Period*. Oxford: Clarendon Press.

Low, Setha. 2016. *Spatializing Culture: The Ethnography of Space and Place*. London: Routledge.

——— and Irwin Altman. 1992. "Place Attachment: A Conceptual Inquiry" In *Place Attachment*, edited by I. Altman and S. Low, 1–12. New York: Plenum.

Low, Setha M., and Denise Lawrence-Zuniga, eds. 2003. *The Anthropology of Space and Place: Locating Culture*. Malden, MA: Blackwell.

MacGaffey, Wyatt. 2013. *Chiefs, Priests, and Praise-singers: History, Politics, and Land Ownership in Northern Ghana*. Charlottesville, VA: University of Virginia Press.

———. 2010. "The Residue of Colonial Anthropology in the History and Political Discourse of Northern Ghana: Critique and Revision." *History Compass* 8/6: 431–39.

———. 2006–07. "A History of Tamale, 1907–1957 and beyond." *Transactions of the Historical Society of Ghana* New Series 10:109–24.

———. 2006. "Death of a King, Death of a Kingdom? Social Pluralism and Succession to High Office in Dagbon, Northern Ghana." *Journal of Modern African Studies* 44 (1): 79–99.

Mahler, Sarah J. 1998. "Theoretical and Empirical Contributions toward a Research Agenda for Transnationalism." In *Transnationalism from Below: Comparative Urban and Community Research*, 8, edited by Michael Peter Smith and Luis Eduardo Gaurnizo, 64–100. New Brunswick: Transaction.

Manboah-Rockson, Joseph. 2007. "Chiefs in Post-Colonial Ghana: Exploring Different Elements of the Identity, Inequalities and Conflicts Nexus in the Northern Region." *Chieftain: The Journal of Traditional Governance*. Retrieved November 12, 2016 from https://prism.ucalgary.ca/handle/1880/44285.

Manoukian, Madeline. 1951. *Tribes of the Northern Territories of the Gold Coast.* (Ethnographic Survey, West Africa). London: International African Institute.
Massey, Doreen. 1994. *Space, Place, and Gender.* Minneapolis: University of Minnesota Press.
Mauss, Marcel. 1990 [1950]. *The Gift: The Form and Reason for Exchange in Archaic Societies* translated by W. D. Halls. London: Routledge.
Mazzucato, Valentina. 2008. "The Double Engagement: Transnationalism and Integration. Ghanaian Migrants' Lives between Ghana and the Netherlands." *Journal of Ethnic and Migration Studies* 34 (2): 199–216.
McCaskie, T. C. 2008. "Gun Culture in Kumasi." *Africa* 78 (3): 433–54.
———.1983. "Accumulation, Wealth and Belief in Asante History. I. To the Close of the Nineteenth Century." *Africa* 53 (1): 23–43.
———. 1972. "Innovational Eclecticism: The Asante Empire and Europe in the Nineteenth Century." *Comparative Studies in Society and History* 14 (1): 30–45.
McIntyre, Norman. 2006. "Introduction." In *Multiple Dwelling and Tourism: Negotiating Place, Home and Identity*, edited by Norman McIntyre, Daniel R. William and Kevin E. McHugh, 3–31. Oxford: CABI.
McWilliam, H. O. A. 1962. *The Development of Education in Ghana; an Outline.* Accra: Longmans.
Menon, A. G. Krishna. 2001. "Thinking 'Indian' Architecture." In *The Discipline of Architecture*, edited by Andrzej Piotrowski and Julia Robinson, 208–34. Minneapolis MN: University of Minnesota Press.
Middleton, John. 1979. "Home-town: A Study of an Urban Centre in Southern Ghana." *Africa* 49 (3): 246–57.
Miller, Daniel. 2010. *Stuff.* Cambridge: Polity Press.
———. 2005. "Materiality: An Introduction" In *Materiality.* edited by D. Miller, 1–50. Durham, NC: Duke University Press.
Mohan, Giles. 2006. "Embedded Cosmopolitanism and the Politics of Obligation: The Ghanaian Diaspora and Development." *Environment and Planning A* 38 (5): 867–883.
Moore, Henrietta. 1986. *Space, Text and Gender: An Anthropological Study of the Marakwet of Kenya.* New York: Cambridge University Press.
Moran, Erin. 2016. "Legal Spaces: Failed Asylum-Seeking Children in the Irish Homeland" In *Identity and the Second Generation: How Children of Immigrants Find Their Space*, edited by Faith G. Nibbs, and Caroline B. Brettell, 191–204. Nashville, TN: Vanderbilt University Press.
Mudimbe, V. Y. 1988. *The Invention of Africa: Gnosis, Philosophy, and the Order of Knowledge.* Bloomington, IN: University of Indiana Press.
Mumuni, Muhammad. 1975. *Succession to the Nam of Yendi – a Legal Analysis and Critique of the Laws and Customs Relating to the Enskinment of a Ya-Na.* LLM Thesis, University of Ghana.
Nketia, J. H. 1953. "Progress in Gold Coast Education: Transactions Of The Gold Coast & Togoland." *Historical Society* 1 (3): 1–9.

Northcott, H. P., W. C. Giffard, W. C. Anderson, and A. L. Walker. 1899. *Report on the Northern Territories of the Gold Coast*. Intelligence Division: War. London: Her Majesty's Stationery Office.

Nyamnjoh, Francis. 2002. "'A Child is One Person's Only in the Womb': Domestication, Agency and Subjectivity in the Cameroonian Grassfields." In *Postcolonial Subjectivities in Africa*, edited by Richard P. Werbner, 111–38. London: Zed.

Nyamnjoh, Francis, and Michael Rowlands. 1998. "Elite Associations and the Politics of Belonging in Cameroon." *Africa* 68 (3): 320–33.

Oppong, Christine. 1973. *Growing Up in Dagbon*. Accra: Ghana Publishing Corporation.

Orozco, Manuel. 2005. *Diasporas, Development and Transnational Integration: Ghanaians in the US, UK and Germany*. Washington, DC: Institute for the Study of International Migration and Inter-American Dialogue.

Osei-Fosu, A. K. 2008. "The Heavily Indebted Poor Countries (HIPC) Initiative Fund Micro-Credit and Poverty Reduction in Ghana: A Panacea or a Mirage?" *Journal of Science and Technology* (Ghana) 28 (3): 94–102.

Osumanu, Issaka K. 2008. "Private Sector Participation in Urban Water and Sanitation Provision in Ghana: Experiences from the Tamale Metropolitan Area (TMA)." *Environmental Management* 42:102–110.

Owusu-Ansah, David, Abdulai Iddrisu, and Mark Sey. 2013. *Islamic Learning, the State and the Challenges of Education in Ghana*. Trenton, NJ: Africa World Press.

Paintsil, David Allan, and Joseph Coomson. 2002. "Ghana: Dagbon Conflict Costs ¢6bn" *The Chronicle*, November 142 2002. Retrieved June 18, 2019 from https://allafrica.com/stories/200211150621.html.

Patterson, Rubin. 2006. "Transnationalism: Diaspora-Homeland Development." *Social Forces* 84 (4): 1891–907.

Pellow, Deborah. 2016. "Logics of Violence Among the Dagomba in Northern Ghana" In *The Management of Chieftaincy and Ethnic Conflicts in Ghana: Complementary Pathways and Competing Institutions*, edited by Steve Tonah and A. S. Anamzoya, 39–66. Accra: Woeli.

———. 2015. "Multiple Modernities: Kitchens For An African Elite." *Home Cultures* 12 (1): 55–81.

———. 2014. "'Everybody Thinks They Can Build': The Architect as Cultural Intermediary in Ghana." *Architectural Theory Review* 19 (1):56–75.

———. 2012. "Chieftaincy, Collective Interests and the Dagomba New Elite." In *Development, Modernism and Modernity in Africa*, edited by A. Agwuele, 43–61. New York: Routledge.

———. 2011. "Internal Transmigrants: a Dagomba Diaspora." *American Ethnologist* 38 (2): 132–47.

———. 2008 [2003]. *Landlords and Lodgers: Socio-Spatial Organization in an Accra Community*. Chicago: University of Chicago Press.

———. 1992. "Spaces that Teach: Attachment to the African Compound." In *Place Attachment*, edited by I. Altman and S. Low, 187–210. New York: Plenum Press.

———. 1991. "The Power of Space in the Evolution of an Accra Zongo." *Ethnohistory* 38 (4): 31–51.

Piot, Charles. 1999. *Remotely Global: Village Modernities in West Africa*. Chicago: University of Chicago Press.

Plange, Nii-K. 1979. "Underdevelopment in Northern Ghana: Natural Causes or Colonial Capitalism?" *Review of African Economy* 15/16, The Roots of Famine: 4–14.

Pogucki, R. J. H. 1955. *A Survey of Land Tenure in Customary Law of the Protectorate of the Northern Territories. Gold Coast Land Tenure*, Vol I. Accra: Lands Dept.

Prato, Giuliana, ed. 2016. *Beyond Multiculturalism: Views from Anthropology*. London: Routledge.

Prussin, Labelle. 1969. *Architecture in Northern Ghana: A Study of Forms and Functions*. Berkeley: University of California Press.

Quist, Hubert O. 2003. "Secondary Education – a 'Tool' for National Development in Ghana." *Africa Development* xxviii (3 + 4): 186–210.

Raffaeta, Roberta, and Cameron Duff. 2013. "Putting Belonging into Place: Place Experience and Sense of Belonging among Ecuadorian Migrants in an Italian Alpine Region." *City and Society* 25 (3):328–47.

Rapoport, Amos. 1982. *The Meaning of the Built Environment: A Nonverbal Communication Approach*. Beverly Hills, CA: Sage.

Rattray, R. S. 1932. *The Tribes of the Ashanti Hinterland*. Vol. II. Oxford: The Clarendon Press.

Republic of Ghana. 2002. *The Commission of Inquiry (Yendi Events)*. C.I. 36/2002 (Wuaku Commission).

Richter, Roxane, Thomas Flowers, and Elias Bongmba. 2017. *Witchcraft as a Social Diagnosis: Traditional Ghanaian Beliefs and Global Health*. Lanham, MD: Lexington Books.

Rubinstein, Robert L., and Patricia A. Parmelee. 1992. "Attachment to Place and the Representation of the Life Course by the Elderly." In *Place Attachment*, edited by I. Altman and S. Low, 139–63. New York: Plenum Press.

Saaka, Yakubu, ed. 2001. *Regionalism and Public Policy in Northern Ghana*. New York: Peter Lang.

Saaka, Yakubu. 2001a. "Introduction" In *Regionalism and Public Policy in Northern Ghana*, edited by Y. Saaka, 1–11. New York: Peter Lang.

———. 2001b. "North-South Relations and the Colonial Enterprise in Ghana" In *Regionalism and Public Policy in Northern Ghana*, edited by Y. Saaka, 139–52. New York: Peter Lang.

Safran, William. 1991. "Diasporas in Modern Societies: Myths of Homeland and Return." *Diaspora: A Journal of Transnational Studies* 1 (1): 83–99.

Sahlins, Marshall. 2000. "On the Anthropology of Modernity, or, some Triumphs of Culture over Despondency Theory." In *Culture and Sustainable Development in the Pacific*, edited by A. Hooper, 44–61. Canberra: Australian National University Press.

Schatzberg, Michael G. 1993. "Power, Legitimacy and 'Democratisation' in Africa." *Africa* 63 (4):445–61.

Schielke, Samuli. 2012. "Surfaces of Longing, Cosmopolitan Aspiration and Frustration in Egypt." *City and Society* 24 (1): 29–37.

Sefa Dei, George J., and Alireza Asgharzadeh. 2002. "What Is to Be Done? A Look at Some Causes and Consequences of the African Brain Drain." *African Issues* 30 (1):31–36.

Senadza, Bernardin. 2012. "Education Inequality in Ghana: Gender and Spatial Dimensions." *Journal of Economic Studies* 39 (6): 724–39.

Seyire, Augustine. 1968. "Dagomba Traditional Religion" Field Notes: Yendi Project. Report, 9. Legon: Institute of African Studies, University of Ghana and Program of African Studies, Northwestern University.

Shack, William, and Elliot Skinner, eds. 1979. *Strangers in African Societies*. Berkeley: University of California Press.

Sheffer, Gabriel, ed. 1986. *Modern Diasporas in International Politics*. London: Croom Helm.

Shepherd, Andrew, E. Gyimah-Boadi, Sulley Gariba, Sophie Plagerson, and Abdul Wahab Musa. 2004. "Bridging the North South Divide in Ghana." *World Development Report 2006*. Retrieved April 7, 2021 from http://siteresources.worldbank.org/INTWDR2006/Resources/477383-1118673432908/Bridging_the_North_ South_Divide_in_Ghana.pdf.

Sibidow, S. M. 1969. *Background of the Yendi Skin Crisis*. Accra: Yenzow.

Simone, Abdoumalique. 2001. "On the Worlding of African Cities." *African Studies Review* 44 (2):15–41.

"Six Injured in Abudu-Andani Clashes." 2010. *Daily Graphic*, September 8, 2010.

Skinner, David. 1976. "Islam and Education in the Colony and Hinterland of Sierra Leone (1750–1914)." *Canadian Journal of African Studies* 10 (3): 499–520.

Soeters, Sebastian Robert. 2012. *Tamale 1907–1957: Between Colonial Trade and Colonial Chieftainship*. Ph.D. dissertation. University of Leiden.

Sökefeld, Martin. 2006. "Mobilizing in Transnational Space: A Social Movement Approach to the Formation of Diaspora." *Global Networks* 6 (3):265–284.

Songsore, Jacob, Aloysius Denkabe, Charles D. Jebuni, and Steven Ayidiya. 2001. "Challenges of Education in Northern Ghana: A Case for Northern Ghana Education Trust Fund (NETFUND)." In *Regionalism and Public Policy in Northern Ghana*, edited by Y. Saaka, 223–38. New York: Peter Lang.

Sowatey, E. A. 2005. "Small Arms Proliferation and Regional Security in West Africa: The Ghanaian Case." *News from the Nordic Africa Institute* 1: 6–8.

Staniland, Martin. 1975. *The Lions of Dagbon: Political Change in Northern Ghana*. Cambridge: Cambridge University Press.

Sutherland-Addy, Essie. 2002. "Impact Assessment Study of the Girls' Education Programme in Ghana." UNICEF – Ghana.
Swart-Kruger, Jill. 2001. "Children in a South African Squatter Camp Gain and Lose a Voice." In *Growing Up in an Urbanizing World*, edited by L. Chawla, 111–133. London: Routledge.
Tait, David. 1963. "A Sorcery Hunt in Dagomba." *Africa* 33 (2):136–46.
Talton, Benjamin A. 2003. "The Past and Present In Ghana's Ethnic Conflicts: British Colonial Policy And Konkomba Agency, 1930–1951." *Journal of Asian and African Studies* 38 (2–3):192–210.
Tamakloe, E. F. 1931. *A Brief History of the Dagbamba People*. Accra: Government Printer.
Thomas, Roger G. 1974. "Education in Northern Ghana, 1906–1940: A Study In Colonial Paradox." *The International Journal of African Historical Studies* 7 (3): 427–67.
Tonah, Steve. 2012. "The Politicization of a Chieftaincy Conflict: The Case of Dagbon, Northern Ghana." *Nordic Journal of African Studies* 211 (1):1–20.
Totoricaguena, Gloria, ed. 2007. *Opportunity Structures in Diaspora Relations: Comparisons in Contemporary Multilevel Politics of Diaspora and Transnational Identity*. Reno: University of Nevada, Center for Basque Studies.
Tsikata, Dzodzi, and Wayo Seini. 2004. "Identities, Inequalities and Conflicts in Ghana" *Working Paper 5*. CRISE (Centre for Research on Inequality, Human Security and Ethnicity) Queen Elizabeth House, University of Oxford.
Tsing, Anna. 2005. *Friction: An Ethnography of Global Connection*. Princeton: Princeton University Press.
Tufeiru, Ahmed. 2014. "The Nexus of Female Capital and North–South Labor Migration in Ghana: A Potential Remedy from Microfinance." *Journal of Developing Societies* 30 (1): 91–114.
UN Habitat. 2009. Ghana: Tamale City Profile. UN Human Settlements Programme.
Van Den Berg, C. 2007. "The Kayayei: Survival in the City of Accra." MA Thesis. International Development Studies, University of Amsterdam.
van der Geest, Kees. 2011. "North-South Migration in Ghana: What Role for the Environment?" *International Migration*. Retrieved October 9, 2017 from http://onlinelibrary.wiley.com/doi/10.1111/j.1468-2435.2010.00645.x/full.
van Hear, Nicholas. 1982. *Northern Labour and the Development of Capitalist Agriculture in Ghana*. Ph.D. dissertation. Centre of West African Studies, University of Birmingham.
Werbner, Pnina. 1997. "Essentialising Essentialism, Essentialising Silence: Ambivalence and Multiplicity in the Constructions of Racism and Ethnicity." In *Debating Cultural Hybridity: MultiCultural Identities and the Politics of Anti-Racism*, edited by P. Werbner and T. Modood, 226–54. London: Zed Books.
White, Bob W. 1996. "Talk about School: Education and the Colonial Project in French and British Africa (1860–1)." *Comparative Education* 32 (1): 9–25.
Wilks, Ivor. 1975. *Asante in the Nineteenth Century: The Structure and Evolution of a Political Order*. Cambridge University Press.

———. 1965. "A Note on the Early Spread of Islam in Dagomba." *Transactions of the Historical Society of Ghana* 8: 87–98.

———. 1962. "A Medieval Trade Route from the Niger to the Gulf of Guinea" *Journal of African History* iii (2): 337–41.

Winters, C. 1977. "Traditional Urbanism in the north central Sudan." *Annals of the Association of American Geographers* 67 (4): 500–20.

Wipper, Audrey. 1972. "African Women, Fashion, and Scapegoating." *Canadian Journal of African Studies* 6 (2): 329–49.

Works, John A., Jr. 1976. *Pilgrims in a Strange Land: Hausa Communities in Chad*. New York: Columbia University Press. Retrieved April 11, 2021 from world populationreview.com/world-cities/accra-population.

Yakubu, Abdulai. 2005. *The Abudu-Andani Crisis of Dagbon: A Historical and Legal Perspective of the Yendi Skin Affairs*. Accra: MPC Ltd.

Yeboah, Ian. 2001. "Structural Adjustment and Emerging Urban Form in Accra, Ghana." *Africa Today* 47 (2):61–89.

Yeboah, Muriel Adjubi. 2010. "Urban Poverty, Livelihood, and Gender: Perceptions and Experiences of Porters in Accra, Ghana." *Africa Today* 56 (3): 42–60.

INDEX

1.5ers, 11, 12, 14, 17, 67, 70, 89, 90, 93, 94, 95, 109, 128, 141, 164, 165, 168, 172, 184, 186, 187, 199, 220, 220, 242
(*see also* bridge generation)

Abdulai, Dr. A. E., viii, 75, 85–89, 119, 122, 135, 156, 179, 183, 187, 193
Abdulai, Dr. David, 66, 102, 116, 156, 204
  chieftaincy, 217
  peace, 217
Abdulai, "Mopson," viii, 87, 88, 89, 181, 183, 187, 188
Abdulai, Salamatu, 87, 92, 125, 187
  auntie, 122–33, 152
  education, 110, 123–24
Abdulai II, chief of Savelugu, 35, 40, 45–46, 50, 110
Abdulai Mahamadu, xv, 197, 228, 230
Accra, viii–ix, xi, xv, 7, 20, 51, 136, 161
  chieftaincy in, 204, 207, 211–13, 216–18, 223 (*see also* chieftaincy)
  Dagomba and, 5–6, 8–9, 10, 13–14, 16, 23–25, 52, 60, 69, 72, 87, 90, 95, 108, 151, 168, 174, 176, 178, 180–83, 187–88, 191–94, 196–199, 220–22, 224 (*see also* elite: Dagomba)
  economic development and, 30–33, 57, 66, 86, 98

  education, 100–4, 107, 109–110, 112–14, 117–18, 124–25, 152, 153, 157–58, 225 (*see also* education)
  journalism (*see also* Adam, Iliasu: journalism), 140, 143
  memory and, 2–4, 64–65, 67
  modernity of, 170–71, 179 (*see also* modernity)
  politics and, 148–49
  shrines in, 78
  suburban, 175, 178, 224
  urban, 56, 169 (*see also* urban)
  Yendi, 229 (*see also* Yendi)
Accra Mail, 143
  Haruna Atta, 143
Acheampong, General I. K., 55, 146
  rice, 55, 137, 138
Action Aid, 184
  Sunson-Na, 184
Adam, Iliasu, x, 22, 26n3, 43, 68, 89, 110, 112, 114, 143, 190, 191, 193, 212, 217
  education, 117
  journalism, 142
Akropong, 195
African Inland Mission, 92
Akan, 5, 16, 154, 213
Alhassan, Abubakari, x, 116, 156–57, 188
Alhassan, Dr. Abubakari, 62, 103, 116
Alhassan, Dr. Ramatu, 23, 86, 126, 129, 138, 153, 159, 193

Alhassan, Yakubu (MP of Mion), 127
Aliu, Mahama (Vice President), 149, 181, 210
Allassani, J. H., 49
Andani, Alhassan, 74, 83, 86, 88
Andani, Dr., 76, 152
Andani, Yakubu, 49–50, 213, 217–18, 228, 230
Andani, Yakubu "Accountant," 188
Appiah, Anthony Kwame, 12–13, 17
Asante (Ashantis), 6, 70, 207, 228
    empire, 30–31
Asantehene, 12, 163, 207–8, 212
Ashanti (region), 6, 31–33, 36, 57, 65, 96, 101, 105–7, 162
Atta, Haruna, 110, 143, 191, 208
Attachment, 1, 14, 47, 165, 199, 226
    affect and, 5, 220
    home and, 15, 23–24, 26, 63–64, 69, 90, 170, 173, 202, 224 (*see also* diaspora: home; hometown)
    memory and, 3, 4, 27 (*see also* Accra: memory and)
    place, xi, 2, 4, 8, 60, 62, 220–21
"Auntie," 121, 157
Avenor, 194, 197

Baba, Fuseini, 8, 53, 69, 89, 92, 107, 111, 112, 127, 150, 151, 160, 188, 189, 190, 192, 193, 194
Bamini, 122–23
Banvim, 87, 103, 122, 206
    Lana, 205
Basel Mission, 97
Belongingness, 20, 169, 178
Bicultural, 1, 10, 11, 12, 14, 172, 224
"Big Men," xii, 23, 24, 47, 128, 200
Blair, H. A. (District Commissioner), 28, 34
Boforo, Mary, 126, 149, 150, 187–88
Boi-Nai, Vincent (Bishop), ix, 51, 74, 180, 198, 216, 217, 218
Bombande, Ernest, 207

Bossman, William, 134
Braimah, J. A., 99
"Brain drain," 166, 167n3
Bridge, 1, 11, 17, 24, 25, 128, 168, 169, 221
    home, 11, 13
    hometown, 220
Bridge generation, 9, 47, 62, 67–70, 89, 90, 94, 109, 120, 126, 141, 150, 165, 168, 186, 187, 199, 220, 226
British, 6, 13, 26n1, 28, 31, 32, 33, 35, 36, 37, 38, 46, 52, 53, 56, 57, 58, 65, 85, 92, 93, 96, 99, 100, 101, 102, 104, 105, 108, 109, 110, 112, 114, 120, 124, 130, 131, 133, 135, 140, 142, 153, 158, 163, 170, 171
    Chief Commissioner, 44, 184, 222
    colonialism, 25, 29, 30, 31, 32, 34, 35, 37, 41, 49, 52, 85, 96, 97, 98, 105, 170, 181, 222
    housing, 56
    Indirect Rule, 28, 34, 37, 46, 49, 99, 100, 102, 105
    underdevelopment, 57
Broadcasting, 143
Brown, Kusum Tahiro, 152
Bugum, xi, xii, xiii, 23, 24, 69, 72, 211
Busia, K. A., 21, 46, 55, 137, 154
    Progress Party, 47, 50–51

Candler, Reverend A. H., 100
Cantonments, 171
Chamberlain, Joseph, 32–33
Chief(s), xii, xiii, xiv, xv, xvn1, 21, 22, 27, 34, 35, 38, 39, 40–42, 44, 46, 48, 58, 60, 61n7, 61n11, 64, 70, 72, 73–77, 78, 80, 83, 87, 88, 100, 102, 105, 109, 122, 123, 124, 130n1, 130n3, 140, 142, 152, 164, 167, 180, 183, 185, 186, 187, 188, 190, 191, 202n3, 202–209, 212, 216, 217, 228, 229–31
    succession, 1, 2, 14, 29, 42, 43, 44, 47, 48, 49, 59, 61n7, 122,

129, 209, 211, 216, 217, 221, 222, 223, 224
Chieftaincy, xi, 5, 7, 14, 16, 22, 25–29, 33, 36, 37, 38, 39, 40–52, 58, 59, 61n8, 62, 64, 70, 73, 74, 87, 90, 129, 149, 164, 180, 183, 184, 185, 186, 193, 195, 198, 199, 200, 202–09, 211, 212, 216, 221, 223, 224, 225, 228
   conflict, 46, 49, 206
   and development, 41, 206, 208, 216
Christianity, 96, 102, 133n3
CMS (Church Mission Society), 92
Civil service, 133, 150–51
Committee of Eminent Chiefs. X, 163, 211–12, 228, 229
Concerned Citizens of Tamale, 207
CPP (Convention Peoples' Party), 35–36, 49–50, 99, 106, 208
Cordon sanitaire, 104, 170
Cosmopolitan(ism), 13, 15, 18, 19, 20–21, 24, 30, 54, 168, 171–74, 179, 203, 222
Coussey, Mr. Justice Henley
   Coussey Commission, 36
CSIR (Council for Scientific and Industrial Research), 155
Crafts, 139
Curfew, xii, xiii

Da Tchuma Luna, Baba Fuseini, 27, 71
Dabali, Basharu Alhassan, 207
Dagara, 18–19, 172
Dagbon Development Plan, 154
Dagomba Constitution, 28, 44, 50
Dagomba State Council, 50
Daily Graphic, 8, 145
Dakpema, 35, 37–38, 60n3, 79, 82, 163–64, 186–87, 196, 198
Damba, 23–4, 69, 70, 72, 73
Denkyira, 30
Development, 1, 15, 26, 54, 58, 128, 150, 156, 180, 182, 215, 220

   in Acheampong, 55, 137, 146
   chief and, 204
   patrons and, 11, 15, 170, 183, 199
   regulation, 30, 33, 35, 55, 132, 142, 146, 160, 181, 220, 225, 226
   underdevelopment and, 6, 30, 33, 57, 206, 216
   unequal, 25, 29, 30, 57, 96, 102, 132, 135
Diaspora, 15, 23, 24
   1.5 generation, 196, 198, 222
   home, 12
   hometown attachment, 21
Drew, Jane, 158
Drummer, 70, 71, 73, 74, 77
   tom-tom beaters, xiii, xiv, 70, 73, 91
   See also luntse
Dwelling place, 3
Dwellingness, 2, 14

ECOWAS (Economic Community of West African States), 68
Education
   chiefs and, 74, 100, 109, 152, 183, 185, 205, 208–209
   colonial, 6, 25–26, 36, 56, 92, 96–99, 104–105, 131–33
   exclusion, 101–102
   government policy and, 7, 10, 57, 60, 94, 106–107, 111, 127, 129, 136–37, 154, 160–62, 180, 182, 199, 224
   identity and, 12, 14, 16, 22, 110, 215
   Makaranta/Quranic and
   primary, 93, 157, 189
   School for Life
   secondary [including Accra Traaining College, TAMSEC, Achimota, Government Girls Boarding School, Tamale Girls,

Wesley Girls, Accra Academy, Adisadel, Mfantsipim], 101, 107, 113–14, 129, 141, 143, 186, 191
secular, 96, 103, 112
status and, 164–65, 167, 172–73, 183, 202, 221–22
university, 113–14, 140, 143, 151
vocational, 149
Western, 24, 47, 128, 146, 225
women and, 16, 82, 95, 108, 114–15, 120–26, 140, 144, 155, 193
See also Chapter Three
Ejura, 101
Elite, viii, x, xi, 6
Accra, 10, 180, 217
Andani, 197
colonial, 171
criticism of, 146
Dagomba, x, xi, xv, 3, 5, 7, 9, 10–11, 22–23, 28–29, 47, 52, 60, 63–64, 68–69, 85, 94, 96, 131–33, 135, 141, 160, 168, 172, 174–78, 182, 184, 191, 198–99, 200, 206, 209, 220, 222, 224
diasporic, 221 (*see also* diaspora)
emerging, 211
indigenous, 102
new, xv, 1, 4, 7, 8, 14, 16–17, 19–21, 25, 56, 65, 67, 69–70, 94–96, 108, 114, 127–28, 131–33, 135, 141–144, 160, 168, 172–75, 180–83, 191, 199, 206, 208, 220, 225–26
non-, 140, 169–70, 193, 196–97
northern, 22, 33, 36, 102, 104
as political force, 48
southern, 24, 57, 169
Soviet trained, 112
of Tamale, 165, 167 (*see also* Tamale)
Enlightenment, 17, 92, 100

Ethnicity, 42, 69

FARA (Forum for Agricultural Research in Africa), 155
Farming, 35, 148
crops, 35, 55, 67, 135, 149–50
education and, 32, 38, 98, 162 (*see also* education)
politics of, 37, 74, 137, 183
work and, 80–81, 122, 136–38, 140, 161, 167, 189, 194
Flashpoints, 215
Foreign Affairs, 149
Fulani, 66, 138
Fuseini, A. B., 132, 145, 164
Fuseini, B. A., 81, 101, 110
Fuseini, "Lawyer Inussa," 148, 155

Ga, 74
Gambaga, 60n1, 97–98
Gariba, Mohammed Adam, 230
State Secretary to Dagbon Traditional Council, x
Gates (clans), viii, ix, x, xi, xiv, 1, 9, 16, 19, 24, 25, 26n3, 29, 43, 44, 45, 47–52, 74, 103, 122, 170, 172, 181, 186, 188, 191, 195–98, 203, 207, 208, 211, 213, 216, 218, 222, 223, 224, 225, 229, 230, 231
Abudu, xi–xiii, xv, 1, 8–9, 24, 26, 28–29, 42, 45–52, 74, 103, 144, 147, 149, 161, 170, 181, 202, 208, 210–15, 217, 223, 225, 228–30
Abudu-Andani split, 24, 151, 165, 169, 172, 190–91, 195–98
Abudu-Andani Yendi skin rotation, 209–10, 221
Andani, xi–xiii, xv, 1, 8–9, 22, 26, 28–29, 42, 45–52, 144, 147, 149, 161, 170, 181, 202, 208, 210–15, 217, 223, 225, 228–30
Gbewa, 27, 39
Germany, 31, 104, 110, 113, 153, 179

INDEX

Gold Coast Legislative Assembly, 36, 105
GBC (Ghana Broadcasting Company), 152
GIMPA (Ghana Institute of Management and Public Administration), 161
Gold Coast
    Asante control of, 30 (*see also* Asante)
    British colonialism in, 31–33, 46, 52, 101, 105, 170
    chieftaincy in, 41 (*see also* chieftaincy)
    education in, 96, 98, 120, 157
    elite of, 56, 92 (*see also* elite: northern)
    transformation into Northern Ghana, 37
Gomda, "Major," 109, 142
Gomda, Dr. Yahuza, 25, 53, 58, 104, 109, 113, 114, 118, 156, 162, 179, 189, 190, 191, 197, 204
Gonja, 31, 34, 37–38, 41–42, 51, 69, 72, 78, 99, 121, 134–35, 212, 228
    Yagbonwura Bawa Dosie, Chief, 212
Guggisberg, F. G. (Governor), 32, 34, 98–102
Gulkpe-Na, 38, 78
GUNSA (Ghana United Nations Student Association), 143
Gushiegu, 75, 107, 195, 216

Hamidu, Joshua, 87–88, 149, 184, 200n3, 210
Hamidu, Mahama Shani, 58, 87, 184
See also Sunson: Sunson-Na
Haruna, Shirazu, ix
Hausa, 13, 15–16, 53, 95, 160, 172, 188, 194
    zongo, 53, 171
Hausa, Dagomba, 16, 24, 25, 64, 128, 154, 196

Hodgson, F. M. (Governor), 6
Home, ix, 2, 3, 5, 6, 9, 10, 13, 16, 17, 48, 53, 66, 75, 113, 114, 118, 121, 123–26, 155, 164, 174, 175, 179, 180, 228
    attachment, 1, 2, 15, 26, 193, 202
    aunt's, 152, 157
    cosmopolitan, 19, 21, 173, 176–78
    memories, 3
    north, 23, 26, 82, 86, 140, 166, 175, 178, 183, 192, 213, 220
Homeland, 15
Hometown, 8, 9, 10, 14, 24, 25, 27, 54, 63, 78, 94, 117, 128, 133, 148, 181, 183, 194, 198, 199, 220, 221, 222, 225, 226
    Akropong, 195
    bond to, 2, 3, 5, 11, 16, 17, 18, 23, 26, 27, 64, 67, 69, 128, 172, 173, 198, 199
    identity, 19, 22, 69, 183, 192
    influence, 1, 14
    as power base, 22, 23
Hunting, 132, 138–39
Hybridity (cultural), 19–20, 63, 172, 177, 179

Id al Adha, xi, 70, 181, 211
Id il Fitr, 70
Identity
    1.5, 11, 12, 16
    collective, 4, 27
    cultural, 2, 14
    Dagomba, 17, 24–25, 36, 52, 170, 206
    ethnic, 11, 12
    language and, 12
    memory and, 3
    middle-class, 174
    place, 5, 178, 204
    primal, 19, 69, 195
    regional, 22, 180
    transnational, 226

urban, 227
Iddrisu, Alhaji Mahama, ix
Iddrisu, Alhassan (*mbadugu*) xvn2
Iddrisu, Dr. Mutawakil (Muta), 9, 25, 53, 64, 68, 85, 108, 113, 153, 156, 179, 182, 187, 188, 192, 198
Iddrisu, Haruna, 59, 66, 70, 73, 145, 147, 206
Iddrisu, Richard Alhassan (*Dakpema* Regent), 38
Imam, xiii, 9, 88, 103, 160, 164, 190, 194, 210–11, 217
Inequality, 1, 23, 30, 47, 106, 120
Infrastructure
  colonial, 93
  economic, 136
  educational, 56, 96, 106, 128–29, 132–33
  modernity and, 170, 174 (*see also* modernity)
  in north Ghana, 6, 32, 34, 53–54, 57, 66
  in south Ghana, 16, 180, 206
  the state and, 58
  sustainability and, 138
Institute of Professional Service, 152
Isaaka, Fati, 66, 157, 159, 186
ISSER (Institute of Statistical, Social and Economic Research), 154–55

Jagbo, 78
Jones, William (Chief Commissioner, Northern Territories), 28
Journalism, 133
  Dagomba in, 142–45
  Institute of, 117

Kaleem, Henry, x, 26n3, 74, 78, 97, 101–103, 105, 109, 110, 114, 163, 167n3, 180, 186
Kaleem, J. S., x, 45, 97, 100, 105, 109, 126, 151, 163, 164, 186–89
Kampakuya-Na, ix, x, 22, 40, 74, 76, 139, 202, 214, 228, 229

Yo-Na Andani Yakubu Abdulai V, Chief, 228
Karbo, J. A., 99
Katariga, 79
Kayayi, 138, 140, 158, 197
Kenney-Herbert, Capt AHC, 31
King (Ya-Na), xi–xiv, 2, 5, 7–9, 13, 42–45, 64, 72, 202–203, 211, 213, 215, 221–22, 224–25
  kingdom, 5, 25, 29, 39, 60, 136
  kingmaker, 190
  kingship, 14, 48, 75, 90, 203, 208, 216, 222
Kintampo, 60n1, 66
Kirby, Fr. John, ix, 61n14
KNUST (Kwame Nkrumah University of Science and Technology), 114
Koenigsberger, Otto, 158
Konbon-Na, 194
Konkomba, 5, 28, 37, 42, 49, 51, 75, 219n5
Korle Bu Hospital, 157
Kpatina, 75
Kufuor, John, 154, 181, 201n3, 212, 219
Kuga-Na, x. 44, 45, 46, 163, 164, 230
Kunbun-Na, 9, 109
Kunbungu, 54

Lamashoggu, 213
Landowner, 37–38, 41, 77
Leadership, 5, 7, 21, 22, 40, 47, 59, 74, 86, 102, 146, 197, 199, 202, 216
  remote control, 5, 47, 202, 225
LI 59 (Legislative Instrument), 50
Literacy, 7, 106, 131, 136, 143, 146, 155, 165, 221
  adult, 109–10, 127, 165
  English, 96, 105, 107
  illiteracy, 54, 94, 127, 225
Livestock, 131, 134, 138
Lloyd, John, 158
Luntse, 8, 70, 71, 72, 73, 74. *See also* drummer

Mahama, E. A., 99
Mahama, "Lawyer" Ibrahim, xv, 21, 22, 26n3, 212
Mahamma, Dr., Mohammed (Dr. M. M.), 51, 78, 156
Mahama, Gifty, 8, 126, 150
Mahdi, Alhaji, 109, 115, 119, 138, 161, 179, 191, 197
Majid, Abdul, 9, 57, 68, 72, 73, 100, 102, 121, 156
Malam Sani, 192
Malgu-Na, 194
Mamprussi (Mamprugu), 30, 34, 39, 48, 72, 204
    Na Yiri-Na Bohuga Shirigu (King), 45
Manhyia Palace, 229
Marakwet, 85, 178
Marriage, 3, 23–24, 40, 64, 69, 77, 90, 153, 165, 191, 194, 216
    and children, 86
    inter-gate, 9
    women and, 120–21, 140
Mate Kole Commission, 50
    Manya Krobo, 61
    Nene Azzu Mate Kole, 61
Materiality
    ancient, 178
    of the home, 20, 63, 173–75, 178, 220 (*see also* home)
    of modernity, 170, 177 (*see also* modernity)
    new, 180, 199
    western, 224
Memories
    childhood, 221
    collective, 2, 27
    and the home, 3, 90
    of the hometown, 67
    recreation of, 4
Methodology, viii, ix, 9–10, 187–88
Migration, 11, 18, 34, 135–36, 170, 172, 182, 193, 221, 226
    internal, 10

international, 10
labor, 139
transnational, 12, 15
transregional, 16
Military, 10, 52, 87, 139, 141–43, 146, 167, 184, 202, 210, 212–13, 217, 223
    colonialism and, 31, 52, 105
    coups, 163
    government, 46, 50, 148
    occupation, 8–9
    recruitment, 6
Millenium Challenge Corporation, 59
Millenium Development Goals, 58
Mion-Lana Abdulai Mahamadu, 228, 230–31
Modernity, 14, 56, 65, 69, 85, 93–94, 96, 132, 143, 164, 166, 169, 172–79, 190
    hybrid, 11, 168, 170, 199, 224
    multiple, 17–20
    traditional-modern binary, 17
    Western, 21
Mohammed, Janet, 58
    Christian Council, ix
Mossi, 134
Mothers, 62, 86, 87–89, 109, 111, 114, 123, 164–66, 177, 180
    step, 88
Mumuni, Bawumia, 99
Mumuni, Mohammed, 23, 57, 75, 104, 113, 115, 117, 161, 231
Munka'ila, Adisa, 54, 143–44, 190
Murder, 38
    of Ya-Na Yakubu Andani II, viii–ix, xi, xv, 1–2, 5, 8, 21, 45, 49, 51–52, 60, 61n5, 68, 72, 76, 90, 144, 147, 149, 154, 161, 164, 181, 190, 196–98, 201n3, 202, 207, 209, 211, 213, 215–16, 218, 221–23, 225, 229 (*see also* Ya-Na Yakubu Andani II)
Muslim, xi, 31, 81, 85, 97, 138
    chiefs and, 39–41, 86

children, 95, 103
    Dagomba as, 78
    in northern Ghana, 69, 102, 160, 171

Naa Nyagsi, 27, 39
Nachin-Na, 140, 194
Nanumba, 39, 42, 51
Naseri, Issa, 118, 162, 179, 199, 215, 218
Nasser, Dr., 68, 81, 89, 112–14, 117, 153, 179, 193, 206
National House of Chiefs, 211
National Security Advisor, 149, 201n3
National Service, 133, 141, 145–46, 152–53, 160, 192
    National Service Secretariat, 151
Native Administration, 34, 99, 100, 102
Native Authority, 34–35, 120
Navrongo, 96, 112, 117, 120, 126, 141, 162
NCCE (National Commission for Civic Education), 162, 199, 215
NDC (National Democratic Congress), 8, 23, 58, 143, 146–48, 151, 155, 161, 177, 181, 208, 211
NGO (Non-governmental Organization), 58, 128, 145, 184–85, 206, 208
Nkrumah, Kwame, 35–36, 49–50, 61n8, 93, 97, 99, 106, 109, 111, 113–14, 120, 127–28, 137–38, 154, 156, 162, 167, 183, 185, 208
NORIP (Nordic Reference Interval Project), 58
NRC (National Redemption Council), 46, 50, 55, 137
Northcott, Lt. Col. development, 31
NPP (Northern Peoples Party), 37, 49, 51, 144, 147, 149, 151, 154–55, 181, 197, 208, 211, 218
Northern Students Union, 143, 145

Northern Territorial Council, 36
Northern Territories, 6, 28, 31–37, 46, 49, 53, 94, 99, 106–107
Nyangse (son of Sitobu), 79–80

Obekyebi-Lamptey, Jake, 51
Ofori-Atta, E., 94
Old Fadama, 194–95
Ollennu Committee, 46
Opoku Ware II, Asantehene, 208
Otumfuo Osei Tutu II, Asantehene, 208, 212, 228, 229

Palace, xi–xiv, 8–9, 38, 40, 46, 48, 51, 55, 64, 73, 85, 87–88, 109, 181–82, 202, 206, 212–17, 221, 223, 229–30
Place, xii, 12, 14–15, 22–23, 38, 41, 45, 64, 68, 71, 75, 81, 84–85, 90, 132, 166, 193, 204, 211, 215, 217, 220, 222, 225–27
    affect and, 47, 220 (*see also* attachment: affect and)
    attachment, 3–5, 16, 60, 63, 199, 221 (*see also* attachment: place)
    cosmopolitan, 54 (*see also* cosmopolitan)
    Dagbon, x, 27–29, 62, 70, 94, 202, 207, 221
    gate, 213 (*see also* gates)
    home and, 1, 202
    memory and, 3 (*see also* memories)
    modernity and, 168–69, 174–75, 181 (*see also* modernity)
    new, 10–11, 19–20, 173, 195
    nostalgia for, 26
    of origin, 168, 204, 224
    shrines and, 77–80
Progress Youth Club, 147

Radio Universe, 143, 208
Rawlings, Jerry John, 128, 146–47, 149, 160–62, 200n3
Red Hunter, 28, 39

Regional Executive, 144, 177, 181, 208
Regional House of Chiefs, 211
Remittance, 57
Resources, 41, 60, 63, 90, 147, 170, 180–83, 206
   colonialism and, 6, 32, 131
   education and, 93, 104, 107, 111, 129 (see also education)
   patrons and, 7, 22
   the state and, 57–59
Rice, 33, 55–57, 64–68, 80–81, 85, 134, 137–38, 149, 161, 167n1, 194
Road Map to Peace, x, 9, 10
Rumania, 113

Sandoh, Walter, 116, 155, 187–88, 205
Salaga, 31, 98
Samori, 31
Sarnargu, 13, 76
   Sarnargu-Na, 76
Sherif, Mahama "Savannah," 118, 161, 191
Seini, Wayo, 57, 92, 103, 148, 153–54, 179
Selection Committee, 28
Shaikh Sulayman Abdallah Bagayugo, 130n2
Shekina Clinic, 130n4. See also Abdulai, Dr. David
Siddique, Alhaji, 143, 208
Sitobu, 27, 39, 79
Skin/stool, ii–xv, 29, 40–48, 50–52, 59–60, 76, 86, 90, 103, 122, 164, 183, 188, 195, 202, 205, 209, 217, 218, 221, 223, 231
Sokoto, 30
Soviet Union, 112–13
Space, 1, 3–5, 19, 25–26, 63, 82, 90, 168, 195, 220–21, 226
   cultural, 168
   domestic, 178
   of intercultural improvisation, 18
   marginal, 54, 136

   modern, 170–73, 175–76 (see also modernity)
   new, 14, 20, 169, 173, 179, 224
   production of, 64
   symbolic, 56
   temporal, 204
Stanbic Bank, 40, 74, 76, 88, 152
State Housing Corporation, 160
State Insurance Corporation, 161
The Statesman, 143
Sule, Alhaji, 115, 153
Sumani, Issifu, 110, 158–59, 165, 188, 196
Sumani, MP Abubakari, 116
Sunson, ix, 58, 183, 184, 195, 200, 208
   Sunson-Na, 73, 80, 84, 87, 183, 184, 185, 200n3
Swazi, 4

Tamale, iii–xv, 3, 6–10, 13, 27, 62, 65–66, 78–9, 81–82, 85, 87, 89, 90, 174, 180, 187, 189, 191–92, 194, 196, 199, 204–207, 211–12
   careers and, 131–167
   chiefs and, 73, 186, 190, 203
   colonialism in, 33–37, 38, 135
   development in, 181–183, 198
   education and, 97–99, 100–129, 132 (see also education)
   hometown and, 67–72 (see also hometown)
   leadership, 21–24
   post-colonial, 52–54, 57–59
Tamale Hospital, 181
Tamale-Yendi Road, viii, 51, 181, 205
Teacher, 36, 67, 97, 110, 127, 129, 148, 162–63, 189, 192, 206
   colonialism and, 93, 99
   Islamic, 95, 103
   northern, 98, 104–107, 119, 141
   primary, 152
   Quranic, 111–12
   university, 153

secondary, 117, 146
southern, 100
TICCS (Tamale Institute for Cross-Cultural Studies), ix
Third Republic Constitution Commission, 143, 144–45
Tijani, Mohammed Habib, xii, 37, 149, 197, 210
Traders, 10, 30, 35, 54, 85, 95, 131, 172
Transnationalism, 10, 16, 23, 206, 226
    internal, 15, 168
    transmigrant, 10, 12, 14, 226
"Tropical architecture," 158
Tuya-Na, 74, 81, 162, 163, 198

UGCC (United Gold Coast Convention), 35
Ukraine, 114
University of Cape Coast, 126, 154, 192
Urban, 4, 20–22, 47, 136, 169, 180, 226–27
    cosmopolitan, 7, 17 (*see also* cosmopolitan)
    modernity and, 18, 170–76, 178 (*see also* modernity)
    in the north, 52–53, 67, 107–108
    peri-urban, 41
    planning, 56
    and rural, 14, 23, 106, 226

Victoriaborg, 170–71
Vteng, 39, 182–83, 191

WANEP (West African Network for Peace), 207
Wangara, 95, 130n2
Washington State University, 126, 155
Water, 43, 53–54, 58, 63, 66, 80, 84–85, 101, 122, 170, 174–76, 184–85, 190
Weapons, xi, 52, 74, 139
Wesleyan Methodist Church Mission, 97

White Fathers (Society of Missionaries of Africa), 96–97
White Volta, 133
Widows, xi, xv, 1, 209, 212
Wives, xi, xiii–xiv, 40, 44, 86–90, 112, 116, 122, 125, 163, 174, 176–77, 185, 187–88, 201n4, 221
Women, viii, ix, xiii, xiv, 1, 9, 10, 16, 54, 68, 75, 191, 195, 216–17, 224, 226
    chiefs and, 40, 205
    in Dagomba compounds, 82–85
    education and, 95, 107–114, 120–123, 126–128, 176, 185, 193 (*see also* education)
    marriage and, 86–90
    shrines and, 78, 80
    work and, 80–81, 132-3, 138–140, 143–45, 150, 152, 155–158, 164–65, 174, 182
World War II, 36, 53, 132, 135, 158
World Bank, 13, 58, 106, 128, 185, 208
Wuaku Commission, 210–11, 218, 223

Ya-Na (king), 50, 51, 72, 73, 74, 111, 139, 203, 205, 207, 210, 216, 221
    importance of, xi, 221
    selection of, 60, 218, 223, 230
    succession of, 42–46, 50, 60, 61, 218, 223
Ya-Na Abdulai II, 35
Ya-Na Abdulai III, 45, 50, 61
Ya-Na Andani, 46
Ya-Na Andani II, 35
Ya-Na Andani III, 21, 46
Ya-Na Andani IV, 50
Ya-Na Darimani, 45, 48
Ya-Na Mahama II, 44
Ya-Na Mahama III, 45, 61
Ya-Na Mahama Abukari II, x, 26, 217, 228, 230
Ya-Na Mahamadu Abdulai IV, xii, 45, 46, 49, 50, 100, 223, 228, 229, 230

burial, 218
death of father, 50
deskinned, 50, 61n5
succeeded, 50
funeral, 51, 229, 230
Ya-Na Mohammed Zangina, 39, 95
Ya-Na Yakubu I, 42, 48, 196
Ya-Na Yakubu Andani II, xii, xiii, 8, 21, 112, 189, 190, 209
burial, 228, 229, 230
death/murder of, viii, xi, 5, 40, 48, 68, 90, 196, 197, 202, 225
enskinned, 50
funeral, 228, 229
Yahaya, Huudu, 23, 67, 97, 138, 145, 146, 162, 177, 181, 182, 186, 187, 208
Yakubu, Abdulai (diplomat), 204
Yakubu, Abdulai ("Sabon Kudi," new money), 103, 160, 190
Yakubu, Bawa, 61n9, 212
Yakubu, Malik, 8
Yakubu Tali, Tolon-Na, 49, 61n9, 130n3
Yendi, viii, ix, xi–xiii, 9, 25, 31, 38–39, 40, 44–45, 48, 50–52, 54, 58, 62, 64, 66, 68–69, 85, 88–89, 97–98, 104, 109, 131, 147, 149, 151, 157, 162–63, 181–82, 185, 188, 195, 197, 212, 223, 226, 228, 231
Bishop of, 74, 180, 198, 216 (*see also* Boi-Nai, Vincent)
chiefs in, 37, 46, 139, 222
crisis, xv, 142
colonialism and, 31–35
dispute, 47
education in, 100, 107–108, 110, 160, 189 (*see also* education)
Imam of, 210
massacre, 213, 229
regent of, 8, 205, 219n3
the seat of Dagbon, 5, 7, 22, 29, 53
skin, 42–43, 45, 47, 49, 51, 76, 90, 122, 202, 209, 221 (*see also* skin)
tragedy, 200, 225
youth in, 28
Yoruba, 16, 52–53, 67

Zibilila, Alida (Zibs), ix, x, 73
Zohe, 210–211, 219n4
Zong, 53, 80, 82–83, 89, 171, 197

www.ingramcontent.com/pod-product-compliance
Lightning Source LLC
Chambersburg PA
CBHW051532020426
42333CB00016B/1891